D0782332

PASCAL THE PHILOSOPHER

An Introduction

#82141-1

GRAEME HUNTER

# Pascal the Philosopher

## An Introduction

UNIVERSITY OF TORONTO PRESS
Toronto Buffalo London

© University of Toronto Press 2013
Toronto Buffalo London
www.utppublishing.com
Printed in Canada

ISBN 978-1-4426-4142-6

Printed on acid-free, 100% post-consumer recycled paper with
vegetable-based inks

**Library and Archives Canada Cataloguing in Publication**

Hunter, Graeme, author
Pascal the philosopher : an introduction / Graeme Hunter.

Includes Infini-rien and the English translation.
Includes bibliographical references and index.
ISBN 978-1-4426-4142-6 (bound)

1. Pascal, Blaise, 1623-1662.  2. Philosophical theology.  I. Title.

B1903.H85 2013      194     C2013-903492-7

University of Toronto Press acknowledges the financial assistance to its
publishing program of the Canada Council for the Arts and the Ontario
Arts Council.

Canada Council   Conseil des Arts
for the Arts     du Canada

ONTARIO ARTS COUNCIL
CONSEIL DES ARTS DE L'ONTARIO
50 YEARS OF ONTARIO GOVERNMENT SUPPORT OF THE ARTS
50 ANS DE SOUTIEN DU GOUVERNEMENT DE L'ONTARIO AUX ARTS

University of Toronto Press acknowledges the financial support of the
Government of Canada through the Canada Book Fund for its publishing
activities.

This book has been published with the help of a grant from the Canadian
Federation for the Humanities and Social Sciences, through the Awards
to Scholarly Publications Program, using funds provided by the Social
Sciences and Humanities Research Council of Canada.

*For Annegret*

*A quest of thoughts, all tenants to the heart*

# Contents

# Acknowledgments

First, I would like to thank the students whom, at different stages of my career, I have been fortunate to supervise, and who have produced excellent theses on Pascal: Mathieu Bras, Monica Izaguirre, and Patrick Moran. We learn much from those we teach.

Special thanks are due to my brother Bruce, who over the years has made generously available his expertise in the craft of publishing, and to my editor, Len Husband, for his gentle tact and encouragement.

A number of people have read parts or all of the manuscript and made helpful comments. Sincere thanks to past and present colleagues in the Ancient Philosophy Research Group at the University of Ottawa, especially Christopher Byrne and Catherine Collobert. Also friends and colleagues from this and other departments, including Roger Ariew, Hilliard Aronovitch, Greg Bloomquist, Fr Paul Cormier, Antoine Côté, George Englebretsen, Peter Gallagher, Daniel Garber, Hugh Hunter, Pierre Hurtubise, Denis Kambouchner, John McDade, and Paul Rusnock. Two anonymous readers also deserve thanks for improvements too numerous to be separately acknowledged.

My wife's sound judgment is exceeded only by her patience. To her this book is dedicated.

PASCAL THE PHILOSOPHER

An Introduction

# Introduction

## Pascal the Philosopher
### ... *philosophie, seule mon sujet* ...

This book is about Pascal the philosopher. Some notable scholars assert there is no such person. Therefore this book is controversial.

## Pascal and Philosophy

Though the range of Pascal's writing is enormous, its quantity is not. His complete works fit nicely between the covers of one not particularly thick quarto volume. They cover mathematics, physics, and topics in religion as well as philosophy. Very few pages of his work are devoted to philosophy as such. And yet, as I shall argue, apart from works dedicated to particular problems of mathematics or physics, the mode of Pascal's writing is philosophical. Moreover, it has greater philosophical authority than its brevity would lead you to expect.

Much of what is written about Pascal passes over his philosophical importance. "At an age when most men have scarcely begun to live," wrote the Viscount de Chateaubriand, "Pascal had already concluded a magisterial survey of the whole range of human science, recognized its ultimate insignificance, and turned his thoughts toward religion."[1]

The picture evoked in these vivid words was already conventional when Chateaubriand published them, and remains so today. It depicts Pascal's youth as marked by precocity and genius, his adulthood by conversion, and his maturity by saintly self-denial.

All true, but, like most big pictures, it leaves things out. This one omits my entire subject: Pascal's philosophy. Chateaubriand makes it look as if Pascal leapt from a pinnacle of scientific achievement and landed on the holy mountain, without setting foot on any philosophical territory in between, even if that territory was only an arid valley.

Was philosophy left out by oversight or design? It's hard to know. Both happen. A few years earlier, Voltaire had portrayed Pascal as a distinguished geometer and literary stylist, but one who lacked "any true philosophy."[2] And over the years other observers have concurred. Recently a distinguished scholar who has done much to further our understanding of Pascal concluded that he "considered philosophy a futile business and did not want to be a philosopher."[3] Such writers see Pascal as deliberately turning his back on philosophy.

Others come to a similar conclusion from the opposite direction. They think philosophy excluded Pascal. They adopt a philosophical standpoint – say that of metaphysical naturalism – and find that from that point of view it is difficult to take Pascal seriously. Dogmatic naturalism, rather than careful study of Pascal's writings, is the likeliest explanation of Pascal's cameo appearance in Bertrand Russell's *History of Western Philosophy* as the man who "sacrificed his magnificent mathematical intellect to his God."[4] Others set up what David Wetsel calls an "artificial dichotomy" between religion and philosophy,[5] and put Pascal on the religious side of the divide.

There are, in fact, limitless ways of arriving at the conclusion that philosophy and Pascal are irreconcilable. Adopt any conventional or limited view either of the discipline or the philosopher and you will likely obtain the desired result.

I won't attempt to hunt down all such accounts and refute them. Happily, a more positive and, I hope, a more readable endeavour lies ahead. The plan is to lay before you Pascal's views about philosophy, God, the world, and the human condition, exhibiting in the course of doing so the exciting way in which Pascal transformed philosophy as he found it, restoring it to a shape in which each man and woman has a duty to practise it, and in which Pascal hoped it would be immensely attractive to his reader.

When we wonder whether to consider Pascal a philosopher, his literary standing is not what is in question. Nothing historians of philosophy say will have the least impact on that. His *Provincial Letters* and *Pensées* are fixtures in the pantheon of letters. Neither work has ever gone out of print in French or English since its first edition. Anyone who believed he could affect Pascal's stature by bestowing or withholding the honorific title of "philosopher" might as well imagine he commands the tides.

The question of whether Pascal is a philosopher is important not to Pascal but to us. He is a literary giant, and we want to know how best to understand him. Are we to read him as we would a philosopher, testing his premises, weighing his arguments, expecting consistency as well as insight? Could we even expect to learn something from him about how to practise philosophy? Or are we to assess him by other criteria, perhaps as a poetic or religious writer?

My answer is that several of the key writings of Pascal yield their deepest insights when they are read with the interpretive expectations of philosophy. If Pascal speaks as a philosopher, he can also speak that way to us, though we read him under different skies and in the light of new philosophical assumptions. This book is intended as an introduction to the Pascal who can speak to us in that way. It is not always introductory in other senses one might attach to that word.

I am not alone in thinking Pascal a philosopher. Far from it. Thomas More Harrington's study, *Pascal Philosophe*, deserves to be mentioned.[6] Harrington presents an inclusive account of Pascal's thought, beginning with his natural philosophy, then adding special studies of his psychology, anthropology, and his use of Christianity as a hypothetical interpretive device. Harrington's work remains useful because it gathers the philosophically relevant bits from Pascal's varied writings and shows the scope of the contribution they can make to the discipline of philosophy once they are brought together.

However, Harrington's book is mainly one of erudition. One could accept all his results and still wonder whether Pascal was himself a philosopher. Writers as different as John Milton and Arthur Koestler also made substantial contributions to philosophical thought, but are not normally taken to be philosophers.[7] But Pascal is more than a contributor of philosophical insights. Harrington does not notice Pascal's way of renewing an ancient way of thinking philosophically, one more in keeping with our real situation in life than were the modes of philosophizing going on around him, and one which prepares us better to understand ourselves. Pascal's philosophy arises out of a philosophical *mission*, as I shall try to explain.

There is another work on Pascal's philosophy, which I would also like to distinguish from my own. Vincent Carraud is dismissive of Harrington, accusing him a little unkindly of missing the point.[8] Carraud's approach consists first in examining many different conceptions of what philosophy is, including those of Pascal's own time, and then in presenting Pascal's contributions (mainly critical ones, in Carraud's view) to canonical parts of philosophy such as metaphysics, ethics, and natural theology. Once again, my own approach will be different. I shall not be concerned with Pascal's piecemeal contributions to mainstream philosophy but instead with what I see as a distinctive attempt on his part to swallow philosophy whole, and then chart a different, though recognizably philosophical, course.

One final caveat: I am not suggesting that only a handful of people read Pascal as a philosopher. That he *is* one is surely the unstated assumption of most philosophers who write about him and of thousands of casual readers who find inspiration in his writing. It is the deniers who are in the minority, though they form a substantial minority, if we count those who tacitly express their dismissal of Pascal by treating the history of philosophy as if he did not belong to it.[9]

Whether large or small in number, however, the deniers form an influential body and deserve to be addressed. They include some distinguished philosophers and historians of philosophy, and they raise deep questions about what philosophy can be. Answering their questions enables us to rediscover a way of doing philosophy that is of the utmost importance, though seldom practised in our time.

This book is about the Pascal the deniers have misjudged. It shows how to read his fragmentary writings *philosophically*.

## Life

Pascal's short life began on 19 June 1623 and ended on 19 August 1662. He was sick through most of it, and often in great pain. Yet he had seen much by the time death came. In the apt phrase of Jean Racine, he died of old age at thirty-nine.

The life can be studied in almost any degree of scholarly depth. Some good summaries are available on the Internet. There are brief accounts of greater authority in encyclopaedias and "companions" of philosophy. Among full-length biographies, the most detailed are in French, but there are also English biographical works of high quality.[10] The interested reader is referred to them.

Religion is too important to Pascal's philosophy to make any sharp distinction between them. But because my focus is philosophical, I will limit my discussion of religious questions to what is needed for philosophical purposes. Most of the unavoidable points are connected with the reform-minded religious movement of Jansenism, to whose rigorous doctrines and practice Pascal converted in 1646.

Jansenists were reformers with a strong "sectarian tendency,"[11] though they never allowed it to mature into schism. Unlike Protestant reformers, Jansenists never contemplated leaving the Catholic Church. On the contrary, as reformers do, they took themselves to be pillars of orthodoxy in a decadent age. Their teachings were inspired by a book called *Augustinus*, a study of Saint Augustine written by the Belgian bishop of Ypres, Cornelius Jansen, but only published in 1640, two years after Jansen's death.

No religious writer is more central to Catholic theology than Augustine, but Jansen caused concern because he emphasized certain harsh aspects of the Augustinian doctrine of grace, which Catholics have traditionally preferred to contextualize. For example, Jansen read Augustine as saying that God's saving grace is not offered to everyone. That doctrine was viewed as too severe by the Catholic establishment, and too close to the Calvinism condemned by the Council of Trent. Jesuits in particular defended the more generous idea that sufficient grace was offered to all.

The Jansenist understanding of grace therefore came under scrutiny. When they could not be persuaded to think differently, scrutiny turned to censure, and ultimately to a (relatively mild) form of persecution. As can easily happen, the perceived hostility of an uncomprehending world caused the Jansenists to circle their wagons. They came to regard themselves as that "invisible Church," whose doctrines are always orthodox, whose lives are lived in the ardour of faith, and who alone are destined for heaven.

Jansenism's base in France was the Cistercian convent of Port Royal, located just a few miles from Paris. Port Royal's Mother Superior was Angélique Arnauld, and its chief defender was her brother Antoine, called "The Great Arnauld." He earned the epithet by his astute objections to Descartes's *Meditations* and his interminable controversies with another celebrity of the day, now read mainly by specialists, Nicolas Malebranche.[12]

Arnauld could be withering as easily as he could be brilliant, and he enjoyed being both. Equal to any academic question, he raised "knock 'em down, drag 'em out" argument to an art form. His technique was to mix one part impeccable logic and two of caustic disdain, and pour the mixture by the treatise-full on anyone who dared disagree with him. Thousands of the pages he left behind in forty-three folio volumes engage the enemies of Port Royal in this fashion.

By 1656, however, Port Royal needed more than Arnauld's theological rigour and fire in the belly if it wanted to save itself. It had come under public scrutiny and needed improved public relations. That is when Arnauld encountered the dazzling writer Pascal. By the time they met, Pascal had experienced a second and even deeper conversion to Jansenist Christianity. He was just what Port Royal needed: someone equipped to write *pour le grand public*, and at the same time dedicated to the cause.

Out of that meeting with Arnauld, and in response to urgent needs of Port Royal, grew the first of Pascal's famous books, *The Provincial Letters*. In these satirical letters, Pascal adopts the persona of a bemused visitor in Paris writing to a country gentleman like himself, trying to explain to him the shenanigans of theologians in the city. The protagonist appears as the voice of bewildered common sense seeking to fathom the hair-splitting Jesuit attacks on Port Royal. To compare the madness of academics to the sound, if plodding, judgments of ordinary people is a fail-safe recipe for comic writing, as many satirists have discovered. But Pascal took it to new heights. His indictment of the Jesuits figures among the great satires of world literature and has never gone out of print.

When it comes to understanding Pascal's philosophy, however, the *Provincial Letters* are not the place to turn. I shall focus mainly on his other bestseller, the *Pensées*. Not that the *Pensées* is any less a religious text than the *Provincial Letters*. But its aim is wider. Though infused with Jansenist ideas, it is conceived broadly as an apology for Roman Catholicism, a fact philosophers sometimes hold against it.

The *Pensées* is undeniably a strange book, consisting of short essays, anecdotes, maxims, aphorisms, and obscure notes the author intended only for himself. Short sequences of these writings sometimes appear to have a kind of order, but it never lasts. The overall impression given by the book is chaotic. Normally its disorganized character is attributed to the fact that Pascal died before completing it. But the existence of more than one fragment mocking the whole idea of order, or questioning its possibility, makes you wonder just how different the *Pensées* would be had the author lived to publish it.[13]

The unfinished and practically formless character of the main piece of textual evidence is a handicap in arguing my thesis, and may prejudice an uninitiated reader against it. How could some chaotic jumble of religiously edifying texts be the basis for a philosophical interpretation of their author? My reasons for thinking so will be unfolded slowly in the chapters that follow, and only definitively stated in the last. I will not weaken them by trying to anticipate them here. But let me at least make clear what my contention is. I could put it this way: When Pascal tells Isaac Le Maître de Saci, his spiritual director, that "philosophy was

[his] only subject," he meant to characterize not just the conversation in which they were at that moment engaged but his entire intellectual temperament and calling.

Though theology filled Pascal's nonscientific writings, it was not his métier. He had for it neither the inclination nor the right cast of mind. In fact he begs Saci's pardon for ever presuming to venture into it.[14] Nor was the theology Pascal defended properly his own, not at least in its nuanced form. In writing it he depended on behind-the-scenes coaching from Arnauld and others.[15] How different matters look when we turn to Pascal's philosophy. *That* is clearly his own. In it are reflections of a brilliant thinker who found himself at the geographical and intellectual centre of many of the major philosophical controversies of his day. Pascal should be seen as a philosophical reformer, a critical virtuoso, and a militant inquirer.

Reform is first on this list, but you cannot reform what you do not first attack. So it is with a careful study of Pascal's *attack* on philosophy, in the profound and imaginative form it takes in his "Conversation on Philosophy with M. de Saci" that I propose to begin.

**Texts**

The translations used in this book are my own. I have mainly used Louis Lafuma's edition of Pascal's works, which appears in the bibliography as Pascal (1963) and is cited as such, followed by a page number, for all Pascal's writings except the *Pensées*. When citing Lafuma's edition of the *Pensées*, I follow scholarly convention and cite it simply as "L," followed by the number of the *fragment* under discussion, only adding the page number in the case of long fragments, as an aid to finding the quoted passage quickly. The famous wager argument, for example, would be cited as L418. Its first paragraph would be cited as L418, p. 550a. (Each page of Pascal (1963) is divided into an a column and a b column.)

There were many editions of the *Pensées* prior to the Lafuma edition, and several important ones have appeared since. Most editions are of less editorial authority than Lafuma's. However, some scholars prefer a more recent edition by Philippe Sellier, based on a different copy of the original manuscript from that used by Lafuma. It figures in the bibliography as Pascal (2000).

Either edition of the *Pensées* would have served my purposes equally well. The most important difference between the two editions is the order in which they present the fragments. In most fragments, the wording is identical. From time to time, fragments that are separate in one edition are joined in the other. Although I take Lafuma as my standard, I adopt the common practice of citing both editions. Occasionally I take note of variants found in Sellier.

When citing fragments from Sellier I once again defer to normal scholarly practice and refer to it as "S," followed by the fragment number, followed again by the page number in the case of longer fragments. For example, the wager fragment in the Sellier edition is S680. Pascal's famous saying, that the heart has its reasons that reason knows not of, has its own number in the Lafuma edition, but in the Sellier edition it occurs as part of the much longer wager fragment. It would therefore be cited as L423/S680, p. 467.

Both editions of the *Pensées* have excellent English translations. Pascal (1966) follows the Lafuma edition, and A.J. Krailsheimer's graceful translation captures much of Pascal's scintillating style. Philosophers need to tread carefully, however, because the Krailsheimer translation is occasionally guilty of blurring the logic of the arguments.

Roger Ariew's translation of the Sellier edition, Pascal (2005), makes the arguments very clear, but is not always as attentive to the beauty of Pascal's prose. A concordance included in the Sellier edition, and in Ariew's translation, enables the reader to navigate easily between Sellier and Lafuma.

## Capitalization

Pascal's Christianity is important not only to Pascal personally and to the historical period in which he lived, but also, in a singular way, to his manner of doing philosophy. I will need to discuss matters relating to Christianity, such as the Christian virtues of Faith, Hope, and Charity. Faith of the Christian kind is not the same as garden-variety faith, nor Hope as hope, nor Charity as charity. In these and other cases, where the point I am trying to establish depends on a term's being given its Christian sense, I capitalize the term. Otherwise, it is left in lower case. I have tried to be parsimonious with capitalization, using it only where I think it will clarify what I mean to say.

# 1 Against Philosophy

## Tournament of Champions

Pascal liked the way sceptics divide philosophy into two parts: theirs and everybody else's. He shared the sceptic's suspicion that too many philosophers overestimate their ability to find *the truth*. For such presumption the ancient sceptic Sextus Empiricus labelled them "dogmatists."[1] It was immaterial what particular dogmas they stood for.

Sextus's book, *Outlines of Pyrrhonism*, is a good place to go for the radical kind of scepticism Pascal liked. It is named after Pyrrho of Elis (ca 365–270 B.C.), the founder of the school, though he is not known to have originated all the doctrines associated with it.[2]

There is also a more moderate form of scepticism, called Academic, because it was practised in Plato's Academy after its founder's death, but Pascal showed little interest in that.[3] When it comes to making his dramatic contrast between scepticism on the one hand and dogmatism on the other, Pascal simply ignores Academic scepticism. There is "an open war among men," Pascal tells us, "in which everyone must choose, siding either with dogmatism or with Pyrrhonism. Anyone who imagines he can remain neutral will be a Pyrrhonist par excellence."[4] On this understanding Academic scepticism becomes a form of dogmatism.[5]

Mainstream philosophers normally see the landscape differently. To them sceptics are marginal figures, parasites on the body of philosophy, whose function is to help decompose philosophy's unfit or moribund parts. Kant is typical when he says that scepticism cannot be taken seriously as philosophy, but serves only to goad dogmatic philosophers into refining their arguments.[6] No doubt he has in mind the way the sceptic David Hume awoke him from his own "dogmatic slumbers."[7]

Dogmatists think sceptics look at philosophy through the wrong end of the telescope, and that's what makes them ascribe so much importance to themselves. Sceptics hold real philosophy at such a distance that its tangled threads appear to form a single dogmatic cloth.

Seen from the middle, though, the place dogmatic philosophers believe they occupy, that cloth is a roiling tangle of loose doctrinal ends. Philosophy is not one thing but many, consisting of unceasing, multilayered struggles of dogmatic philosophers among themselves. The scissors of scepticism are always snipping at the fringes to be sure, but scepticism rarely figures as a leading force in mainstream metaphysics, logic, ethics, political philosophy, and so on ... even in epistemology, though Descartes's *Meditations* are a glorious exception. The living modes of philosophizing, those close to philosophy's heart, are rarely sceptical in outlook.

So, at least, complacent dogmatists would have it. Pascal did not agree. Though not himself a sceptic, he refused to see scepticism as a docile underlabourer in the philosophical enterprise. He thought dogmatic philosophers should view sceptics not as useful parasites but as foes. This picture of implacable opposition makes an excellent point of entry into Pascal's unusual conception of philosophy.

What interests him about the immemorial standoff between scepticism and dogmatism is not its contingent history but the logical reality he believes underlies that history and explains it. And that is, no doubt, why he feels free to sidestep historical questions altogether and simply anoint one champion to represent each side of the conflict.

As a literary move, the idea of designating champions is ingenious. Two debaters in a showdown are more manageable than a free-for-all in many voices. The story becomes more focused, the conflict more compelling. The truth is not what captivates our interest, Pascal once observed, "to take note of it with pleasure we have to see it arising out of a dispute."[8] He is also careful to choose champions with whom readers will easily identify because of their engaging conversational style.[9]

The use of champions is also dialectically astute. It permits the argument to escape the death by a thousand details that would inevitably overtake anyone confronting all of philosophy – for that is Pascal's gigantic ambition – one philosopher at a time. His use of champions prefigures the analytic philosopher's preference for dealing with philosophical *types* rather than with details of particular philosophers' thoughts.[10]

Not that Pascal egregiously misrepresented the thought of his two protagonists. The opinions he explicitly attributes to them can be documented,[11] but there is necessarily some sculpting of the two figures, and it is bound to draw criticism.

Historians of philosophy are going to be critical of the use of champions, as they are of the use of types. They will not like seeing their entire domain abbreviated to just two philosophers. Can any thinker represent bodies of thought as complex as either scepticism or dogmatism, they will wonder? And even if they were prepared, for the sake of argument, to allow for the possibility – even if they agree that, for Pascal's purposes, it is inevitable – they will still quarrel with the particular champions he selects. To represent Pyrrhonism, for example, Pascal chose not Pyrrho or Timon, or even Sextus Empiricus. No ancient philosopher, Greek or Roman, no sceptic of early, middle, or late antiquity is chosen. Instead Pascal picks the sixteenth century's brilliant essayist, Michel de Montaigne.

Some might think Montaigne too murky a figure or too insignificant to serve as a representative of so vast a school of thought as scepticism. Frederick Copleston, for example, sees Montaigne as a bit of a dabbler, someone who indeed "revived the ancient arguments for scepticism" but who did so in the manner of a "cultivated man of letters," adding to his scepticism a dash of "the moral ideal of Socrates" and "the Stoic ideals of tranquility and of obedience to nature."[12]

Copleston's faint praise has not gone down well with specialists, however. Hugo Friedrich, in his meticulous study of Montaigne's thought, concludes that Montaigne reached "the outermost point" to which scepticism could be developed.[13] More recently Marcel Conche calls Montaigne's scepticism "radical and universal."[14] But Richard Popkin, the historian of scepticism, responding explicitly to Copleston's account, outdoes all Pascal's other defenders. "The occurrence of Montaigne's revitalization of the Pyrrhonism of Sextus Empiricus," Popkin says,

coming at a time when the intellectual world of the sixteenth century was collapsing, made the "nouveau Pyrrhonisme" of Montaigne not the blind alley that historians like Copleston ... have portrayed, but one of the crucial forces in the formation of modern thought. By extending the implicit sceptical tendencies of the Reformation crisis, the humanistic crisis, and the scientific crisis, into a total *crise pyrrhonienne*, Montaigne's genial *Apologie* became the *coup de grâce* to an entire intellectual world. It was also to be the womb of modern thought.[15]

Popkin's reading of Montaigne also meets with criticism, however, especially from those who base their judgment more on what Terence Cave has called Montaigne's mode of "presentation" than on the "content" of the *Essays*.[16] These commentators see Montaigne's eclectic form of writing less as an endorsement of Pyrrhonism than as "a movement of transvaluation that allows one to hold successively, in the same trajectory of thought, two or more radically different attitudes."[17] This volatility of thought, which they think became possible in the sixteenth-century context, was consistent even with a denial of Pyrrhonism itself.[18] In the light of such an understanding of the *Essays*, Richard Scholar accuses Popkin of draining Montaigne's encounter with Pyrrhonism of its adventure, straightening out the twists and turns it takes, and subduing "its antiperistatic volatility."[19] Only with caution, therefore, can we use Popkin's Montaigne as a bridge to Pascal's critique of scepticism.[20]

There seems to be, then, a Montaigne who is too sceptical for Pascal – sceptical of scepticism itself – and another who is not sceptical enough, because he entertains some dogmatic positions as seriously as he does Pyrrhonism. Fortunately, for present purposes, it is not necessary to come to any conclusion about how to read Montaigne. It is enough to remember that he figures as a *type* in Pascal's writings and to pay attention to what Pascal took from him and what he left aside.

Academic sceptics, as already mentioned, were too close to dogmatism to count as sceptics for Pascal. They forfeited his interest by recognizing some doctrines as more probable than others. According to Cicero, they "allow some things to be 'probable' and almost like truth, and ... this provides them with a rule in the conduct of life as well as in inquiry and discussion."[21]

Pyrrhonian sceptics, on the other hand, insist on what they call *isostheneia* or "equipollence," according to which for every argument with the conclusion *p* there is always an equally good argument with the conclusion *not-p*. If follows, then, that no proposition can be preferred to its negation on grounds of probability. And therefore, more generally, no proposition is more probable than any other.[22]

It is no more probable that I am alive as I write these words than that I am dead, if the doctrine of equipollence is correct. It is no more probable that you are reading these words than that you are not. No doubt you will say that the doctrine of equipollence is what is improbable here. If you are a dogmatic philosopher, then that is what you are bound to say.

Pascal disagrees. He took particular delight in Montaigne's way of expressing equipollence, believing it so clever that it would frustrate dogmatic criticism altogether. And not only that. It wins this immunity to criticism by being so extreme that it cannot even be weighed on normal scales of probability. How did Montaigne accomplish such wonders?

First, he avoided expressing equipollence as a doctrine. Doctrines are too much like dogmatism and are not in vogue with sceptics. Better yet, for Montaigne equipollence is not even a proposition. He expressed it instead as a visual image and proclaimed it in the form of a coat of arms.[23]

The genius of the thing, Pascal tells his spiritual director, M. de Saci, shows Montaigne to be a "pur pyrrhonien."[24] The device he displayed on his proposed escutcheon was *a balanced scale*, and its accompanying motto was no affirmation but a question.

"Que sais-je?" is the unsettling provocation on Montaigne's coat of arms: "what do I *know*?" With that, Pascal says, "[Montaigne] quietly evacuates all that passes among men for most certain. His object is not at all to establish any contrary thing with certainty, for he is the enemy of certitude. He only wishes to show that, appearances being equal on all sides, no one knows where to bestow his belief."[25]

If sceptics promise their followers nothing in the way of knowledge, how did they attract followers in the first place? They did it by offering something else that was in high demand. Sceptics told their disciples that once scepticism becomes a habit of the intellect, it releases the mind from heavy burdens and gives it rest. The selling point of scepticism, according to Sextus Empiricus, is that it leads us "first into a state of suspense (*epoche*) and at last into *ataraxia*," which literally means a mind free of trouble.[26] Once we realize that reason cannot answer the questions that trouble it, including those rooted most deeply in human existence, we can come to view our former concerns and vexations as mere shadows in the world of appearances, and so find rest for our souls.

Pascal believed such peace of mind was unachievable in the present life. Moreover for his dialectical purposes, he needed a scepticism that fell short of providing it and thought he found that in Montaigne. As Pascal read him, Montaigne settled for a lesser, but more realistic, kind of mental quiescence. To Saci, Pascal describes it as "naive, familiar, pleasant, jolly." He quotes Montaigne himself as saying that "ignorance and incuriosity are two soft pillows for a well-made head," meaning that the only answer to the weakness of reason lies in taking our shift-less ease, but does not entail achieving a mental quietude of intrinsic value.[27]

It is likely that Pascal represents Montaigne's outlook as bleaker than it was,[28] a distortion that may involve more than just massaging a particular sceptic into the shape required for him to represent the entire Pyrrhonian *type*. The suspicion that Pascal is somehow underestimating his adversaries has occurred to more than one commentator. At bottom, the question is whether he appreciated the tectonic shift towards *secularization*, whose first alarming tremors prompted the writing of Pascal's apology.[29]

Pascal's vantage point was, after all, not an ideal one. Huge and prolonged social, religious, and intellectual transformations, such as secularization involved, are not best viewed from the beginning. But that was where Pascal stood, and he responded to what he feared as much as to what he saw. To that historically limited perspective most of what may strike us as distortions in Pascal's characterization of unbelief could be attributed. But I shall stress the far more important, even astonishing, degree to which such condescension is unnecessary – the uncanny way in which Pascal's response to nascent secularism remains admissible in later contexts, including our own.

On an interim basis, however, and merely for the sake of argument, let us take Pascal's picture of Montaigne as we find it, with whatever private reservations we think necessary. Montaigne is made to represent all of scepticism and especially its negatives. That will allow the other champion – the one Pascal appoints for dogmatism – to represent philosophy's affirmations.

If finding a single representative of scepticism was difficult, what will it be like to find one for the limitless field of dogmatic philosophy? Dogmatism is the logical complement of scepticism. It includes every philosophical position scepticism leaves out. How can he find a single figure to represent *that*?

In a general way, the answer is he cannot. We will not understand his choice of a dogmatic champion unless we agree once again to see it from the point of view of the literary and dialectical purpose it serves. Montaigne's scepticism swallows all the purported achievements of reason, both theoretical and practical, in "universal doubt."[30] Pascal wants a dogmatic champion who stands up bravely for certainty and knowledge. The dogmatist he is looking for will have the highest possible regard for reason. He will say that through the exercise of reason we can arrive at the most recondite truths about God, man, and the world while also achieving perfect contentment of spirit.

In the light of these constraints upon his search, it is not surprising that Pascal chose a Stoic to represent dogmatic philosophy, for Stoics are the historic enemies of scepticism. In theory he might have chosen an Epicurean philosopher, but Pascal scarcely expresses any opinion about them.[31] And outside of Hellenistic philosophy, it would be difficult to find one with a sufficiently high opinion of philosophy's practicality, even its self-sufficiency, to suit Pascal's purposes.

Nevertheless in this case, as in the case of scepticism, even if we allow Pascal the unusual liberty of appointing a champion dogmatist, whomever he settles on is bound to seem controversial to historians of philosophy. He chooses neither the Greek fathers of Stoicism, Zeno of Citium or Chrysippus, nor their famous Roman descendants such as Marcus Aurelius or Seneca. Pascal seems to have known Stoicism mainly through another late Roman representative, though one who expressed himself in Greek, Epictetus.

Like Socrates, Epictetus wrote nothing. Unlike Socrates, however, he had a secretary who composed what purport to be transcriptions of Epictetus's actual conversations, and also a brief summary of his principal teachings.[32] These Pascal read in a French translation, and they seemed to him to put the case for dogmatic philosophy as well as it can be put.

Any choice of champion would narrow the field. The question is whether this particular choice is a travesty of it, as might at one time have been thought. "For much of the nineteenth and twentieth centuries," A.A. Long tells us, "Epictetus was not a central figure. He was largely treated as a Stoic popularizer, lacking depth and creativity."[33] But things have changed. Long argues that Epictetus deserves the more exalted status he enjoyed prior to the nineteenth century as "an author, stylist, educator and thinker" who deserves to be read alongside Socrates and Plato.[34] Epictetus's continuing ability to function as a guide to the perplexed even in situations of direst tribulation has recently been documented in a memoir by Vice-Admiral James B. Stockdale and imaginatively portrayed by Tom Wolfe in his novel *A Man in Full.*[35]

If there is to be a champion for dogmatism, then, Epictetus is at least not a travesty. But neither can he be taken to do justice to the field. Pascal realizes this. In fact, Epictetus is a figurehead behind whom other dogmatists are barely concealed. Perceptive readers have noted that the most serious dogmatist of Pascal's time, Descartes, is often the target more than Epictetus is, especially when it comes to the purely theoretical pretensions of reason.[36]

Whatever weaknesses it may have, Pascal's way of abbreviating the history of philosophy as a contest between two champions makes a good point of entry into his thought. In Pascal's eyes, philosophy is a battle in which every person must take sides. I already cited something he says to that effect in the *Pensées*, but we find the same idea in the "Conversation with M. de Saci":

> I cannot hide from you, Sir, that in reading [Montaigne] and comparing him with Epictetus I have found them to be assuredly the two greatest defenders of the two most famous sects in the world. They are the only ones conformable to reason, because we have no other choice than to take one of these two routes.[37]

## The Boast of Dogmatism

According to Sextus Empiricus, you are a dogmatist if you think you know something. We all think that, of course, unless we're sceptics. It's the healthy outlook on the world of ordinary men and women, as common as cabbage and as uninteresting to most philosophers.

Pascal is interested, though. Not only does he agree we know things, he believes there are things we can't avoid knowing. They're instinctive in character and arise from what he famously calls *the heart*. Heart and instinct are the foundations on which the whole edifice of reason is erected, though reason often fails to perceive its dependency on them, or even denies it.[38] The knowledge these foundations supply is not just trivial either. Through the heart we know God; through it we also know all that is axiomatic in the sciences or intuitively felt about the world.[39]

Heart knowledge is therefore both significant and impossible to set aside. Its weakness is that it has no unassailable theoretical defenses. That's why the sceptic is dangerous. He has powerful criticisms, and he aims them like arrows at the dogmatist's heart. The criticisms hit home often enough for him to be declared the winner of the tournament of champions ... at least in theory.

In practice, though, things look different. In their ordinary lives sceptics find themselves under the humiliating necessity of imitating the behaviour of the same simple dogmatists to whom they feel theoretically superior. Sceptics may be giants in argument, but ordinary life cuts them down to size. When it comes to preparing a meal, for example, reason gives the sceptic no certain grounds for preferring meat to manure. Yet unless he wants to be a dead sceptic, he has to act as if he knew which was better. Hence he regulates his behaviour according to the habits and following the customs of ordinary people, just as he would if he were acting from what ordinary people call knowledge.[40] For that reason, the sceptic's rejection of laymen's dogmatism looks hypocritical.

So laymen's dogmatism looks good again, even if it has no unassailable argument in its favour. Pascal, no sceptic, has nothing against it. He praises "simple people" who believe without reasoning, God having inclined their hearts.[41] What he dislikes, and what makes him lean towards scepticism, is the incautious dogmatism of *philosophers*. He is critical of philosophers who believe there is plenty of truth to be found and for whom truth is also instrumental to attractive things that lie beyond it. The most tantalizing of these attractions are godlike felicity on the one hand and godlike power on the other.

That is where the dogmatists' champion, Epictetus, comes in. As Pascal paraphrases him to Saci, Epictetus holds "that man can, by his own strength (*puissances*), know God perfectly, love him, obey him, please him, cure himself of all his vices, acquire all the virtues, make himself holy, and so become a friend and companion of God."[42] And again in the *Pensées*, Pascal has Epictetus say, "lift up your eyes to God ... behold the one whom you resemble and who made you to worship him ... Wisdom will make you his equal, if you are willing to follow him. Free men, lift up your heads."[43]

Neither to Saci nor in the *Pensées* is Pascal misrepresenting the Stoic philosopher. The words he uses are either Epictetus's own or a faithful paraphrase of them.[44] What, then, does this position amount to?

Moral perfectionism is what Epictetus chiefly has in mind. The mental rest called *ataraxia* – moral perfection's fruit – beckons seductively from every page. Pascal denies we can find such peace of mind and writes against it. When he does so, Epictetus is the philosopher he has in view, though sceptics and Epicureans could have been attacked for the same thing.

But what about intellectual perfectionism? Though not explicitly mentioned in the attributions to Epictetus I just quoted, it surely must be part of the package. Can we know God perfectly and lack other knowledge? Does one who acquires all virtues lack the intellectual ones?

Intellectual perfectionism is implicit in Epictetus all right, but Pascal is not thinking of him when he comes to criticize it. Epictetus represents generic dogmatism, but the supreme intellectual perfectionist, the target of Pascal's criticisms, especially in the *Pensées*, is, as I have already mentioned, Descartes. Sometimes Pascal leaves us in no doubt about whom he means, as comes out so well in a note to himself included in the *Pensées*: "Write against those who go too deeply into the sciences. Descartes."[45]

People today are likely to side with Pascal on this point. Descartes's giddy confidence in science is at best a relic of his age, at worst an embarrassment. We don't need help from Pascal to view it with caution. Recall, for example, the famous passage in the *Discourse on Method*, just after Descartes presents his four-step methodology. He directs our gaze upward to the bright future of science and writes:

> Those long chains of reasoning, simple and effortless, which geometers habitually use to arrive at their most difficult demonstrations, prompted me to imagine that all things knowable by men are inter-connected in the same way. And so, provided we abstain from receiving anything as true that is not so, and provided we always maintain the order necessary for deducing one thing from another, there can be nothing so distant, that we will not ultimately get to it, nor so hidden that it will not be discovered.[46]

You can still find science boosters who talk that way. But few informed readers today would feel confident of the linear model of scientific development Descartes takes for granted, or of the completeness and consistency he supposes even the largest systems of knowledge to be capable of.

But these reservations are mild compared to those that would greet Descartes's still more flamboyant hopes for science, which he unveils near the end of the *Discourse*, where he is trying to win new collaborators for his project. Prospective colleagues are promised that if science is well conducted, it could make them "like masters and possessors of nature," shower them with "an infinity of inventions," and allow them to enjoy without effort the fruits and commodities of the earth, curing unnumbered maladies of mind and body and even, perhaps, the debility of old age.[47]

Those are heady words; Descartes is an accomplished stylist; and no one doubts the sincerity of the hope with which he is imbued. Yet he rarely transmits much of it to contemporary readers. Why not?

No doubt we are partly at fault. Like spoiled children, we take for granted the almost miraculous way in which the promises of science have been kept. Technological and medical wonders are no sooner performed than assumed as entitlements. Failure of imagination can make us as deficient in gratitude as in awe.

But we also have some good reasons to be wary of Cartesian scientism. He can easily come across as "the new Prometheus," the subtitle Mary Shelley gave to her book, *Frankenstein*. At least since the nineteenth century, we have been aware of Frankenstein's shadow on the sunny uplands of science. It has been our mixed fortune to live through the fulfilment of what, for Descartes, were only dreams. We are aware of the inevitable costs that reduce the benefits of science. He never guessed there were any. We have seen nuclear bombs as well as nuclear energy, polluting effluents as well as efficient mass production, busts and booms. We know how often "a bliss in proof is proved a very woe."

In a word, we are unresponsive to Descartes's dogmatic fantasies because we have learned to regard them as utopian. Knowing Pascal is critical of them makes Pascal sound modern to our ears, while Descartes and Epictetus in this respect seem dated. But it would be a mistake to get too cozy with Pascal. His criticisms of utopian dogmatism are different from ours and go deeper. They are not born of the historical hindsight we possess. Pascal grew suspicious of moral and scientific utopias not by witnessing their repeated failures but a priori, by reflecting on the corrosive questions of the sceptics. He uses these questions to blow up the whole edifice of dogmatic utopianism.

## Sceptical Questions

In the "Conversation with M. de Saci," Pascal tries to overcome some of the wariness with which his spiritual advisor approaches Montaigne. Pascal would like to persuade Saci that Montaigne is worth reading even for Christians. He's worth it, Pascal thinks, because he vindicates something Christians believe. Montaigne shows how unfounded are the judgements of those who "voluntarily strip themselves of all revelation" and so abandon themselves "to their own natural lights."[48] In other words, Montaigne makes us aware of how untrustworthy human understanding becomes when its only guiding star is reason.

True, more is offered Saci than only Montaigne. Just as other dogmatists were represented by Epictetus, so, as Richard Scholar points out, in this place Pascal uses Montaigne to represent the whole field of scepticism, including that of Descartes in the *Meditations* and even of

Pascal himself.[49] Pascal assembles the whole arsenal of scepticism for his assault on those who overvalue reason.

Later in the seventeenth century, bumptious scientistic people would be called "strong minded" (*esprits forts*), a name that reflected simultaneously their high opinion of themselves and the different opinion others understandably formed about them. "Do these strong-minded ones," La Bruyère would ask in 1688, "not realize we call them so ironically?"[50]

Self-knowledge is still not universal among the learned, however. A group of contemporary philosophers and scientists has recently taken to calling themselves "the brights," not suspecting their name might likewise evoke more amusement than awe.[51] Pascal has much to say against such people, but he gives them no particular name. He almost used the term *esprit fort*, but never did.[52] Since the target of his criticism is overreliance on reason, I shall simply call their point of view *rationalism*.

What Pascal finds so impressive in Montaigne's critique of rationalism is his thorough scrutiny of its first principles. First he winkles those principles out of rationalism, Pascal says approvingly, and then examines all of them.[53] Naturally Pascal doesn't go into all the details of Montaigne's lengthy and colourful investigations. He contents himself with a representative selection of about two dozen of the main questions Montaigne poses, selecting those that are so well formed as to leave Saci in little doubt about the answers.

The bulk of the questions concerns philosophical psychology, a natural place to begin because it is the mind[54] rationalists take to be so powerful. Does the mind know itself, Montaigne asks. Does it know its body? If it is material, how can it reason, and how can it be united to its body, if it is not material? Does the mind make errors? If so, how can it know that it does, since making them presupposes not knowing they are errors, and since falsehoods are as firmly believed as truths?

Other questions concern epistemology. They are very basic, but not for that reason easy to answer. Montaigne asks whether, in the strong sense demanded by rationalism, we know anything, and whether we can define the truth we say we know in a way that is universally acceptable. Since neither is the case, he inquires how we can know whether we have ever grasped anything true.

He also raises awkward metaphysical questions such as what matter is, whether substance, accident, body, and spirit are exhaustive categories of being, and whether, since any definition we propose for the concept of *being* must inevitably be a circular one, we can properly be said to understand what being *is*.

Next, what we now call philosophy of science is given a short, stiff examination. Montaigne is curious whether rationalists think they can define space or motion or unity or time in such a way as to win universal acceptance. He also wonders whether they can prove that the propositions they adopt as axioms are true. Few readers will anticipate any but negative answers to these questions.

Even humble common sense – just in case any rationalist dares elevate that to the level of philosophy – comes in for scrutiny. Montaigne asks whether unaided reason can teach us what health or sickness or life or death or good or evil or justice or sin are. And since it is plain that no one possesses knowledge of these matters through reason alone, rationalists must be impostors, if they pretend otherwise.

Summing up Montaigne's attack on reason, Pascal says he,

> examines all the sciences and geometry as profoundly as can be, disclosing the uncertainty in its axioms and undefined terms, such as extension, motion, etc. Physics even more thoroughly. Medicine in an infinite number of ways. And the same with history, politics, morality, law and the rest. In the end we remain convinced that, apart from revelation, we wouldn't know whether we were dreaming or not. For we think no more clearly in our present state than in some of our dreams. Or is life itself a dream, from which we awaken only at our death, and which, while it continues, allows as feeble a grasp of true principles as we have during ordinary sleep?
>
> This is how Montaigne devours reason so thoroughly and cruelly, when it is divorced from faith ... giving it no room to act except to recognize its weakness in sincere humility, instead of exalting itself in stupid insolence.[55]

## Failure

The sceptic wins this round in his struggle with dogmatism, but, as we have seen, his victory appears in an ambiguous light. The sceptic crushes everything except what he set out to destroy – the dogmatist's cheerful assurance that he knows. Sceptical arguments may conquer rationalism, Pascal points out, but they have no effect upon that dogged grasp of intuitive and axiomatic things Pascal attributes to the heart. In the *Pensées'* most famous one-liner, "the heart has its reasons that reason knows not of."[56] An elegant epigram puts it this way: "No dogmatism can overcome our powerlessness in supplying proofs; yet our idea of the truth can never be conquered by Pyrrhonism."[57]

Each champion is thus successful in his own way – the dogmatist in preserving heart-knowledge, the sceptic in undermining reason. But trouble arises when we try to combine them in the same category: philosophy. That is the next point Pascal wants us to see.

We must combine scepticism and dogmatism, of course, if we are to understand the historic meaning of philosophy, which has always involved sceptical inquiry into dogmatism on the one hand and dogmatic resistance to scepticism on the other. But according to Pascal, those two activities do not fit together, and any attempt to bring them together fails. In a word, he thinks philosophy fails. The discipline Cicero called "the guide to life, the explorer of virtue, the expeller of vice, the concern without which human life amounts to nothing,"[58] fails. That great good thing, taken as a whole, proves unwholesome even to itself. It consumes itself, leaving only dust and ashes. Philosophy fails because it consists both of arguments and refutations of arguments, each of which succeeds only in making the other fail. How did it come to this?

As Pascal presents them, Montaigne and Epictetus each stand for everything the other does not, each representing half of what philosophy is. Together they account for the entire field – unfortunately a field of failure.

Pascal's critique contains an important logical dimension. Scepticism and dogmatism bear the relation to each other that a predicate bears to its complement, or logical contrary. Pascal exploits that analogy in presenting the logical character of the standoff to Saci.[59] It is natural for Pascal to draw on the logic of terms as a device to help Saci, since every educated person of his day would understand it. It is less useful to readers today, because the logic of terms is less studied. So I shall make explicit some of the logical points on which Pascal's argument depends.[60]

Term negation is narrower in scope than sentential negation and is an important element of the logic of terms. For present purposes, however, just three points about term negation are essential. The first is that a term bears to its complement the same relation of *mutual exclusion* as we have seen scepticism and dogmatism bear to each other. For example, nothing can be both red and non-red (where non-red means being either some other colour than red, or else colourless).

The second essential point about terms and their complements is that, jointly, they account for the whole of what modern term logicians call a *category* of things. Thus, the disjunctive predicate "red or non-red" applies to everything we can sensibly say to be coloured. In the same way, Pascal understands sceptics and dogmatists between them to account for the whole category of what, in the Conversation with Saci, he calls *philosophy*.

The third logical point with application here is that some categories include others. Thus, the category of things mathematical includes the category of things prime(in the mathematical sense) but is not included by it. Diagrams, for example, may be mathematical, but it would be a category mistake to call them prime or non-prime.

Now each of these features of the logic of terms helps in understanding the philosophical significance of Pascal's tournament of champions. Sceptics and nonsceptics (or dogmatists) divide the category of philosophy between them. But unlike such terms as *red* and *non-red*, they do not peacefully coexist. They cannot coexist, because philosophy is not merely a concept. It is an activity. Dogmatists and sceptics interact. They criticize one another. They are at war, each succeeding in demonstrating the untenability of the other. In Pascal's colourful words, "[Dogmatism and scepticism] smash and annihilate each other."[61] Each half of philosophy is proved defective by the other, and they are jointly incoherent. Philosophy is an inconsistent whole made of untenable parts. That is the *logical reason* why philosophy is a failure and needs to be transcended.

In the second place, scepticism and dogmatism, like any term and its complement, jointly exhaust the category of philosophy. Therefore, when they destroy one another, as Pascal says they must, there is nothing left of philosophy. The disparaging remarks about philosophy and philosophers that Pascal will scatter throughout the *Pensées*,[62] and that many interpret as a rejection of philosophy in any form, are grounded in this implosion of the *category* to which traditional philosophy belongs.

It is on the basis of that categorial collapse that Pascal draws a conclusion gratifying to M. de Saci but alienating to many of his readers. Dogmatism and scepticism "smash and annihilate one another," we have just seen him say. But he continues, *"in doing so they make room for the truth of the Gospel"* (my italics).[63]

"Sometimes there is God *too* quickly," we might say, with apologies to Tennessee Williams. God's abrupt appearance in the Conversation with Saci presents a challenge to anyone attempting to understand

Pascal as a philosopher. Some commentators take it as evidence that Pascal intended to abandon philosophy and turn to religious thought.[64] And the logical character of the argument I have depicted so far seems to warrant that interpretation: philosophy is the volatile combination of scepticism and dogmatism. They consume each other. Maybe religion is all that's left. Despite the prima facie plausibility of that reading, however, there are good reasons to resist it.

First, there is a problem of self-reference. What kind of argument is Pascal making in the tournament of champions? How should we classify it? Is it not recognizably philosophical? It is based, as I have shown, on the logic of terms and is concerned with the nature of philosophy itself. But no philosophical argument can refute philosophy, any more than there can be a sound argument in English proving that the English language does not exist. At best it can refute parts of philosophy, which is the most Pascal can be said to have achieved.

Second, Pascal's words to Saci are less dismissive of philosophy than people tend to think on first reading. He says that scepticism and dogmatism smash and destroy one another, making way for the truth of the Gospel. But he does not say their destruction *establishes* the truth of the Gospel. Establishing it is what Pascal intended to do in the *Pensées*,[65] which he conceived as an apology for Christianity. He wanted to win non-Christians over to Christianity by making them think it offered the most reasonable and also the most attractive explanation of their lives and of the world. That project seems to me to involve philosophy, as does Pascal's assurance that he is not looking for "blind faith."[66]

You may ask how in Pascal's own terms the larger project of the *Pensées* could be philosophical, when it presupposes the literary reenactment of philosophy's self-destruction in the form of the tournament of champions. The point is a good one, but it is only terminological, not conceptual. It is only about the word 'philosophy'.

Recall the third point I mentioned about the logic of terms – namely, the possibility of broader categories containing narrower ones. That possibility can explain how Pascal might still be a philosopher, even though he accepts the result of the tournament of champions. For there may be a category wide enough to include scepticism, dogmatism, and something more – something not reducible to the first two elements. I think there is such a category, and in English, if I wanted a neutral name, I would call it 'inquiry.' When Pascal speaks about it, he often uses the verb *chercher*, as when he calls those people who have not found God "reasonable," provided they spend their lives *inquiring* after him.[67]

These people are reasonable, Pascal says, but they are clearly not rationalists. They accept the outcome of the tournament of champions. Therefore, they do not expect proof of God's existence, nor will they be deterred by philosophical arguments for his nonexistence. There may very well be some valid sceptical arguments or some true dogmas left behind in the debris after the dust of the tournament settles. But they will not distract inquirers like these. Those who understand the implications of the tournament have lost their relish for what once seemed to them to be philosophy. The kind of inquiry they now pursue is neither sceptical nor dogmatic. They seek reasons for believing Christianity true, and they do so because they have come to *hope* that Christianity is true. They see that their happiness depends on its being so, and they want to discover it to be so indeed. Once sinners recover from their blindness, Pascal says, they "begin to search for the true good."[68] Traditional philosophy sets out in that direction, but never arrives.[69] Those who discover the root of philosophy's failure have no alternative but to become post-philosophical inquirers. There is a quick preview of where the argument of this book is going.

**The Scope of Failure**

Just how troubled should we expect philosophers to be by the tournament of champions, even if we admit it to be formally valid according to the logic of terms? They might, of course, quibble about the reduction of all philosophy to a choice between Montaigne and Epictetus. But when Montaigne and Epictetus are considered as types, that reason for disregarding the tournament falls away. It then has sufficient generality to be troubling.

Still, it is difficult to imagine any professor of philosophy thrown into an existential crisis by reading the Conversation with Saci. Philosophers will not resign their positions in philosophy departments or burn their philosophical libraries. Even unstable people are unlikely to resort to suicide. It is easy even to imagine a philosopher chuckling over Pascal's demonstration of the futility of his discipline, accepting the argument against it as valid and possibly sound, and then wondering where to go for lunch.

Such readers would be rationally inexplicable, but they are still easy to imagine. The psychology of their position is quite transparent. Even if the argument as I presented it looked sound, it will be unpersuasive because it seems incommensurate with the object it is trying to displace.

Surely no argument so brief, and no logic so thin, can undo a discipline as old and venerable as philosophy. Pascal's argument may fail to persuade not for lack of logical cogency but for lack of what I will call *mass*.

When candidate arguments present themselves before the court of our mind, asking to be believed, they may or may not be equipped with mass. They possess it when they are not only intuitively clear and plausible but also anchored in the assumptions and practices of ordinary life and connected to habitual pathways of thought. We easily bestow belief upon arguments that are in tune with our established convictions and conventions. Arguments that do not fit in so easily, however, lack mass and are unlikely to be believed. Pascal's tournament of champions is paradigmatically lacking in mass.

On the other hand, it is more cunningly constructed than most unpersuasive arguments. It is designed to prosper without mass. For if the tournament of champions fails, it will then serve to illustrate another of the fundamental weaknesses of traditional philosophy that greatly interested Pascal: the fact that proof has no necessary connection with persuasion. If philosophers read with indifference Pascal's argument against philosophy, their attitude illustrates by other means what the tournament set out to prove: that philosophy fails. Pascal's allegation of philosophical failure is thus in the happy position of either being proved by his argument or evidenced by its failure.

Arguments for the existence of God exhibit the same gap between proof and persuasion, according to Pascal. Suppose there were a sound argument for the existence of God. Even the few people sufficiently well trained to recognize it as demonstrative will wonder, an hour after working through to its conclusion, whether they have not been deceived.[70]

Pascal may be the first nonsceptic to argue for philosophical failure, but he is not the only one to do so. Some contemporary philosophers have independently taken up the same line of reflection. A few years ago Robert Nozick introduced the subject as a way of motivating a kinder, gentler approach to philosophy, which he called "philosophical explanation." The kind and gentle part, at least, struck a nerve. It soon became, if not the dominant philosophical attitude among Anglo-American philosophers, at least the cool one.

What Nozick wanted to get rid of was what he called "coercive philosophy."[71] Not only was it overbearing, and therefore uncouth; he also found it pointless. After all, Nozick mockingly asked, how much coercion can we philosophers really exert? Anyone who doesn't mind hearing us call him irrational is free to reject our soundest arguments.

Nozick shames coercive philosophers even further by making us aware of violent wishes we conceal behind apparently peaceful poker faces. "Wouldn't it be better if philosophical arguments left the person no possible answer at all," we are presumed to wonder. "Perhaps philosophers need arguments so powerful they set up reverberations in the brain: if the person refuses to accept the conclusion he *dies*. How's that for a powerful argument?"[72]

Nozick thinks we should abandon our sanguinary daydreams and resign ourselves to a more amiable philosophy that only seeks to *explain*. Like Pascal, he thinks coercive philosophy is a failure.

Peter van Inwagen has recently taken what he calls "the depressing topic of philosophical failure"[73] one step further. He begins the third of his Gifford Lectures on the problem of evil by announcing that, when it comes to substantive philosophical questions, "[t]he idea that there are proofs in philosophy as there are proofs in mathematics is ridiculous," though he concedes that it is, nevertheless, "an all but irresistible idea."[74] What makes it irresistible is that, *pace* Nozick, we have no other way of writing philosophy than in the form of purported proofs.[75] What makes it ridiculous is that none of our proofs is any good.

It sounds rash to say that no philosophical argument is any good, so let us consider the evidence. Suppose, for example, we were to say that a philosophical argument would be considered a success if it starts with premises almost no sane, rational person would doubt, and proceeds by logical steps whose validity almost no sane, rational person would dispute, to the conclusion that *p*. If we said that, we would have a nice strong definition of philosophical success. It is just that by that definition, van Inwagen points out, "almost no argument for any philosophically substantive thesis would count as a success."[76]

Why not? Because we philosophers know that "leaving aside those philosophical theses that almost everyone would accept *without argument*, there are no philosophical theses that are both substantive and uncontroversial."[77] The most likely explanation for that discouraging fact is that our arguments are unconvincing.

It will not be necessary to follow van Inwagen through the progressively weaker definitions for success, which he considers in an effort to find one that would allow for philosophical success. For even if we adopted one of them, which he shows we cannot, there would still be no substantive arguments about which almost all philosophers agree, and therefore there would still be none we could uncontrovertibly hold up as a philosophical success story.

One of my teachers used to say that the purpose of philosophy was to replace opinion with knowledge. (I think he may have got that from Plato.) The vehicle by which we try to accomplish this task, he would tell us, is argument. It is a pleasing, muscular view of philosophy. But my teacher was not aware of the rebuke to that picture van Inwagen represents. For if none of our arguments succeeds, then the vehicle of rational argument has flat tires and is out of gas. And that means philosophy is a failure. It is a melancholy thought, as van Inwagen notes, but Pascal recorded it first.

The doubts about the cogency of philosophical argument neatly expressed by van Inwagen and Nozick help to make intelligible the idea that Pascal's argument in the tournament of champions could be sound and yet fail to convince. But a historical example of philosophical failure will make the point clearer still.

## The Ontological Argument

What I have in mind is a substantive philosophical argument of great longevity, one that is often studied as a paradigm of philosophical reasoning and "finds new defenders among the ablest thinkers in every generation."[78] The so-called ontological argument for the existence of God may be able to teach us some of the practicalities of philosophical failure, whose theory Pascal and van Inwagen have led us to consider.

### Anselm's Version

Saint Anselm first propounded the ontological argument in the *Proslogion*.[79] Although the full presentation ran to seven or eight pages, the core of it went like this:

> If that than which a greater can never be thought can be thought not to be, that very thing than which a greater can never be thought is not that than which a greater can never be thought, which is unthinkable.[80]

Admittedly, the argument appears on first reading to be a caricature of medieval reasoning: a brain buster and tongue twister combined. It looks as if, as soon as the grammar is untangled, it will be easy to discover its fallacy. Closer attention, however, brings a careful reader face to face with a shocking lucidity to which reason tamely surrenders. Then comes further reflection. The shock and awe wear off, and the reader smiles again. It is not the amusing fallacy he first took it for, but it now amuses in a new way: the ontological argument is a fascinating logical conjuring trick: pulling the greatest conceivable rabbit out of a merely conceptual hat.

I will not linger over the many excellences of Anselm's version, but fast-forward to two of its weaknesses. They led subsequent philosophers first to criticize the argument, then to amend it.

Anselm's proof turns on the idea of a being than which no greater can be thought. But that idea goes beyond what the bare logic of the argument requires in two ways. In the first place, it raises metaphysical questions about God's greatness that turn out to be irrelevant to the argument's logical success. Second, it introduces irrelevant psychological questions about what we human beings can and cannot conceive of.[81]

## Descartes's Version

Descartes's most elegant statement of the ontological argument, as of so much else, is found in his *Meditations*. There he streamlined Anselm's version by avoiding the psychological question of what can be thought. He also made structural changes to the argument, transforming it into a syllogism. In the major premise Descartes replaced Anselm's subjective notion of conceivability by a more concrete principle of *conceptual analysis*. Descartes's new principle proved to be so plausible to his contemporaries that it soon was accepted as axiomatic.[82] The principle-cum-major premise runs as follows:

> Consider how I have only to draw an idea of any given thing from my thought and it follows that everything I clearly and distinctly perceive to belong to that thing really does belong to it.[83]

Why do I call Descartes's principle more concrete than Anselm's? You might say that Descartes does not escape from the psychology of conceivability at all, but only replaces it with an equally subjective appeal to what is clear and distinct. But consider it another way. We often have the linguistic competence to know whether concept C entails or does not entail C' without fully grasping, the concept C. You needn't be expert in jurisprudence or ethics, for example, to know that justice is good.

The principle Descartes is proposing is psychologically modest because it demands of us only ordinary linguistic competence of that kind. It is nevertheless powerful. In the simplest terms it says that:

> Whatever the idea of X clearly and distinctly implies about X can be said about X itself.

Is such a principle reliable? Descartes explains it by means of a well-chosen example. Suppose you are thinking about triangles. It follows, according to Descartes's principle, that *the things* you are thinking of, triangles, have all the properties you clearly and distinctly perceive them to have. So, for example, if you clearly and distinctly perceive triangles to have interior angles equal to two right angles, then triangles really have interior angles equal to two right angles and you are therefore entitled to say so. And that seems right.

The example was well chosen because it holds whether or not any material object ever was perfectly triangular. Let triangles be spatiotemporal objects or merely conceptual beings or inhabitants of a Platonic heaven. In each case, we are entitled to affirm about triangles whatever is clearly and distinctly implicit in the idea of them. The Platonist, the conceptualist, and the physicalist may dispute about the ontological status of triangles, but they agree that triangles have interior angles equal to 180 degrees.

Even clearly nonexistent entities, such as unicorns, are subject to Descartes's principle. For although there has never been a unicorn, we still speak truly if we say that unicorns resemble horses, except in having a single long horn growing from their foreheads.

After stating the principle that will shortly serve as his major premise, Descartes immediately raises the crucial question: "Does that not furnish us with an argument for God's existence?"[84]

The answer is yes. The principle furnishes us with an ontological argument provided we use it as a major premise together with a minor that makes God an instance of it. The required minor premise is carefully formulated and doubly illustrated by Descartes as follows:

> Existence can no more be separated from the essence of God than can the sum of a triangle's three angles equaling two right angles from the essence of a triangle, or than the idea of a mountain can be separated from that of a slope.[85] Thus it is no less[86] absurd to think of God (that is the completely

perfect being) lacking existence (that is, lacking some perfection) than to imagine a mountain lacking a slope.[87]

The principle (major premise) and the application (minor premise) taken together validly yield the conclusion that God exists. For if whatever an idea of a thing entails about it can be truly affirmed of that thing, and if existence truly belongs to the idea of God, then God can truly be affirmed to exist.

How many philosophical arguments have you seen, dear reader, in all the years you have been reading philosophy, as compelling as this one? Very few, if your experience is anything like mine. Many pages would be required to praise it as it deserves. Yet if this argument has ever persuaded anyone not already convinced of its conclusion, his name is lost to history. On the contrary, I am aware of a number of philosophers who did already believe the conclusion and yet were not convinced by the argument. The most interesting one was Leibniz.

*Leibniz's Version*

Leibniz discusses Descartes's ontological argument on many occasions. Though he makes a number of criticisms of it, he is famous for only one of them. That criticism, sometimes wrongly referred to in the singular as his "contribution" to the development of the ontological argument,[88] faults Descartes for failing to prove that the most perfect being is possible.

It is a good point and worthy to be called a contribution. Leibniz thought so, too, to judge by the frequency with which he repeats it. Descartes's argument "is not a fallacy," Leibniz concedes,

> but is an imperfect demonstration which takes for granted something that ought also to have been proved in order to attain to mathematical self-evidence. Its defect is tacitly to take for granted that this idea of a greatest being, or a most perfect being, is possible, and does not imply a contradiction.[89]

On the occasion of writing the words just quoted, Leibniz goes on to give Descartes's version some praise. He is not always so courteous.

In one uncharacteristically grumpy text he leads off with a general objection to all of Cartesian philosophy. It depends, he says, on "the way of ideas," something he dismisses as "a refuge of ignorance."[90] And that leads him to object to Descartes's principle of conceptual analysis in particular. While not contesting the principle's theoretical truth, he thinks it resembles counsels of perfection, empty maxims that tell you what you ought to do but not how to do it. "I see," he writes in his "Meditations on Knowledge, Truth and Ideas":

> that men are no less abused by that principle bandied about in our time – *whatever I clearly and distinctly perceive concerning any thing is true, or assertable of that thing.* For often things that are obscure and confused appear clear and distinct to men who are judging rashly. The axiom is therefore useless, unless *criteria* of what is clear and distinct are brought in.[91]

Descartes's improved version of the ontological argument is not so compelling after all. And it gets worse. Not only does it omit what is necessary (the possibility-proof) and introduce what is useless (the conceptual analysis principle), it also retains one of the chief defects of Anselm's original. Anselm's argument depended on appealing to what is *greatest* (*id quo maius nequit cogitari*) and something like it remains in Descartes's version.

Leibniz notices how Descartes quietly substitutes the most perfect being (*ens summe perfectum*) for Anselm's greatest being.[92] His objection is that the change leads to no improvement. To bring either greatness or perfection into the argument only obscures its logical force:

> [A]n even simpler demonstration could be given by avoiding altogether this talk about perfections. Then we would not be detained by those who would contrive to deny that all perfections are compatible, and, consequently, that the idea in question is even possible.[93]

Anyone who has ever taught the Cartesian version of the ontological argument will recognize that Leibniz's rejection of the notion of perfection is justified on what logicians call *pragmatic* grounds. Pragmatic, in this sense, applies to informal matters affecting the persuasive force of argument. When people encounter Descartes's argument for the first time, they may be delighted (or more often appalled) at its apparent cogency. But their first line of defence against its disturbing conclusion is almost always to raise the question of whether anything can be perfect, or whether perfection has any univocal meaning.

Leibniz is the first proponent of the argument to notice that perfection is a red herring. He also sees how to get the conclusion we want without it. Once you remove all the Cartesian distortions, the argument becomes:

> a modal proposition that [is] one of the best fruits of all Logic, namely that, *if the necessary Being is possible, it exists.*[94]

No praise seems too lavish for Leibniz to bestow on that single modal conditional, so lean in its logical form, so replete with metaphysical consequence. "That is undoubtedly the most beautiful and most important proposition of all modal teachings," he says, "because it permits us to go from potency to act. It is the only place in which moving from possibility to existence is valid."[95]

The ontological argument is not going to get any leaner. Leibniz has reduced it to bare logical bones. And he is right in seeing in it the unique case in which we can move validly from mere possibility to actuality (or, in the technical terms Leibniz borrowed from an earlier age, in which *a posse ad esse valet consequentia*).

We're meant to be startled by that Latin tag. We're to think he misquoted a Scholastic commonplace which runs, of course, "*a posse ad esse non valet consequentia.*" It should *never* be valid to move from possibility to actuality! When Leibniz asserts that there is a special case in which we can move in that direction, it is meant to amaze us. You can't appreciate what is so exciting about the ontological argument unless you know why the possible does not generally imply the actual.

The reason is this. If possibility implies actuality, then possibility can be shown to mean the same thing as actuality, which reduces the assertion to a pointless tautology. Not only that, but if possibility and actuality mean the same thing, then necessity also becomes indistinguishable from either. Modal logic simply collapses into ordinary extensional logic, and the concepts of possibility and necessity are lost in the process.[96] That's why you are not normally allowed to go from possibility to existence.

Yet Leibniz was the first to see you can do so in this special case without causing any logical problems. You can add the statement, *if a necessary being is possible, it exists*, to a system of modal logic without vitiating modal thinking. He's not just right about this, he's right in spades! It's even better than he says. A properly modalized version of Leibniz's proposition[97] – let us call it L – is not just some weak and therefore harmless proposition, the last theorematic gasp of some modal system. On the contrary, L is a system-defining proposition. Taken as an axiom and added to a basic propositional modal logic, L defines the most powerful and useful modal system, the system most reflective of our ordinary modal intuitions, which normally goes by the clunky name of S5.[98]

Now here is a mystery. Leibniz simply could not have known of the formal significance of L for S5, since S5 was not explored and understood before the twentieth century. No formal tools comparable to those we now possess for modal logics were available to Leibniz for investigating L. Yet the correspondence between his ontological argument and S5 is far from coincidental. Both derive from the more basic intuition that possibility and necessity are absolute characteristics of things, not relative to what we are capable of conceiving, nor to any contingent circumstance of our world.[99]

It was exceptionally clever of Leibniz to capture the whole ontological argument in a single modal insight. Everything superfluous in Anselm's and Descartes's versions has now been peeled away. All we need accept is an assertion that can double as a logical axiom. How good is that!

Some say too good to be true. The argument is now so lean and light that it runs into the same problem of *mass* that affected Pascal's tournament of champions. The more you trim the logical form, the less capable it seems of supporting its enormous conclusion. Leibniz's version of the ontological argument looks like a trick, like some illusionist lifting himself by a single hair. The logic is fine. It forces you to say the words "the necessary being exists," but even while you pronounce them, you may be in serious doubt as to whether any necessary being really does exist. You wonder whether instead you have fallen for some undetected fallacy.

What I say about the argument's mass is not conjecture. In an article on Leibniz's system of thought, Jean-Claude Dumoncel ably sketched the connection between S5 and Leibniz's ontological argument about which I have been speaking.[100] But that did not deter another gifted logician, the Thomist Georges Kalinowski, from Thomistically wondering in print whether (a) the S5 version is in the strict sense an *argument* at all and (b) whether, if called an argument in some looser sense, it is not a circular one.[101] He accuses Dumoncel's argument of establishing its conclusion in a way Kalinowski called "weakly analytic." It was circular, Kalinowski said, to go from the weakly analytic truth that a necessary being exists, if it is possible, to the stronger claim that such a being exists in fact, even if it is conceded, as Kalinowski did concede for argument's sake, that a necessary being is possible.[102] Dumoncel replied.[103] But although Kalinowski never to my knowledge responded to that reply, that is no indication that he was satisfied with Dumoncel's answer.

I shall enter no further into the details of the controversy, which, after all, was meant only to serve as an example of philosophical failure. The excruciatingly subtle exchange between two contemporary logicians about Leibniz's absolutely minimalist version of the argument must at least make you wonder whether there is not some merit in the idea of philosophical failure, to which, in different ways, van Inwagen and Pascal point. Arguments for the existence of God, says Pascal, or substantive philosophical arguments of any kind, say both Pascal and van Inwagen, persuade us at best momentarily. In the case of the ontological argument, even when it is stripped of everything inessential and expressed with complete logical rigor as a theorem of S5, and even when the possibility of a necessary being is conceded, the strange insufficiency that has always haunted that argument returns. And if Pascal is right, then the same is true of philosophical argument in general.

Thus, if Pascal's tournament of champions fails to persuade us, then its author cannot be surprised. Why should this substantive argument be more successful than any other in compelling our assent? The only way Pascal can supplement what he has displayed in the tournament is by offering us something resembling what Nozick calls an *explanation* of why arguments fail.

Neither Nozick nor van Inwagen provides such an explanation. Pascal does. He develops a far-reaching account of philosophical failure, rooting it ultimately in his pessimistic theory of the Fall.

# 2 Failure and Fall

You are invited to read a paper to a learned audience. In the opening paragraph you announce the startling proposition you are going to defend. It is controversial, but you state it with brevity, wit, and exceptional clarity. You go on to offer arguments of glasslike transparency in its defence. The logic of your arguments contains no surprises. Every move is as simple and invincible as *modus ponens*. For these reasons, as your talk approaches its conclusion, you must work to suppress a triumphal feeling close to euphoria. You expect the audience to gaze at you some little time with wonder, and then to forsake the conventional discussion period in favour of something resembling a coronation.

Things, however, turn out otherwise. Your audience is unimpressed. The discussion is perfunctory, and there is not a single allusion to your paper in the sparsely attended reception that follows.

I admit to having more than one of these deflating experiences on my résumé. When I was young, I blamed them on my limited grasp of clarity and logical rigour. As I grew older, I began seeing audiences as the culprits. I surrendered to the surly satisfaction that comes from cursing an uncomprehending world. It did not occur to me to wonder whether a lucid, valid argument necessarily produces conviction in its hearer. What *causes* philosophical failure, I should have asked myself, and what does it take to make people believe?

In the previous chapter, Robert Nozick and Peter van Inwagen were enlisted to bring the problem of philosophical failure into focus. But apart from acknowledging it as a "depressing topic" (van Inwagen's term), they leave the matter there. They never connect philosophical failure to the dark landscape of human desolation to which, as Pascal argues, it properly belongs.

Pascal's account of the logic of philosophical failure, outlined in the previous chapter, is only a prologue to exploring its cause and character. His investigation of it goes well beyond what can be learned from Nozick and van Inwagen. Before turning to Pascal, however, it will be useful to gather whatever we can learn about philosophical failure from other places. It will lead to greater appreciation of Pascal's comprehensiveness.

## Confabulation

First there is 'confabulation,' a concept now brandished as a technical term in the gleaming laboratories of philosophers of mind. I have not seen anyone using it to explain philosophical failure, but one has only to encounter the concept to recognize that possibility.

As psychologists, cognitive scientists, neurologists, and other specialists in the philosophy of mind explain it, confabulation is a mental disorder some people exhibit in which, without intending to deceive, they make up explanations that sound rational but are based on insufficient knowledge. It has been characterized as "a sort of pathological certainty about ill-grounded thoughts and utterances."[1] Confabulations resemble lies, except that they are believed by the teller and told without intending to deceive. And they are not like ordinary mistakes either, because the confabulator is in a position to see without difficulty that what he is saying is false.

It does me no credit to admit that the idea of confabulation first interested me for the light I thought it might shed on at least some of my own philosophical failures. If philosophical confabulators had been attending my lectures, what but failure would ensue? They didn't have to be stupid or ornery or opinionated. For my part, I cannot remember speaking to any audience that did not represent an ordinary cross-section of the genteel and sophisticated philosophical profession. But even audiences such as these may be full of confabulators, providing the disposition to confabulate is sufficiently common. It is a hypothesis public lecturers will take to their comfort, even though it would be difficult to offer hard evidence in its favour.

Compelling examples of confabulation can likely only be gathered under clinical conditions. But there, at least, some illuminating ones have been recorded. Among them are confabulations observed in connection with split-brain surgery, an operation performed on some epileptics to lessen the frequency and severity of their seizures.[2] Split-brain surgery partly or wholly severs the connection between the brain's left and right hemispheres. In a normal brain, the two hemispheres specialize in different tasks but pass information back and forth between them in ways that maximize processing power. Splitting the hemispheres limits or interrupts that transfer of information.

For present purposes, what is important is that split-brain patients can often be brought to confabulate. First they are induced to undertake some action through a stimulus to the less verbal (right) hemisphere of their brain. Then the more verbal hemisphere is engaged, and they are asked to account for what they are doing. The results are instructive. M.S. Gazzaniga found, for example,

> "When 'laugh' ... was flashed to the right hemisphere, the subject commenced laughing, and when asked why, said 'Oh, you guys are too much.' When the command 'rub' was flashed, the subject rubbed the back of his head with his left hand. [The left hand is controlled by the right hemisphere. GH] When asked what the command was, he said 'itch' ... When the command is 'walk,' a subject typically pushes her chair from the testing table and starts to walk away. You ask, 'Why are you doing that?' The subject replies, 'Oh, I need to get a drink.'"[3]

On the one hand, such experiments reassure us that we are indeed rational animals, loving to give reasons for what we do. The disturbing thing is that we seem capable of inventing reasons ad hoc, reasons no more authoritative in connection with our own actions than our most flippant conjectures are about the actions of others.

Split-brain subjects are not the only confabulators. The phenomenon has been clinically investigated in connection with syndromes including Alzheimer's disease, schizophrenia, and half a dozen other more exotic afflictions such as Korsakoff's syndrome and anosognosia for hemiplegia.[4] To my knowledge, confabulation has never before been considered in connection with philosophical failure.

You have only to hear confabulation defined, however, to see how it could have a philosophical application. William Hirstein, one of the researchers in the forefront of investigating it, defines confabulation through a set of necessary and jointly sufficient criteria. The same criteria can be applied in a straightforward way to philosophical failure. To set the stage a little, suppose you have just presented a sound, simple, and lucid argument against $p$ to a philosophical audience. Then suppose that Professor Jones, a trained philosopher who has just heard your talk, and whom you know to be an earnest man of settled convictions, rises in the question period to dispute your conclusion.

You will not deny, I suppose, that such scenes have been enacted in the long history of philosophical disputations. Well-argued conclusions have from time to time been challenged by the likes of Professor Jones. Ask yourself, therefore, whether even one of Hirstein's criteria for confabulation fails to apply to Jones.

1. Jones claims that $p$.
2. Jones believes that $p$.
3. Jones is confident that $p$.
4. Jones's thought (that $p$) is ill-grounded.
5. Jones does not know that his thought is ill-grounded.
6. Jones should know that his thought is ill-grounded.[5]

At the risk of being tedious, let me briefly review the points in order. By hypothesis, Jones is denying your conclusion (not-$p$). Therefore, as criterion 1 demands, he is claiming that $p$. It is true that after lectures we sometimes get questions that are merely sceptical about our conclusions, or merely exploring alternative possibilities. But from earnest men of conviction like Jones we get outright denials. Therefore, let Jones be making an outright denial of not-$p$ in this case.

His earnest character implies that he is not merely pretending to believe $p$. He really believes it, so that criterion 2 is also satisfied. And Jones shows he is confident that $p$ (criterion 3) by the fact that he is undertaking to refute you in a public setting.

Serious though he is about $p$, his thought is nevertheless ill-grounded (criterion 4) because, by hypothesis, your argument was sound. The fifth criterion is also met. Jones does not know that his thought (that $p$) is ill-grounded, because if he knew that, he would not believe $p$, which, by criterion 2, he does. Yet he *should* know that his thought is ill-grounded (criterion 6) as the following two considerations show: first, your talk was simple and lucid. Therefore, a trained philosopher like Jones should have had no trouble in following it. Second, your argument was sound. Therefore Jones's training should have made him unable to reject its conclusion.

Perhaps he did not know that the premises of your argument were true, you will say. But again let us suppose that the premises are such that he ought to have known them to be true. Suppose them such that any person with a good education and a functioning imagination could be expected to recognize them as true. Under these conditions, criterion 6 will be satisfied.

Of course, when I speak of what Jones *should* have known I am citing an epistemic, not a moral obligation. To reproach Jones for not knowing what he should is to make him epistemically, but perhaps not morally, culpable. Separating epistemic and moral 'oughts' is not always easy, but I shall do my best to keep them separate in discussing philosophical failure.[6]

To return to the epistemically culpable Jones, all criteria are now satisfied. By Hirstein's definition, Jones is confabulating.

You may think I have cooked the books and my account of Jones's rebuttal is inconsistent. If so, you must believe it impossible for all six of Hirstein's criteria to be simultaneously satisfied. However, clinical experiments reveal that they *can* be simultaneously satisfied. Worse still, they seem to be satisfied so easily and so frequently that some researchers now think confabulation plays a larger role in ordinary life than philosophers have guessed.[7] If confabulation is so ubiquitous, and philosophers for the most part have not even noticed it, have we any good reason to suppose them exempt from engaging in it?

Promising as the idea of confabulation is in making philosophical failure more understandable, it must be rescued from its place in contemporary brain science if it is to fulfil its promise. The scientific context in which confabulation is usually discussed, on which I have been gratefully drawing thus far, understands itself to be developing a "naturalized epistemology,"[8] in which behaviour is taken to be explained when it is correlated with operations, regions, or traumata of the brain. Present interests being more conceptual, we must look elsewhere for further light on philosophical failure. It would be desirable to find a philosophical rather than a physiological cause of confabulation.

We should hope philosophical causes, or reasons, can be found. Outside a clinical setting, it would be rash (and possibly actionable) to accuse those who disagree with us of suffering from brain lesions or schizophrenia or worse. And the charge of confabulation would amount to that, if these were its only known causes. But there is at least one plausible philosophical candidate for being a cause of confabulation. Is it not likely that philosophers confabulate about a sound argument when what in Chapter One I called the argument's *mass* is decidedly smaller than the mass of the obstacle it is trying to remove?

For example, in Chapter One we considered Pascal's short, careful, logical argument *against philosophy*. Even if that argument is sound, we might expect philosophers, when confronted with it, to confabulate. Won't it seem to them that nothing as massive, as diverse, as ancient, and as venerable as philosophy (or even that part of it which consists of dogmatism and scepticism) can be brought down by a single argument drawn from the largely forgotten logic of terms?

Or suppose for a moment that Leibniz's version of the ontological argument for the existence of God is sound. In that case, the protagonist of all theology, God, can be demonstrated to exist, with all the theological, ethical, and existential consequences his existence entails. Atheism and agnosticism are confuted; a good part of the Enlightenment is abolished; the separation of church and state is called into question. Life in the secular Western world is turned upside down. And it all comes about from a single modal sentence expressible in eight words: *If the necessary being is possible, it exists.*

Leibniz's argument is so simple. If it were also sound, would there be any way to evade its consequences except by confabulating? If it is sound, must not the exquisitely recondite criticisms that have been levelled against it, of which I gave an example in Chapter One, be confabulations? "We know you confabulate," we would explain to such objectors, "because the mass of the ontological argument is tiny, and the combined mass of atheism, agnosticism, and secularism is great."

What would happen next, if confabulating were admitted into the arsenal of philosophical invective, taking its place alongside invalidity, fallacy, unsoundness, confusion, and the other epithets philosophers hurl at mental delinquents? Less would happen than you may think. If in my zeal for the ontological argument I were permitted to accuse skilled philosophers of confabulating, they would be entitled to the exasperated reply that it was I who confabulated in my obtuse response to their objections, which, when properly understood, were lucid and sound. Neither side would derive any unfair advantage from the term.

The advantage would lie in the clarity brought to the idea of philosophical failure. Confabulation clearly belongs in the part of logic that deals with the reception of arguments rather than with their construction (syntax) or their soundness (semantics). Confabulation is a failure at the level of what logicians call *pragmatics*. It exposes human epistemic weakness without putting in question the existence of sound, substantive arguments.

If it turns out that even philosophers confabulate, then something has been explained that van Inwagen only draws to our attention and deplores. If confabulation is a real phenomenon in philosophy, it shows us why capable philosophers sometimes cannot be convinced, no matter how excellent the argument we offer them.

There is a further question about philosophical failure, however, that confabulation cannot answer. It won't explain why philosophical arguments fail more frequently than mathematical ones do, even though philosophy is sometimes as rigorous as mathematics. Why are even the best philosophical arguments almost never received as proofs, while mathematical arguments, unless they are unconventional in their methods, almost never fail to be? Van Inwagen relies on that difference, as you may recall, in motivating his discussion of philosophical failure. "The idea," he says, "that there are proofs in philosophy as there are proofs in mathematics is ridiculous, or not far short of it."[9]

It can't be just that confabulators prefer philosophy to mathematics. They may, but why do they have that preference? Why does philosophy, but not mathematics, make confabulators feel at home? The difference must depend on qualities of the disciplines themselves.

Is it that philosophical arguments collide with beliefs of great mass, whereas mathematical arguments don't? It can't be that, for some mathematical arguments displace massive beliefs without experiencing much resistance. Cantor's Diagonal Argument or Gödel's Incompleteness Theorems, for example, are normally viewed as proofs, and cause no confabulation, despite upsetting some of our deepest philosophical convictions. So we need something more than confabulation to explain why philosophical arguments regularly fail and mathematical arguments do not.

### Descartes on Philosophical Failure

Few philosophers are better qualified to compare mathematics and philosophy than was Descartes, for he was pre-eminent in both. When circumstances forced him to reflect on philosophical failure, he was predisposed to see it in the light of mathematical success, and his account of it brought new causes of philosophical failure to light.

Philosophical failure became an issue for Descartes around 1640, when he arrived at the point of launching his *Meditations on First Philosophy*. He knew they were dynamite. On their surface they contained a radical new approach to metaphysics. Beneath the surface they concealed a depth charge designed to explode on contact with traditional (Aristotelian) physics. Descartes spent more than a decade crafting the arguments that went into the *Meditations*, and he was determined they should succeed. The point that worried him most was what we might call the *marketing* of his ideas. As a practised controversialist, he knew the difference between making a good argument and getting a fair hearing.

Yet even his unusual determination to engineer a favourable reception of the *Meditations* does not fully explain the bizarre step he took in attempting to secure it. In what looks like Descartes's strangest lapse of judgment, he dedicated the *Meditations* to the *theologians* of the Sorbonne and used the dedicatory letter to request that they support his logical arguments with their authority. The strange tale of this dedicatory letter is the backdrop of his discussion of philosophical failure.[10]

Descartes begins his letter by telling the theologians that the arguments of the *Meditations* are "at least equal if not superior in soundness and self-evidence to those of geometry."[11] Such impeccable arguments, you'd expect him to continue, can look after themselves. What he says instead makes your jaw drop. Though the arguments in the *Meditations* are exemplary in every way, he tells the theologians, "I have no hope of getting much mileage out of them, unless you assist me with your patronage."[12]

You may be wondering what I think is so surprising. Descartes knew he was in theologically dangerous territory and asked for the protection of the Sorbonne. What is so surprising about that?

Nothing about it would be strange if that were what Descartes did. But the protection he asked for was philosophical, not theological. It is as if he had asked a society of accountants to endorse his physics, or poets to approve of his epistemology. Appeals to authority are invalid at the best of times, but in philosophical matters theologians have none to offer. What could have made Descartes think that sound philosophical arguments with self-evident premises will fail, unless theologians (who lack the relevant authority) fallaciously buttress them? How could a thinker of Descartes's genius go so far astray?

His desperation, he says, stems from the fact that his arguments are philosophical rather than geometrical. At this point, suddenly, despite the absurdity of its premise, this letter becomes philosophically interesting. It is about to offer an explanation of philosophical failure going beyond confabulation. Here is what Descartes says:

> The difference between [geometry and philosophy] is that in geometry everyone thinks whatever is asserted has a sound demonstration. Hence

the inexperienced more frequently err on the side of agreeing to what is false, because they wish to appear knowledgeable, than on the side of disputing what is true. The opposite is the case in philosophy. Since everyone believes it is possible to argue either side of every philosophical question, few investigate the truth, and many more, because they dare to deny even the most perfect demonstrations, seek fame as ingenious thinkers.[13]

Descartes's analysis of philosophical failure takes us beyond confabulation, where arguments may fail for lack of *mass*. Descartes suggests three additional reasons for failure. First, he tells us, they may fail because people thoughtlessly adopt a common (though unjustified) belief that philosophical arguments are always disputable. Just as a spittoon has been wittily defined as a receptacle *around* which people spit, so, Descartes suggests, the popular imagination conceives of proof as an ideal *below* which philosophical arguments invariably fall.

Such thoughtless disqualification of sound arguments is not the same thing as confabulation. It derives from inattention rather than conviction, and so fails of Hirstein's third criterion (that the confabulator have a confident belief in what he says).

In the second sentence of the passage quoted, Descartes introduces another explanatory factor: the vanity of inexperienced philosophers. The inexperienced (*imperiti*) are not confabulators, because, being inexperienced, they lack epistemic guilt, and so do not meet the last of Hirstein's criteria (epistemic obligation to know the contrary of what they say to be true).

Two kinds of inexperience are possible, which Descartes does not take time to distinguish. When a philosopher's inexperience is innocent in itself (as it may be in the young, for example), he is both epistemically and morally blameless, provided he keeps silent. But he is morally at fault if vanity prompts him to deny the force of an argument he has not properly understood.

There is also culpable inexperience. Mature philosophers may have had opportunities they never seized to remedy their inexperience. In that case, they are morally (though still not epistemically) at fault when sound arguments fail to convince them. And they also exhibit the further moral weakness of vanity if, on the basis of their misapprehension, they make public their rejection of a sound argument.

In the last sentence of the passage quoted, Descartes recognizes a third philosophical weakness – the culpability of trained philosophers who put their training to bad use. Once again they are not confabulators, because they speak against arguments they *know* to be sound. Thus, they satisfy neither Hirstein's second nor his fifth criterion. (They have neither belief in what they are saying nor exculpatory ignorance of its falsehood.) The fault of these philosophers is clearly a moral one. They are not seeking truth, but rather fame as ingenious thinkers. Their moral failing is to view arguments as instruments of self-advancement rather than as opportunities for instruction. And so they remain unaffected by the power of right thinking.[14]

A cloud of uncertainty surrounds the motivation of Descartes's dedicatory letter. But there is value in his etiology of philosophical failure, for it provides three reasons for failure that go beyond confabulation: mental sloth, inexperience, and venality.

## Evil

All four reasons considered so far – Descartes's three plus confabulation – connect philosophical failure with personal defects of some kind. Confabulators fail to exhibit an ability they are epistemically obligated to have – the ability to understand and accept an obviously sound argument. Descartes alerts us to three different kinds of philosophical impostors: slothful minds who uncritically accept the canard that philosophical arguments never establish their conclusions; inexperienced ones who, out of vanity, judge patently sound arguments to be inconclusive; and, finally, venal ones, who subordinate truth to self-advancement and epistemic diligence to precipitancy.

Confabulation, sloth, inexperience, and venality are probably not the only causes of philosophical failure, but they do suggest a profile. They all derive from personal defects.

They all belong to the family of what philosophers used to call *deficient causes*. It is an aptly paradoxical name, for defects, while having nothing positive about them, seem yet to possess causal powers. They are like a shadow in a garden. Though shadow is only the absence of light, it nevertheless affects the whole system of the garden. It can lower the temperature of the air in its vicinity and limit the growth of plants that take root within its perimeter. Inability, sloth, inexperience, and venality are likewise defects with causal powers. They can affect people's thinking and action in measurable ways, as Descartes reminds us.

Traditional philosophy also called deficient causes by another name: *privations*. To speak of a privation is to draw attention to something that, while absent, is more than merely absent. Privative absence is unnatural absence. A privation is something *missing* rather than something that is simply not there. For example, Aristotle calls blindness "a privation not in general, but when sight fails to come to those who would naturally have it."[15] A sightless eye thus differs from a sightless stick or stone. Sticks and stones are not expected to see, and so their sightlessness is no privation. The eye's sightlessness is a privation, however, because it is the nature of eyes to see.

The notion of privation occupies an important place in traditional Catholic philosophy. It is the indispensable centre of the Catholic account of evil.[16] Ever since Augustine found in privation a way of overcoming Manichean dualism,[17] evil has been conceived by Catholic philosophy not as itself a positive reality but as the absence of some good thing that ought to be present. The notion of privation has been used to explain both *natural evils*, such as illnesses, earthquakes, and floods, and *moral evils*, such as murder, theft, and deception.[18]

Privation and the defective causality that goes with it look as if they might also help to explain philosophical failure. Sound arguments fail with a given audience, we might say, when the habits of mind, character, or judgment they ought to exhibit are not in evidence.

With the privative aspect of philosophical failure in mind, consider once more its ubiquity. Van Inwagen conjectures that there is not one philosophically substantive argument that could infallibly convince any randomly chosen jury of astute, philosophically trained people, even if we grant them plenty of time to examine the arguments. (Perhaps especially then!)

Van Inwagen's conjecture is not implausible. If it is true, then there can be only two possible explanations. One would be that every substantive philosophical argument is intrinsically unclear or unsound. But that way paradox lies. For if there are no sound, substantive arguments, then there could be no sound argument to demonstrate van Inwagen's conclusion, which is clearly a substantive one. And if nothing can be both substantive and clear, then the substantive point van Inwagen is making about the nature and limits of philosophy would have to be itself unclear. But van Inwagen's point is not unclear. Therefore, it would have to be unsound and we would land in paradox.

If the argument of the foregoing paragraph is sound, then the reason for philosophical failure cannot lie in arguments at all. It must lie instead, as suggested above, in pragmatic territory, in the all-too-human, petty epistemic and moral vices of those who hear and read arguments.

The reason that no philosophical jury would be unanimous about any substantive argument must arise from the prevalence of defects of mind, such as inability, sloth, and the rest. So prevalent must these vices be that human beings regularly, even habitually, resist sound philosophical arguments.

Human philosophical inadequacy on this scale is cause for regret, because it means that we regularly fall short of the rationality that supposedly defines our species. But it also makes our behaviour puzzling. Why should we resist clear, sound arguments the way we do? Are we, perhaps, by nature unbelieving beings?

Far from it. Human beings are normally prepared to believe almost anything. Our credulity is legendary. Think of cults, gurus, nostrums, fads, investment bubbles, advertisements of all kinds. They all draw on the same bottomless reservoir of human credulity, which no number of disappointments is sufficient to stanch. What perverse circumstances, then, bring it about that well-trained philosophers, who may from time to time lose their savings in investment bubbles or fall prey to manipulators in the marketplace, can nevertheless offer impermeable resistance to sound arguments, even when these have been devised with the utmost skill by renowned members of their own philosophical tribe?

Surely our condition is worse than mysterious. It is no exaggeration to call it perverse. Are sound arguments about substantive philosophical questions not among the intellectual artefacts it would do us most good to accept? Yet on many occasions we seem more fortified against them than we are against the transparent manipulators of the hustings or the marketplace. It is as if there were a design flaw in human beings.

A design flaw in human nature is a fanciful suggestion, yet a simple chain of thoughts leads us there. Philosophical failure involves the absence of assent in cases where assent ought to be forthcoming. It's a privation. Privations are never normal. They are the absence of what is normal. Philosophical failure therefore cannot be the norm. It has to be the exception. Yet we have just seen that, statistically at least, it is the norm. So there must be a design flaw in human nature. Our natural propensity towards philosophical failure must derive from some second nature, acquired after some adventitious corruption of an original human nature that functioned properly.

Roman Catholic philosophy does not regard this line of reasoning as fanciful. The idea of an original meta-failure, an *ur*-catastrophe at the beginning of history, is a traditional Catholic doctrine called the doctrine of the *Fall* or of *Original Sin*. Through it we approach at last the gloomy territory of Pascal.

## The Fall

The doctrine of the Fall occupies a central place in Pascal's thinking. Though he describes it sincerely and unaffectedly as resulting from the sin of Adam, his understanding of it is not limited by any narrow biblical literalism. He moves easily between literal meaning and figurative interpretation, in a hermeneutic pattern established in the Bible and long accepted by the Roman Catholic Church. Take, for example, one of the *Pensées* in which God is depicted as speaking to us through the Christian religion:

> I created man holy, innocent, perfect. I filled him with light and intelligence. I communicated to him my glory and my wonders. The eye of man beheld at that time the majesty of God. He was not then in the shadows that blind him now, nor in the mortality and wretchedness that afflict him ...
>
> Behold the state of men today. They retain from their first nature a certain impotent instinct for happiness, but they are plunged into the wretched blindness and concupiscence that is their second nature ...
>
> [God] desired to leave them in the privation of a goodness they did not desire.[19]

Pascal's purpose in this passage is not to acquaint his reader with the Fall as history, but to make him think about its explanatory power. Both the utopian circumstances preceding the Fall and the condition of wretchedness that followed it contribute to clarifying the human condition. The Fall is to be looked at as the *ur*-catastrophe, a formative privation at the origin of things as we know them. It is responsible for more than just human wretchedness. The Fall also evacuated much of the goodness that originally was in nature, leaving behind the perplexing mixture of good and evil in which human experience consists, intensified by a melancholy remembrance of paradise lost. "Nature's perfections show her to be the image of God," Pascal writes, "and her defects show her to be only the image."[20]

As for ourselves, in the Fall we forfeited the innocent but perfect human nature with which we were created. Its successor was the mortal, blind, and miserable nature that is now our prison, though it trails vestigial clouds of its former glory. English readers know Pascal's conception of the human consequences of the Fall better through some famous lines of Alexander Pope than through the *Pensée* from which Pope lifted them. They portray man as:

> Chaos of Thought and Passion, all confused;
> Still by himself abused, and disabused;
> Created half to rise, and half to fall;
> Great lord of all things, but a prey to all;
> Sole judge of Truth, in endless Error hurled:
> The glory, jest, and riddle of the world![21]

One effect of the Fall, according to Pascal, and not its least devastating one, is the ubiquity of philosophical failure, hinted at even in the lines just quoted. For one thing, custom (*la coutume*) has the power to persuade our fallen minds even against the verdict of reason. In many cases, "custom is what persuades us," Pascal says, "dragging behind it the unthinking spirit."[22] But persuasion has more tools to work with than custom alone.

Failure and Fall are linked most clearly in a work called "The Art of Persuasion," probably written in 1659 or 1660, thus at the same time as Pascal was writing the *Pensées*.[23]

The first thing to know about Pascal's treatise on persuasion is that in a perfect world it would not exist. In an unfallen world, persuasion would always be chaperoned by reason. Our beliefs would all be *convictions*. No one would be able to persuade us of anything without first convincing us.

The root of the word 'persuade' is the Latin *suavis*, meaning 'sweet.' Persuasion is the art of sweet-talking. It is concerned with winning consent without necessarily engaging the intellect. The root of the word 'convince,' by contrast, is the Latin verb *vinco*, meaning 'to conquer.' To convince me of something, you must conquer my objections to it by the logical power of your argument.

It is a "low, unworthy and alien," quality of the human mind, Pascal says, that it can be persuaded without first being convinced.[24] A mind functioning as God intended would consent only to those propositions that logically overwhelmed it. Every belief would be like geometrical truths which are either themselves self-evident or a demonstrable consequence of propositions that are.[25]

But the Fall intervened, and our minds were partly disordered as a result. That is why there now exists an art of persuasion that "consists as much in delighting as in convincing. For men are governed more by caprice than by reason."[26] Where there ought to have been only one way by which human beings consent to arguments, now there are two. There is the "natural" (though statistically exceptional) way of conviction. And there is the statistically "ordinary" (but unjustifiable and unnatural) way of persuasion. "No one is unaware," Pascal says,

> that there are two gates through which opinions are received into the mind (*âme*). They are its two principal powers, *intellect* and *will*. The most natural is the intellect, because the only right thing is to agree to demonstrated truths. However the most ordinary [mode of entry], although it is contrary to nature, is through the will. For in almost all cases almost everyone is brought to believe not by proofs, but by delight (*agrément*).[27]

Because the way of delight is low, unworthy, and alien, Pascal tells us, "everyone denies acquaintance with it. Each professes to believe, and even to love, only what he knows to be worthy."[28] In our own eyes we are pillars of epistemic probity, and we work hard to establish that image of ourselves in others. In practice, however, almost everyone almost always believes what he wants. This is what Pascal means by "the civil war between reason and the passions" which he says characterizes all our lives.[29]

What Pascal has begun to outline here promises a more comprehensive explanation of philosophical failure than is offered either by the brain states of the philosophers of mind, or by the privations of Descartes, or by the metaphor of argumentative 'mass' I invoked to account for confabulation. On Pascal's view all or almost all of us are host to incalculably large numbers of false beliefs masquerading as certainties. They have entered our minds through the low, unworthy, and alien gate of our will. Frequently he calls that gate "concupiscence."[30] Will, combining with concupiscent passions on the one hand, and intellect on the other, function in much the same way as the right and left hemispheres of bisected brains in classic confabulation experiments: our intellect rationalizes for public display what passion whispers to the will.

In Pascal's vocabulary propositions persuade by delighting us. We mistake the delight they give us for conviction, deceiving ourselves, and often thereby contributing to the deception of other people. To the extent such pseudo-convictions inform our conversation, or guide our conduct, we bear epistemic guilt.

The postlapsarian world is to some extent God's new creation. In an uncharacteristically murky turn of phrase, Pascal says God altered the world after the Fall "supernaturally" in a way "completely contrary to the order he intended to be natural for men among natural things."[31]

God's judgment on Adam and Eve after their sin can give us an idea of what Pascal intended to say. God explained to Adam and Eve how he had changed the natural order as a result of their sin, and then sent them out of Eden to live in the altered world. Here is God's explanation:

> To the woman [God] said, "I will greatly multiply your pain in childbearing; in pain you shall bring forth children, yet your desire shall be for your husband, and he shall rule over you."
>
> And to Adam he said, "Because you have listened to the voice of your wife, and have eaten of the tree of which I commanded you, 'You shall not eat of it,' cursed is the ground because of you; in toil you shall eat of it all the days of your life; thorns and thistles it shall bring forth to you; and you shall eat the plants of the field. In the sweat of your face you shall eat bread till you return to the ground, for out of it you were taken; you are dust, and to dust you shall return."
>
> ...........................
>
> Therefore the Lord God sent him forth from the Garden of Eden to till the ground from which he was taken. He drove out the man; and at the east of the Garden of Eden he placed the cherubim, and a flaming sword, which turned every way.[32]

These new conditions are harsh: sweat and toil for Adam; pain and obedience for Eve; death for both. But those are only the surface conditions of our suffering. By themselves they still do not exclude moderate human well-being. To achieve it man must only toil and woman obey. However, these conditions are even less palatable to the man and the woman than was the utopia of Eden. And because our minds were partially disordered by the Fall, we are worse equipped than before to discern what is really in our interest. Thus it happens that when we intervene in the new order with the hope of improving it, we sometimes make it worse. This is what I think Pascal means in the elliptical sentence that follows the ones I have just been commenting on:

> [Men] corrupted this [new] order by treating profane things as they should have treated holy ones, because in effect we believe almost only what we like.[33]

The sentence is unclear because it does not explain the connection Pascal sees between confusing profane things with holy ones and believing what we like. But the connection is a close one. The paradigm of it, for Pascal, though it is not mentioned in this place, is the Jesuits' pastoral doctrine of *casuistry*.

Casuistry in itself is innocent enough. It is an approach to ethical questions that recognizes the weakness of fallen beings and sees how mitigating features of individual cases may sometimes trump ethical principles normally held to be universal.[34] However, Pascal took issue with a Jesuit casuistical principle according to which a course of action could be deemed morally permissible (or, in the technical vocabulary of the day, 'probable') if even a single clerically recognized authority supported it. According to Pascal, one Jesuit author even claimed, "You can do whatever you think is permitted by one probable opinion, even if the contrary opinion is more certain. The opinion of one serious [ecclesiastical] doctor is enough."[35]

Pascal was scandalized by the moral laxity implied in such a doctrine. One of his greatest ambitions in writing the *Provincial Letters* had been to expose the dangers of it. The moral problem it would pose to a Jansenist puritan is not difficult to see. If a single ecclesiastical authority can justify my conduct, then I will be justified in doing almost anything I please. To return to the difficult sentence from "The Art of Persuasion," casuistry is an example of the way profane wishes can be elevated to sacred duties, and we are allowed to believe what we like.

What is philosophically objectionable about the Jesuits' use of 'probabilities' in casuistry is that, in excusing all our conduct, they mask the scandal of *moral weakness*, which philosophers have long discussed under the name *akrasia*. It is no surprise that it should prove interesting to Pascal. *Akrasia* is the moral counterpart of philosophical failure.[36] Philosophers call moral weakness that self-destructive ability men and women have to recognize a certain course of action as the right one and still go wrong.

"I see better ways," says Ovid, "and approve of them. Then I follow worse ones." St Paul's version is even better known: "The good that I would I do not; but the evil I would not, that I do."[37]

Nothing is more universally recognized than the existence of moral failure. Try quoting Ovid or St Paul to an audience, and then requesting anyone who has never detected such moral failures in himself to raise his hand. If a hand goes up, it will be in fun. With rueful smiles or nods people acknowledge the familiarity of the experience you are asking them to notice.

Uncontestable as the existence of moral failure is, however, it is difficult to account for its possibility. "How can a man fail in self-restraint," Aristotle asks, "when he believes correctly that what he is about to do is wrong? Some people say that he cannot [fail in self-restraint] when he *knows* the act to be wrong ... [but] this theory is manifestly at variance with the plain facts."[38]

We all know how prevalent moral weakness is, and Pascal is right to blame the Jesuits, if they papered it over with moral indulgence. We are far less aware of our epistemic weakness, however. By a kind of casuistry made natural to us by the Fall, we disguise our epistemic weakness from ourselves. Which is to say we confabulate.

Prior to the Fall, Pascal thinks, it would have been different. In its original condition, the intellect would only have assented to demonstrated or self-evident truths, though even then the intellect did not rule alone. God placed revealed (or "divine") truths directly in the heart "to humble the proud power of reasoning." But the contents of the intellect cohered with the reasons of the heart, and the will loved both, for it loved the truth. Love was as good a guide to truth as reason was in the prelapsarian state, though now that condition can only be recovered by the saints.[39]

How the well-balanced minds of Adam and Eve could ever have been induced to sin is irreducibly mysterious. Pascal, following Augustine, explains it through the gift of freedom, but I shall not attempt to expound or defend his account.[40] What is important for present purposes is how the Fall explains philosophical failure. By the Fall man's original nature was corrupted but not destroyed. Demonstrable truths continue to enter into our minds through the intellect, as they were meant to do. And revealed truths continue to enter through the heart. However, the will has experienced a morbid form of growth. It has developed a power it should not have. It is now capable of installing meretricious certainties in the mind to rival the convictions of the intellect and the reasons of the heart. Worse still, will dominates the mind. Fallen men and women "adopt hosts of [opinions] through the bold caprices of the will, without the counsel of the intellect."[41]

"It can happen," Pascal says:

that what people are trying to prove (*faire croire*) follows from well established, known truths, which, at the same time, are contrary to our most cherished pleasures. Such proofs are in great danger of providing an all-too-familiar experience ... Our imperious mind (*âme*), which brags of acting only through reason, leans instead to what its corrupt will desires.

It pursues this shameful, bold course no matter how much resistance the most enlightened spirit (*esprit*) can offer it.[42]

If Pascal is right about the weakness of our fallen minds and the widespread incidence of philosophical failure, he is also right to look for a way of arguing philosophically that avoids a lofty, but naïve, reliance on demonstration alone. In later chapters we will see how he thinks arguments of this kind can be constructed.

There will, of course, be those who think that no such thing as the Fall ever happened. To miss the pertinence of Pascal's account of the Fall on that account, however, would be to succumb to the very literalism from which Pascal was free. It would be to fall prey to an attitude of mind the literary lion G.K. Chesterton found amusing: "Certain new theologians dispute original sin," Chesterton wrote in 1908,

> which is the only part of Christian theology which can really be proved ... The strongest saints and the strongest sceptics alike took positive evil as the starting-point of their argument. If it be true (as it certainly is) that a man can feel exquisite happiness in skinning a cat, then the religious philosopher can only draw one of two deductions. He must either deny the existence of God, as all atheists do; or he must deny the present union between God and man, as all Christians do. The new theologians seem to think it a highly rationalistic solution to deny the cat.[43]

Pascal could say of philosophical failure what Chesterton says about the cat. Its existence is undeniable and it requires explanation. Yet its ubiquity can only be explained if there is a way the mind is supposed to function but rarely does. Nozick, van Inwagen, Descartes, and my own explanation based on confabulation get that far. But that only explains a failure by a mystery. Pascal does better because he moves the mystery back one further step and answers a question other explanations do not: what is the ultimate *cause* of philosophical failure? According to Pascal, philosophical failure arises because the mind's second nature readily rejects propositions its original nature would have accepted, and readily accepts propositions on grounds whose inadequacy its original nature would have easily discerned. To become aware of our penchant for failure is to judge the behaviour of our second nature by the standards of the first. It also establishes the need for a different conception of philosophy from the one defeated in the tournament of champions.

The Fall is understood as historical by Pascal, but its explanatory power is independent of its historicity. Nothing would have prevented Pascal from treating the Fall as Plato treats some of his myths and as all of us treat metaphors. They are devices for organizing our thoughts about a topic and assigning explanatory features to things needing explanation. Once that has been accomplished, the user can be left to form his own judgment about the literal truth of the myth, story, or metaphor that provides this useful service. We can all recognize that man is a wolf to man without denying the limitations of the likeness.

Theories can be treated the same way if we keep their empirical adequacy and consequent explanatory power separate from their truth.[44] Biblical literalism is convenient for stating Pascal's position. It is also philosophically innocuous as long as it is optional.

## Wretchedness (*Misère*)

Where philosophical failure is ubiquitous, certainty is rare. It is the first casualty of the Fall as Pascal reviews them in one of the *Pensées*. "We wish for truth, but find in ourselves only uncertainty," Pascal says, before descending to deeper reaches of human wretchedness:

> We hunt for happiness, but find only misery and death.
>     We cannot stop wishing for truth and happiness, and yet are incapable of finding either.
>     We are allowed to retain the desire of them as much to punish us as to make us feel from what height we have fallen.[45]

In this fragment the decline into wretchedness involves three stages. First, there is the truth we long for in vain. Next comes the misery that requites our search for happiness. Yet even uncertainty and misery might be bearable if by some spiritual discipline we could reconcile ourselves to our low condition, if we could achieve stoical or sceptical peace of mind. But that is just what we cannot do. We are tormented by the high aspirations God has left in our hearts, both to remind us of our original condition and punish us for throwing it away.

In another fragment Pascal calls what afflicts us a "natural unhappiness," belonging of course not to our first, but to our second, or fallen, nature. Still, the wretchedness that is now natural for us has become inescapable by natural means. Our unhappiness arises from the fact that "we are feeble, mortal and ... inconsolable, if we consider things carefully."[46]

Why inconsolable? Another fragment explains:

> Imagine a number of men in chains, all condemned to death. Every day some are butchered in full view of the others. Those who remain see their own condition reflected in the treatment of their fellows. Hopeless, exchanging tormented looks, the survivors await their turn. That is an image of the human condition.[47]

Impending death is sufficient cause for misery, but it is only the external cause. We bring innumerable smaller torments on ourselves while life lasts. "Our will is depraved," Pascal says with Augustinian severity, and "all the military, political, economic and even bodily disorders of the world" are caused by our depravity.[48]

This deepest cause of our wretchedness – the depraved will – points back to original sin, that first seed of depravity whose tendrils are our present actions. Depravity is now our second nature, and it overpowers us. Self-absorption (*la pente vers* soi) cuts us off from any sustaining objectivity that could right our course. We befriend our worst enemy – ourselves. Self-gratification – that natural, unquenchable appetite – is the engine of self-destruction.

## Science

Many seventeenth-century thinkers shared Descartes's hope that the new science would mitigate, or even relieve altogether, the human wretchedness caused by the Fall. Pascal was not among them, however. He was sure such hopes would be disappointed. Far from curing wretchedness, the natural sciences were one of its clearest expressions.

As one of the scientists on whose work the scientific revolution was based, Pascal spoke with a certain authority, but his critique of science has not received much attention. Pascal's critique of Cartesian *scientism* may be a bit passé. There is no novelty today in calling Descartes's claims about science extravagant, or naive, or even dangerous. Few of us believe that science will produce only good, or that it will perfect mankind, or abolish labour, or cure death. Many disapprove of the arrogance they imagine to be lurking in Descartes's promise that science will make us "like masters and possessors of nature." We don't need Pascal's say-so to dismiss all that as scientism.

Pascal sees more to criticize in science than scientism, however. Like Hume, he goes farther out on the critical limb than most readers are prepared to follow. Pascal's "remarkable brilliance," as one writer terms it, "lies in the fact that at the very beginning of the modern era he had already recognized that modern science's self-confident belief that it possessed a secure method is illusory and a pretension."[49] Pascal differs from Hume, however, in placing his critique of science within a general account of human wretchedness.

Like other leading scientists of his day, Pascal regarded the universe as infinitely vast. Borrowing a phrase from Nicholas of Cusa, he called it "an infinite sphere whose centre is everywhere and whose circumference is nowhere."[50] But our mind is no more equal to that infinity than our body is. Our body occupies only a minute part of the universe, and no human mind can grasp more than a finite amount about anything. In the disparity between our finite selves and our infinite dwelling place Pascal sees the ruin of the grandiose dreams of science. The quantitative disproportion between the universe and our minds entails a qualitative disproportion also.

It is not that science can make no progress. It can. In a short methodological reflection written in connection with his work on the vacuum, Pascal sketches an account of the history of science as a progressive discovery of nature. Newton can still claim to have stood on the shoulders of giants. The careful work of our predecessors enables us, with only a little effort, to see further than they could. We are not like the animals, Pascal says, who are only able to repeat what instinct equips them to do. "It is not the same for man, for he was made for the infinite."[51]

Being made for the infinite exalts us above the animals, but it also fixes us in our place in the great chain of being, lower than God and the angels. Suppose we do explore or understand some finite region in our immediate surroundings. When compared with the vast unknown, the region explored is barely distinguishable from nothing. In itself our knowledge may be something, but in regard to the whole it is nothing.

The beauty of the Copernican revolution was supposed to lie in rescuing us from earthbound provincialism. But only try to lift your gaze to the infinite and eternal, and you will see not everything, but nothing. The new science points you nowhere. Sound empirical theories about the universe are not possible, because we never are able to assemble sufficient samples either of its constituents or of their operations. This empirical shortfall will continue no matter how much telescopes or space travel enlarge the range from which samples are chosen. "The whole visible world," Pascal says,

> is but an imperceptible dot in the ample bosom of nature. No idea even approaches it. In vain do we inflate our conceptions beyond the imaginable spaces. What we give birth to are only atoms when compared with the reality of things.[52]

Even if we cannot obtain definitive knowledge of the universe as a whole, we might wonder why that should prevent us from understanding objects of middle size, including ourselves. But even such a modest view of science as a body of knowledge concerning middle-sized objects is too ambitious, according to Pascal. Science will fail to understand middle-sized objects because it knows nothing of the undetectable, infinitely small objects of which visible things are composed.

It is interesting that Pascal should make this point. Though the microscope had already been invented, the great microscopists had not yet written. Nothing was known of Leeuwenhoeck's "little animals," nor of Swammerdam's *Bible of Nature*. Malpighi's work on the viscera was not even begun. But the point Pascal made is not affected by the finite enlargements of our knowledge microscopy was about to afford. Pascal viewed such potential enlargements as feeble lights, serving mainly to accentuate the infinite blackness into which they would have to be directed. He compares the objects we are familiar with, including our own bodies, to spots of light travellers sometimes see from a distance. On closer approach the lights reveal themselves to be villages, then clusters of houses, each made of rooms, full of furniture, made of parts, reticulating downward forever.[53] What if each thing is like the cosmos in miniature, Pascal wants to know, each token as manifold within itself as its type is multiplied into numberless varieties, and endlessly scattered through trackless infinities of space?

If things are as Pascal says, our knowledge will not merely be limited. In absolute terms, it will be nonexistent. Not even a mite will be fully knowable. Not even a microscopic bump on one tiny leg of a single mite. Just as we can never reach the limits of the universe, so we can never find the smallest parts of individual things. There are no atoms. Nothing is indivisible, but there are always further and further subatomic particles. "What is man then in nature?" Pascal asks. And the answer he gives is a memorable one:

A nothing with regard to the infinite. Everything with regard to nothingness. A middle point between nothing and everything, infinitely far from understanding the extremes. The ends and beginnings (*principes*) of things are invincibly hidden from him in impenetrable secrets.[54]

Our problem isn't just that we can't know everything. We ourselves are obstacles to knowing:

Consider, then, how far we can reach. We are something and we are not everything. The something we are blocks us from knowing the beginnings (*principes*) of things, which come from nothing. And the minuteness of our being hides the infinite from our view.[55]

The limitations of science begin at the level of what we can observe. Nothing very much smaller, or very much bigger, than we are is detectable by us. So we can never expect to know what things are ultimately made of. Ultimate constituents are too small. Neither will observation ever tell us anything about the larger constellations into which observed objects fit, including ourselves. Great magnitudes outstrip our ability not only to observe but to comprehend. We will always be lost in the cosmos.

Pascal's assumption of the two infinities is itself a scientific hypothesis about the world and therefore may be mistaken. But the force of his critique would not be entirely lost, even if his hypothesis were wrong. The universe need only be sufficiently large and its parts sufficiently small that neither human mental power nor any of its cybernetic extensions can cope with it. We are still limited in both directions today. And for as long as our limitations endure, we will not vanquish the ignorance that makes us wretched.[56]

Philosophers who deceive themselves and others with grandiose scientistic promises are therefore ridiculous. The very title of Descartes's *Principles of Philosophy* angers Pascal. Even more absurd are the extravagant promises Descartes makes in the work itself. Not only will he deduce everything from first principles, he pretends, but he will also lift his readers to the heights of wisdom, perfect their lives, and crown them with felicity.[57] Pascal can hardly find enough irony to pour on this kind of foolishness. "It has given rise," he says

to such modest titles as *On the Principles of Things*, *The Principles of Philosophy*, and the like. Which are equally fatuous in fact, though less in appearance, than that jaw-dropper, *Of All That Can Be Known*.[58]

Most of our universe is transmitting on a frequency we can't receive, and that is limitation enough. But even what we do receive is limited by the quality of the receiver. Our senses are so made, Pascal observes, that they limit and change the given. "Our senses perceive nothing extreme. Too much noise deafens us. Too much light dazzles. Too much distance, like too much proximity, dims the view ... We cannot feel either extreme heat or extreme cold." Corresponding problems exist with the intellect: "The observer's mind is hindered as much by youth as by age. Too little learning holds it back. So does too much."[59]

We have limited knowledge of external objects, not only when they are very great, or very small, but even when they are proportioned to our senses. We have even less understanding of ourselves. Like Descartes, Pascal believes we are composites of mind and body.[60]

> Who would not think, to see us composing everything of mind and matter, that that particular mixture must be comprehensible to us. Nevertheless it is the very thing we understand least. Man is to himself the most prodigious object in nature, for he cannot conceive of what body is, even less of the mind. Least of all can he conceive of how a body can be united to a mind. There lies the very summit of his difficulties, and yet it is his own nature.[61]

The inability of science to produce certain knowledge does not mean that technology cannot improve our lives, you might reply. Pascal, the inventor of the first calculating machine and the first system of public transit, would be the first to agree. But he saw clearly what eluded Descartes: that technology without science is blind. "Man's nature is not always to go forward, but back and forth ... So it is with man's inventions from age to age. So with good and evil generally in the world."[62]

Could contemporary science furnish some splendid rebuttal to Pascal's attack? Perhaps, if it has certain knowledge of big or small or middling things. Or certainties about mind or body. If it has established beyond correction any substantive empirical claim concerning either the world or ourselves. But, except in the bubbly prose of scientistic popularizers, science pretends to no such achievements.

On the other hand, science does not need to achieve perfect certainty in order to show its conclusions to be more probable than the ones it rejects. Theories and demonstrations are the eyes of the mind, and many of our theories are like eyes enhanced with microscopic or telescopic lenses relaying information to computer-enhanced minds. We have properly formulated, well-attested theories, and scientific realists believe them true. Those who believe our current theories also believe that by their means we are at last beginning to understand ourselves and our world. With what they intend as modesty scientific popularizers will say we are *just beginning* to unravel the mystery of X or Y. A quick Google search of the phrase "just beginning to unravel" showed us to be on the point of understanding the brain, La Niña, global governance, human metabolism, sex, and dreams. It was an average day.

But Pascal sees further evidence of our wretchedness precisely in the comfort current theories tend to provide. There always are current theories, and they would not be current unless they seemed just about to unravel the mystery of things. The difficulty is that they never seem so for long. The sad epistemic ambiguity of our condition, Pascal says, lies in our being "incapable of either knowing for certain or being completely ignorant."

> We row in mid-ocean immensity, always uncertain. Drifting. Listing from one side to the other. Fixtures bend and elude us. Just when we thought to catch hold and steady ourselves they slip away, forever receding from us. Nothing stops for us. Motion is our natural state, yet the one most contrary to our inclination.[63]

Pascalian caution about the claims of science seems wiser than Cartesian exuberance, and wiser than the scientism that has been with us since the Enlightenment. Yet Pascal would not be surprised if his critique of science were met with scepticism. It is one of his tenets that people believe mainly what they want to believe. The last thing our modern secular society wishes to hear is that science is not a reliable guide, for we permit ourselves no other. No modern liberal democracy, for example, can justify its policy initiatives without some appeal to science.[64]

## Justice

The limitations of science have profound social consequences. "Justice and truth," Pascal says, "are points of such subtlety that our instruments are too blunt to draw them exactly."[65] How can it be otherwise? Modern politics rests on science. Science is too weak to furnish truth. To depend so much on what is undependable cannot but affect our attempts to achieve justice.

"[J]ustice has been understood across cultures and historical periods to be a secular and a rational virtue," a contemporary writer on distributive justice informs us,

> whose demands can be explained and justified without appeal to religious beliefs; to be a virtue that governments can and should enforce, and that indeed ought to be the prime norm guiding political activity.[66]

Pascal is not prepared to consider justice as a secular virtue. He thinks our idea of justice is religious in origin and for that very reason sets a standard that earthly polities recognize but cannot meet.[67] We would be lucky if the only impediment to justice was the defectiveness of our understanding. If that were so, rulers might occasionally devise just policies, if only by blundering into them. But our political situation is even less hopeful. Injustice is overdetermined, as we would put it nowadays. It is bound to occur. Pascal's account of it makes a succinct, if depressing, primer on distributive justice.

Some of the few pages Pascal devoted to political philosophy are contained in his brief work, "Three Discourses on the Condition of the Great."[68] Much of his political thought must be gleaned from isolated fragments of explosive character, scattered like landmines throughout the *Pensées*.[69]

His brevity is intentional. Long-windedness is a sign of levity in political philosophers, Pascal thinks. Philosophers like Plato and Aristotle, who wrote a lot about politics, were not serious in doing so. It was "the least philosophical and least serious part of their life ... They wrote about politics as they might have devised rules for an insane asylum."[70] Pascal, therefore, will be earnest and brief. But he is also paradoxical: "fundamentally conservative," Laurent Thirouin calls him, "hostile to any attempt to question the established social or political order, yet radically critical of that order."[71]

Distributive justice concerns the allocation of goods to those who deserve them. But what goods? Pascal follows tradition in thinking that the goods in need of distribution are *offices*, and the persons considered deserving are those who exhibit merits appropriate to the office they receive.[72] Plato takes this view in the *Republic*, which looks for ways of ensuring that rulers are wise, soldiers brave, and so forth. Contemporary readers are surprised by the indifference of classical political philosophers towards the just distribution of material goods.

But the difference in outlook is not difficult to explain. In his influential work, *De officiis*, Cicero strictly differentiates the demands of justice (*iustitia*) from those of charity (or what Cicero called *beneficentia*).[73] The material well-being of our neighbours, according to Cicero, is not a concern of justice, but only of charity. Charity goes beyond justice and is therefore not subject to legal enforcement.

Good people of course act charitably. That is part of what makes them good. But had their charitable acts been forced upon them, those acts would not have counted as charitable and would not have contributed to the moral stature of the agents who performed them.

Recent theories of distributive justice begin by collapsing Cicero's distinction between justice and charity. Next they invert his priorities. Whereas Cicero believes we must take a person's moral merits into consideration even in our acts of charity,[74] to us it seems that even the bare demands of justice would be unsatisfied, if a substantial part of the population were left in material want, whatever might be the probity or depravity of their lives.[75]

Contemporary readers are often unaware that the traditional view of justice went almost unchallenged until the Enlightenment. Only gradually, beginning in the late eighteenth century, did our default position on justice move to where it is today. First we began to take for granted that *material goods*, rather than offices, are what call for distribution. And only after that did we come to believe that mere existence, rather than merit, entitled someone to a share in these goods.

Even a writer as late as Adam Smith barely recognized the idea of a universal claim to material well-being, raising it only for the purpose of refuting it.[76] We must therefore beware of distorting Pascal's brief political reflections by retrojecting present conceptions of justice onto them. When he sets out to prove that justice is never done, he has in mind justice as traditionally conceived.

Why, then, can offices never be assigned by merit? In an age of affirmative action, that aspiration may appear to be out of date. But Pascal's answer is, I think, still of interest. Office cannot be assigned by merit, he says, in his "first discourse on the condition of the great," because merit itself is a fiction.

No doubt his dismissive view of human merit is derived from Jansenism, but Pascal does not think you need religious revelation to understand it. He demonstrates it with arguments drawn from both nature and nurture.

First, how can anything come to us by merit when our character itself is the result of "infinitely chancy" circumstances?[77] Your genetic makeup, for instance, is the contingent result of alliances and misalliances, stretching back into your family's shadowy (and perhaps at times shady) past. Every living being is the outcome of so many improbable contingencies that each is a statistical miracle. No one therefore can take any credit for the nature with which he is born.

Neither can you claim responsibility for the nurture you received. The material and social circumstances into which you were born were brought about by the prudence, folly, or sheer luck of your ancestors, for which you deserve no credit. If they were prudent, it was only possible because of the stable society on which they relied, for prudence is impracticable without the law. But your ancestors had no hand in creating the social order on which they relied.

Does the rule of law itself not imply the existence of meritorious lawmakers, you might wonder. Not a bit, says Pascal. "Natural right" never guides legislators, he says. They are always guided by "naked will."[78] If they make good laws, it is because it suits them to do so, not because they recognize the natural right and act upon it.

This sweeping condemnation of lawmakers looks ridiculously glib. But that is partly because it has in mind a premodern notion of natural right. A long tradition in philosophy and jurisprudence, with both Stoic and Christian roots, claims that there is a natural law of justice written on our hearts. Though in our particular actions we can fail to observe this law, the tradition teaches, its general precepts cannot fail to be known.[79]

"There no doubt are natural rights," Pascal allows, in a broad concession to the Catholic tradition from which, despite his Jansenism, he does not wish to stray too far.[80] But whatever role they play, they cannot override the fact that "our beautiful corrupted reason has corrupted everything."[81] Philippe Sellier is right to say that, for Pascal, man is not so corrupt as to be incapable of perceiving what is right, but Pascal also thinks our reason corrupt enough that we can be unconscious of the natural law when we act, or, at best, only intermittently conscious of it.[82]

Legislators, concerned as they are with enacting particular laws, therefore may have no regard for natural law. They may be guided, as Pascal claims they are, only by their naked will. "Kings of concupiscence," Pascal calls them in the third of his discourses.[83] It would be reassuring if he included in his censure only legislators who have happened to come to power up to the present. Then one could hope for better things in the future. The political system could be modified, as utopians dream of doing, to ensure that virtuous people ruled.

But justice of that kind cannot happen except by the grace of God, which in the postlapsarian world is only selectively given. Augustine's famous contrast between the City of God and the city of man is influential in the thought of Pascal. The City of God would be one established by charity, but the city we know in daily experience, the city of man, is established by what Pascal, following Augustine, calls concupiscence.

Concupiscence is a wrongful attachment to earthly things. It is the most conspicuous and the most toxic characteristic inherited from the Fall. Together with self-love, it works to dethrone God from his place as the natural object of all our love.[84] Because concupiscence is inseparable from our fallen condition, we, who so plainly see the manipulative chicanery of our legislators, would act no differently if we were in their place. All voluntary human acts are touched with concupiscence. The only acts that are free from it are those we are forced to perform.[85] And even actions we perform under duress are concupiscent if some other person forces us to do them. In performing them we merely operate under another concupiscence than our own. Where secular politics is concerned, every act is concupiscent.

The corollary is that every political order is unjust. Our rulers discover "they have no way of satisfying their concupiscence that does not involve wronging others."[86] And again, "We use concupiscence as best we can to establish a public good. But it is only fakery, a simulacrum of charity."[87]

What world is Pascal describing, you may wonder. Things are simply not that bad. Surely admitting we are all prone to self-love, or concupiscence, does not entail that there is no justice in political life.

Pascal admits that appearances are against him. He sees how the political order can be "beautiful" and "admirable," even if it is only a simulacrum of charity.[88] If his jaundiced view of justice is to make any sense to us, it is probably necessary to see it in the context of his time – that is, addressing Europe in the aftermath of the Thirty Years War.[89] With that war's conclusion in 1648 came also the end of Christendom, with its hierarchical system of international justice, presided over by Pope and Emperor. A venerable administrative structure passed away and was replaced by a community of sovereign nations. For that reason the peace of Westphalia, with which the war concluded, came to stand for a new era in international law. Pascal's diffident theory of justice can be seen as a response to that new era.

Though post-Westphalian Europe was only in its infancy, Pascal was alert to its dangers. The community of sovereign nations that replaced Christendom had no mechanism for resolving disputed questions of law. The very phrase "community of nations" can be construed in two different ways, reflecting two incompatible conceptions of justice. If the nations compose a true community, then the laws they promulgate should have an objective basis reflected in an international consensus. Some saw Westphalia that way, drawing on the old idea of natural law still found in Grotius. Others, however, stressed not the community but its component nations. Law, to these theorists, meant absolutism, the unfettered will of the sovereign. Both conceptions existed together for a time, but absolutism was stronger. The inevitable result was "the weakening of the notion that all states form and are a part of an international community":

> Instead of creating a society of states, the Peace of Westphalia, while paying lip service to the idea of a Christian commonwealth, merely ushers in the era of sovereign absolutist states which recognized no superior authority. In this era the liberty of states becomes increasingly incompatible with the concept of the international community.[90]

Pascal looks to Montaigne for tools with which to understand his time,[91] but he goes beyond Montaigne when he pronounces the political tension of his day, arising out of the Westphalian settlement, to be beyond remedy:

> On what will [a ruler] found the economy of the people (*monde*) he wants to govern? Will it be on the caprice of each particular person? What confusion! Will it be on justice? He does not know what it is. Certainly if he knew what justice is he would not have established that most general maxim current among men, that each should follow the mores of his own country. Instead the light of pure equity would have subjected all people to itself. Legislators would not have cast enduring justice aside in favour of Persian and German fantasies and caprices.[92]

Sometimes a thinker's views may be placed in the context of his time as a polite way of declaring them obsolete. That is not my intention in drawing attention to the Westphalian setting of Pascal's political thought, however. Instead my intention is to bring out its enduring character. When we question the effectiveness of the United Nations today or debate about globalization, we struggle with the same moral question, often using the very same terms.[93] That question is whether there is some objective moral basis on which universal justice can be founded. Or are there only vehement assertions of culturally given norms and values, without universal significance, imposed locally and by force?

Pascal's view was that, because we do not know the natural law, voluntarism prevails. While it may be impossible not to know natural law in theory, as Aquinas held, Pascal emphasizes how elusive such knowledge is in practice. Yet rulers still have to rule. So what can they do?

> Being unable to enforce what is just, they make it just to obey what is enforceable. Having no power to fortify justice, they use power to justify force. The point is to bring force and justice together so that peace triumphs, which is the greatest good.[94]

Pascal does not mean that peace is really the highest good, but only that it is the greatest consolation prize available when the negotiating parties are not just.[95] There are times when peace may appear to be the greatest good, as it did after the devastation of the Thirty Years War, but then a glass of water appears to be the greatest good after a long walk on a hot day.

Though peace is of course highly desirable, it is only a relative good. When we take it as such, it furnishes an example of how something can be on one hand a mere simulacrum of charity and yet on the other hand both beautiful and admirable. Wars result from conflicting interests, and wars are usually worse than the injustices out of which they arise. Sooner or later there must be peace. But how to preserve peace in a world of invincible concupiscence? Peace presupposes justice, and it is beyond the power of politicians to bring about a political order that is just. Therefore they must impose an order that is politically achievable and try to make people believe it is just. The more stable the peace they create by these means, the more it is admirable and beautiful, simulacrum of charity though it is.[96] As Nicholas Hammond puts it, "man's very fallen nature, his *concupiscence*, has achieved a certain coherence which amounts to a form of justice."[97]

Our corrupt will is the source of political order. Even if we are able to bring about peace, which is a good thing, the achievement is always a temporary one. Peace is always precarious because it results not from justice but from equilibrium among the concupiscent wishes of those who negotiated it.

Politics is dirty, many are prepared to concede, but with the tacit proviso that political theory is clean. That is another commonplace that Pascal stands on its head. At least dirty politics gives rise to political order, he thinks, but out of political theory comes first dissent and then, at last, disaster. There is a straightforward reason for this. Political theorists examine the political order in an attempt to ascertain whether it is just. But no order can withstand such scrutiny because all are unjust.

> The art of political criticism, of overthrowing states, is to upset established customs by sounding them to their very source and showing their want of authority and justice. They say we must get back to the fundamental and primitive laws that some unjust customs have abolished. It's a sure bet for losing everything. Weighed in that balance nothing will be just.[98]

Political theory is dangerous particularly when its complaints are justified. People will recognize that they are justified, and revolution will result. Though political theory can never produce real justice, it can destroy whatever simulacrum of it exists:

> The people easily lend their ears to such harangues. When they see the truth, they throw off the yoke. The great ones profit by their ruin and by the ruin of those who examine our received customs with curiosity.[99]

Revolutions spare only the rulers, Pascal cynically observes, though it presumably forces these rulers to devise some new simulacrum of charity by which to rule (and fool) the people.

But the upshot is this: We neither have nor ever will have a just political order. That is the final chapter in Pascal's tale of human wretchedness.

The aftermath of the Thirty Years War was a setting in which brooding pessimism about human prospects could be justified. But as the memory of war faded, so did the plausibility of such dire reflections on the human condition. Time has done nothing to restore Pascal's outlook on life, yet the passage of time has also not entirely extinguished its appeal. In the next chapter I shall show that Pascal's ponderous pessimism is still useful as a critical philosophical tool.

# 3 His Critics' Critic

Pascal's unsparing depiction of human wretchedness makes fascinating reading. Philosophical failure takes its place as a single feature in a setting of unspeakable bleakness. Natural science, anthropology, psychology, social and political philosophy all founder in that mythic ocean of human anxiety, guilt, and uncertainty known as the Fall.

It is an uninviting picture. Yet Pascal's words rarely have the sobering effect on readers their author seems to have intended. One reader may grow agreeably pensive at the arguments of the preceding chapter, another may be a little amused. We may tire of them, or, like the philosophers of the Enlightenment, grow indignant at them. However, it is very difficult to imagine the reader who would tremble and grow pale at Pascal's words or be plunged into despair, as if some dire medical verdict had just been rendered on his health. Yet, if Pascal is right, we are even worse off than we would be if our only concern were some terminal disease.

Common sense does not easily recognize itself in Pascal's dismal sayings. We are not *that* uncertain of everything, we can't help thinking, nor *that* unjustly treated. "*I* don't normally exchange tormented looks with people I meet on the street," normal folk will think. And they have a point. Well-adjusted people, enjoying ordinary health and prosperity, don't think they have much in common with chained convicts awaiting execution. Ironically, they may even find Pascal's sour rants about human wretchedness diverting, just as satires on mankind are amusing to those who feel above them.

Scholars often comment on how unconvincing Pascal's anthropology is, and attribute its lack of traction to different causes. On one point, however, they agree. They recognize that a new, more optimistic conception of man began forming in the early Enlightenment, and think that Pascal's simply failed to grasp its importance.

Thus Hugo Friedrich thinks Pascal distorts the fresh view of man found in Montaigne by forcing it back into the Christian framework from which Montaigne pried it loose:

> Pascal re-Christianizes what Montaigne had wrenched free of Christian accusations. Though the motif of human wretchedness (*Erniedrigung*) occurs often in the *Essais*, its echo always sounds as well: human beings just are that way.[1]

To Friedrich, Pascal's heavy-handed use of a Christian critical framework suggests that he either overlooked the embryonic conception of man found in the essays of Montaigne or downplayed it as some erroneous and unimportant fad. Instead of taking Montaigne's anthropology seriously, Pascal treats his own framework of Christian moralism, and the wretchedness he uses it to display, as if they were among the ground floor facts of life. They are not facts of life at all, however, but only a severe, narrow, and now outdated and implausible view of the facts. That is why Pascal's assertions about human wretchedness are bound to be rejected by a post-Christian world.

Friedrich would no doubt find additional evidence of unworldly naiveté in the shock Pascal professes "that something as obvious as the vanity of the world is so little known" or "that it should be so strange and surprising to mention the folly of seeking greatness."[2]

The historian of ideas René Pintard points out that Pascal missed almost completely the challenge of *le libertinage érudit*. He was deaf to the provocations of philosophers like Gassendi or La Mothe le Vayer, with whom he ought to have been familiar.[3]

Some scholars have been led by the apparent insufficiency of Pascal's arguments to embark on the historically fascinating, but philosophically futile, quest to find an opponent superficial enough to be confuted by the arguments Pascal makes.[4]

Perhaps it would be better simply to concede that Pascal's anthropology is a dead end. Before concluding that it is so, however, it would make sense to get a better idea of what the new conception of man is, the one Pascal is supposed to have had such trouble understanding. It would also be good to know at what historical point Pascal's alternative became obsolete or whether any Pascalian rejoinders are possible to the criticisms levelled against him.

## Voltaire

If common sense rejects Pascal's pessimism, serious intellectuals often find it disagreeable, as did the *philosophes* of the eighteenth century. "This message – 'you are miserable' – more than anything else irritated the great writers of the French Enlightenment," Leszek Kolakowski tells us.[5]

Voltaire's reaction typifies what Kolakowski has in mind. "It seems to me," wrote Voltaire,

> Monsieur Pascal wished to depict man in an odious light when he wrote these *Pensées*. He is determined to paint us all as evil and unhappy. He writes against human nature in more or less the same spirit that he wrote against the Jesuits. He imputes to our essential nature characteristics that apply only to certain people. With eloquence he insults the human race.[6]

Voltaire's words show insight as well as impatience. The link he makes between Pascal's attack on Jesuits and his depiction of human nature is perceptive. Pascal was not a dogged apologist for the Christian status quo of the kind Voltaire delighted to pillory.[7] Voltaire recognizes in Pascal a fellow critic.

A new and liberating vision of human possibilities was blowing throughout the modern age, and Voltaire was eager to let it fill his sails. Pascal seemed somehow to stand in the way, and Voltaire felt the need to address him. Voltaire treated Pascal not as a reactionary in need of enlightenment so much as a dangerous fellow critic whose opposing vision had to be engaged. The breathless rhetoric of Voltaire's assault betrays his apprehensions concerning the advocate for the other side.

What could the motivation be, Voltaire wonders in print, for Pascal's gratuitous attack on human life? "Why make us horrified at what we are? Our existence is not as unhappy as he would have us believe. To regard the universe as a dungeon and all men as criminals on death row is the idea of a fanatic."[8]

To Voltaire Pascal's provocations are as a gauntlet thrown down. Rising to defend human nature against the attacks of this "sublime misanthrope," Voltaire undertakes to prove that "we are neither as evil nor as unhappy as [Pascal] says."[9]

We find the most trenchant of Voltaire's reflections on Pascal in a strange place. They constitute the last of his *Lettres philosophiques*. That is strange because the preceding twenty-four letters in that collection are devoted to watering the seedlings of rationalism, deism, and unbelief Voltaire found growing in England on his visit there in the late 1720s. Neither the English setting nor the antireligious theme is calculated to bring Pascal to mind. Why, then, does Voltaire turn in his last and longest letter from praising eighteenth-century English progressivism to attacking a backward-looking seventeenth-century French religious writer?

So incongruous does the closing letter seem that some editions have simply omitted it. Yet Voltaire was keen enough to include the twenty-fifth letter that he gave up his original title, *Letters Written from London, on the English and Other Subjects,* in favour of the more general *Philosophical Letters.*[10] Why would Voltaire see a systematic attack on the *Pensées* as the best way to conclude his reflections on the progressive English?

Scholars have naturally looked for thematic connections between the last letter and its predecessors, and little by little some have emerged. Roland Desné shows that Pascal's writings were popular in England and were receiving renewed attention during the period of Voltaire's visit. From that he concludes that opposing Pascal, as Voltaire did, amounted to "taking a stand in a debate."[11]

What debate? On the surface it concerns the philosophical credentials of unbelief. But Desné rightly looked deeper. The bedrock issue lies in Voltaire's "affirmation of a view of man," Desné says, in "a moral conception that could find its full meaning only in the living example of the mores and thought of the English."[12]

Voltaire's excitement about a new anthropology is especially striking in his dismissal of a fragment mentioned earlier in this chapter (L421/ S680) in which Pascal traces "every disorder" – economic, political, even corporeal – to the depravity of our self-seeking will. Voltaire's rejection of this idea is categorical: "For a society to be formed and to subsist without self-love (*amour-propre*)" Voltaire tells us,

> is as impossible as it would be for babies to come about without lust, or self-nourishment without appetite, and so forth. Love of ourselves is a precondition for love of others. Our reciprocal needs make us useful to the human race. Such needs are the foundation of all commerce and the eternal bond among men. Without them not a single art would have been invented, nor a society of even ten persons formed. Self-love is nature's gift to every animal. It alerts us to respect the self-love we see in others.[13]

The new anthropology is naturalistic rather than moralistic. It takes man as he is, concupiscence, self-love, and all. And the world is his oyster. His function is not to wallow in misery and self-criticism but to pursue an active life in quest of his own happiness. Societies form from the bottom up, as a by-product of self-seeking, not from the top down, by the machinations of legislators, as Pascal supposes. Society arises when we all pursue our own ends, each one's acquisitive egocentrism being, on balance, beneficial to all. Life is exciting and good. Things are not nearly as bad as Pascal makes them out to be.

Voltaire did not have to invent this alternative to Pascal's Christian pessimism. He encountered it in early-eighteenth-century England in the form of a prospering and increasingly articulate style of life. Self-seeking had even been controversially defended there as a basis for individual and political life in Bernard Mandeville's famous satire, *The Fable of the Bees*. Mandeville argued that the marketplace is the best regulator of morality, and that "private vices" make "public benefits."[14] Despite admitting "that a state based on selfishness is corrupt, and that luxury is contrary to the Christian religion," Mandeville cheerfully shows that, nevertheless, "all society must be based on selfishness and that no state can be great without luxury."[15] The mantle of the most hated British philosopher, worn by Hobbes in the seventeenth century, passed to Mandeville in the eighteenth.[16] As with Hobbes, however, Mandeville's influence was even greater than the odium he had to endure.

More lasting than Mandeville's cynicism was the naturalism with which he sought to explain moral and economic life. It allowed for the thought that economic and moral self-improvement could go hand in hand. This is the line of thinking planted in Voltaire by his English sojourn, and it continued to mature in Britain throughout the Enlightenment. The greatest thinkers of the Scottish Enlightenment, David Hume and Adam Smith, who were later to become Voltaire's friends, would give classic expression to it in their influential defences of the civilizing effect of commercial life. Though neither saw any need to reply to Pascal, his outlook on life continued to be a *negative* point of reference. Smith classes Pascal's account of human wretchedness among the efforts of "whining and melancholy moralists" who "seek to render a certain melancholy dejectedness habitual among men."[17]

Voltaire is not able to dismiss Pascal so easily. He sees the need to answer him, that is, to treat Pascal as a philosopher. A distinctive merit of philosophical theories is that they can grow old without becoming obsolete. If to be old were the same as to be disqualified, then Voltaire would gain no advantage from criticizing Pascal. Moreover, his own position would soon be disqualified, as would any of its successors. Historicism of that kind makes all philosophical positions insignificant. It accepts the absurdity that the soundness of an argument depends on the date it is asserted rather than on the validity of its form and the truth of its premises.

A factual error would also be involved in dismissing Pascal's account of wretchedness as an artefact of his age. It is true that the Thirty Years War offered particularly good reasons for despair, and Pascal was undoubtedly responding to the monumental suffering that war brought about. But he never tries to tie what he says about wretchedness to that war in particular, or to any other contingent event.

The Thirty Years War simply brought into effect the kind of circumstances in which it is easy to recover the immemorial attitude of *contemptus mundi* (contempt for the world), that disparagement of this corrupt world or age (*kosmos* or *aion*), which the New Testament frequently compares unfavourably to the world or age to come.[18]

*Contemptus mundi* was thematic in early Christian ascetic writing and returns like a hardy perennial, whether as religious polemic or as satire, during periods of upheaval and reform.[19] The theme was already old when Pascal took it up and made it the protean explanatory matrix of his account of human wretchedness.

Not every period is receptive to such an idea. Pascal's generation could find in *contemptus mundi* an explanation of life, as the generation of Voltaire no longer could, and as few can today.[20] But although *contemptus mundi* is not felt in every age, its logic is bound to no particular time any more than is the understanding of man that sprouted in Montaigne and was putting forth its tentative blossoms in England during the visit of Voltaire. Each depends on an implicit anthropology it treats as fact. The centuries that separate Pascal and Voltaire from us have neither proven these two anthropologies obsolete nor ended their struggle with one another.

Voltaire's attempt to depict Pascal's account of our wretchedness as anachronistic should therefore be viewed as a dialectical one. It is a move against a critic in the game of inquiry. Voltaire's interlocutor in this case, being dead, can offer no rejoinder. But the reader can. Pascal left behind plenty of critical ordnance. A reader can often see without much difficulty how to use it.

Pascal might have compared the easy-going self-assertion admired by Voltaire to something less flattering. Perhaps to what the renowned American emancipationist and former slave, Frederick Douglass, called "stupid contentment," a condition he often witnessed in slaves. Only through much study had he risen above it himself. "The more I read," Douglass said, "the more I was led to abhor and detest slavery." In lively words he describes the changes that came over him as he learned to see his own enslavement realistically:

> I was no longer the light-hearted, gleesome boy, full of mirth and play, as when I landed first at Baltimore. Knowledge had come; light had penetrated the moral dungeon where I dwelt; and, behold! there lay the bloody whip, for my back, and here was the iron chain; and my good, kind master, he was the author of my situation. The revelation haunted me, stung me, and made me gloomy and miserable. As I writhed under the sting and torment of this knowledge, I almost envied my fellow slaves their *stupid contentment*. This knowledge opened my eyes to the horrible pit, and revealed the teeth of the frightful dragon that was ready to pounce upon me, but it opened no way for my escape. I have often wished myself a beast, or a bird – anything, rather than a slave. I was *wretched and gloomy, beyond my ability to describe*. I was too thoughtful to be happy. It was this everlasting thinking which distressed and tormented me; and yet there was no getting rid of the subject of my thoughts. (my italics)[21]

Douglass was already an abolitionist when he wrote these lines. Denouncing "stupid contentment" had for him a double aim. First, he hoped it would show those in slavery how much they were deceived, and so inspire them not to tolerate it any longer. And, second, he hoped it would confront slave owners with the iniquity of their practice, and so put an end to their attempts to extenuate their conduct by appealing to the apparent happiness of slaves.

Today we would describe what Douglass was doing as 'consciousness raising.' He was trying to open everyone's eyes to the "horrible pit" of slavery, and reveal "the teeth of that frightful dragon." He was not interested in how things subjectively appeared, but in what they objectively were.

Pascal saw himself as doing something similar – raising consciousness about chains less visible, but no less imprisoning, than those of the American slaves. We could understand Pascal to mean that people like Voltaire, who mock the very idea that they are in chains, are twice fettered: first by their true condition and second by their failure to recognize it.

They would resemble people who treat the fables of Lafontaine as childish things, never considering how their own lives are put in question by the moral maxims with which the fables conclude. Or they would resemble the readers of *The Aeneid*, whom Augustine pities, because they weep for the fate of Dido while they move inexorably to their own life's tragic end.[22]

What "incomprehensible enchantment," we might ask, using Pascal's words, permits people to quibble about the literal truth of their wretchedness, and so miss its moral truth. These people must surely be in some "supernatural coma."[23]

Pascal's "incomprehensible enchantment" or "supernatural coma" are akin to Frederick Douglass's "stupid contentment." There is a more recent name for what all these ideas are getting at. It is 'false consciousness,' a term introduced at the end of the nineteenth century by Friedrich Engels.[24] Pascal's answer to Voltaire might be that his uncritical acceptance of the new man, as he came to understand it in England, was simply an instance of false consciousness. It is a piece of wishful thinking that conceals, without removing, the wretchedness at the heart of the human condition.

To accuse Voltaire of false consciousness would be a fine move for Pascal to make in this imaginary, anachronistic debate. But responses seldom go unanswered, and it is not too hard to imagine Voltaire responding to Pascal. When Engels, whom anachronism also permitted to join the conversation, introduced the term 'false consciousness,' he coupled it with ideology. False consciousness arises, Engels says, when we embrace some ideology for reasons that appear convincing to us, but actually rest on an untenable view of our real material situation.

For example, a factory worker who accepts as 'natural' the exploitative conditions in which he works would be a victim of bourgeois ideology, at least in the eyes of a communist. He would therefore be living in false consciousness. Similarly, a radical feminist consciousness-raiser might accuse a housewife who claims to be happily married of living in false consciousness. Marriage, the consciousness-raiser might say, is in reality a form of enslavement.

As these examples illustrate, the charge of false consciousness can be laid with at least some plausibility in a variety of circumstances, and from the point of view of a variety of ideologies. However, to be effective, it must not be seen as rhetorical. It must be taken as *true*. That is why consciousness raising is harder than it looks.

The reality of false consciousness is very difficult to prove, especially in an atmosphere of competing ideologies. In fact, even to level the charge of false consciousness against someone else involves a pragmatic fallacy, unless you are plainly clear of ideology yourself. The accused in any of my examples may be wearing ideological blinders, but if the accuser has only some different set of blinders to offer, what incentive is there to change? Why should the worker who is glad to have a job or the housewife who likes her marriage accept rebukes that rest on nothing but some *other* ideology? Pragmatically speaking, you can only appeal to false consciousness effectively if your own position is in the clear, and is seen to be so by the person you criticize.

Let us call that the *pragmatic requirement of objectivity*. That requirement is not likely to be met when (waving the wand of anachronism) we allow Pascal to accuse Voltaire of false consciousness for denying the wretchedness of human existence. Voltaire could object, as Hugo Friedrich did on behalf of Montaigne, that Pascal arrives at his own view by passing life through the sieve of Christian ideology. That sieve, Voltaire would no doubt say, holds back everything grand and attractive, letting through only what is tiny and vile. Adding the weapon of false consciousness to Pascal's arsenal will do him no good, then, unless he can also meet the pragmatic requirement of objectivity.

Of course Voltaire is no more able to meet the requirement of objectivity than Pascal is. Neither side can do better than offer evidence in its own favour. Each, if he is honest, must acknowledge that there is some evidence on the other side. However, Pascal does acknowledge it. As he puts it in connection with his famous wager argument, "reason cannot decide the matter either way."[25]

The stalemate the adversaries reach in this imaginary debate is favourable to Pascal in at least one point: it allows us to understand him as a philosopher. He does not have to win the exchange to be recognized as his critic's critic. He occupies a dialectical position that is not ruled out by new anthropologies merely because they evolved at a later date. Pascal has marshalled evidence for human wretchedness; he has supplied analogies, anecdotes, and arguments that can be used to examine alternative conceptions of life.

Pascal's position is neither tautological nor indefeasible. It is empirical and subject to refutation. Pascal contends that mankind's fallen nature prevents him from finding happiness. Therefore, he would be refuted if a natural recipe for human happiness could be found. He would stand refuted if such a recipe were even shown to be possible.

There are two logically possible conditions under which even Pascal would admit that man could be happy. We would be happy if our nature could be transcended in such a way that our misery was overcome, or if our wretchedness could be mitigated by some therapy that allowed for fulfilled acceptance of our present state. Neither condition would have to be achieved to refute Pascal. It would merely have to be possible, for then our wretchedness could in principle be left behind. It would not be our second and inescapable *nature* as Pascal maintains it is.[26] Transcendence and therapy have each had utopian supporters, and so we should consider whether Pascal could engage them critically.

## Nietzsche

Friedrich Nietzsche thought human nature could be transcended. He also avowed an extravagant admiration for Pascal, claiming not only to "love" him,[27] but to have Pascal's blood flowing in his veins.[28] Nietzsche enthusiastically embraced Pascal as an interlocutor, even while setting himself up as Pascal's sternest critic. Eduard Zwierlein summarizes Nietzsche's mixed assessment of Pascal:

> Pascal typified a certain psychological type for Nietzsche, one with which he identified. It combined the sharpest insight, the most brilliant eloquence, with impatient radicalism. The heroic one-sidedness of these qualities breathed new power and resolution even into what Nietzsche normally held to be sick Christianity, with its motif of "vanitas," and its theory of wretchedness as the basic pattern of the world. Pascal was a Titan of the spirit. Unable to master the world in its present form, he suffered from it so much that he became "the prodigious logician of Christianity." His thought fashions a religious attitude out of despair and internal hatred. Out of powerful mockery he makes comedy and tragedy. Or rather, putting even the art of moralism aside, Pascal created a universal, erroneous religious theory.[29]

It is fitting to consider Nietzsche's attitude towards Pascal just after concluding with Voltaire's. Nietzsche admired both men and took something from each. But he combined their views in a way neither would recognize or accept. He agrees with Pascal about human decadence[30] while divorcing it from the Fall. He embraces Voltaire's hostility to

Christianity but not his championing of human legitimacy. It wasn't only fallen man that Nietzsche rejected, but man as such. He dreamt not of rehabilitating man but of transcending him. Man was destined to disappear in order that the *Übermensch*, or superman, could flourish.

Nietzsche's idea of the superman is never unambiguously defined, but Charles Natoli offers an admirable characterization of it all the same. The superman is

> noble, lofty of spirit, and perhaps most important he is radically autono-
> mous, a value-creator, a law unto himself. In his hardness and greatness
> of spirit he says "Yes!" to life no matter what terrors it may hold. He is a
> *briseur d'obstacles* who delights in enemies worthy of himself. He is master
> of himself.[31]

The superman will somehow rise above both the self-hatred Nietzsche thinks he sees in Pascal[32] and the self-satisfaction he deplores in the modern *homo economicus*.[33] Both of them are human, all-too-human, and therefore contemptible in Nietzsche's eyes. Unfortunately, the way leading from them up to the superman is long and steep.

Too long and too steep it seems. More than a century after Nietzsche's death we are no closer to arriving at it. Even the necessary intervening stage that Nietzsche called "preparatory men" seems not yet to have been reached.

Nietzsche may have expected too much even of preparatory men. That at least would account for the fact that, although admirers of Nietzsche are today as abundant as sand on the oceans' shores, it is difficult to name one among them who would count even as a prepara-tory man, let alone a superman. Just recall the job description and con-sider how few people aspire to it, even among Nietzsche's professed admirers: "I welcome all the signs of a more manly, warlike era begin-ning," Nietzsche writes in the piece called "preparatory men,"

> one that will bestow honour first and foremost on bravery. For that era
> must prepare the way for an even higher one, and store up energy nee-
> ded for that new age, an age that will lift heroism into the sphere of
> knowledge, waging wars because of ideas and their consequences. To get
> there we need for the time being lots of brave men to prepare the way.
> They cannot come from nowhere, any more than they can come from the
> sand and slime of the present civilization and its big-city education. They
> must be men who know how to be alone, silent and determined. Stable

men, content to go about their business unnoticed. They will be men with an inner propensity to assess every situation with a view to how it can be *overcome*. Men to whom hilarity, patience, smoothness, and contempt of the great vanities, are as natural as generosity in victory, and indulgence of the petty vanities of the conquered. Men who judge all conquerors freely and shrewdly, seeing the role coincidence plays in every victory and in fame. These men will have their own festivals, their own working days, their own times of mourning. They are accustomed to giving orders and equally ready, when appropriate, to obey. They will remain equally proud, whether in obedience or command, and never lose sight of their goal: to produce endangered men, more productive men, happier men! For believe me, the secret of achieving the greatest productivity, and of harvesting the greatest pleasure from existence is to *live dangerously*. Build your cities on Vesuvius! Send your ships into unexplored waters! Live at war with your neighbours and with yourselves. Be predators and conquerors, O knowing ones, until you can be rulers and possessors. The time when it was sufficient for you to live hidden lives, like shy deer in the woods, will soon be past. At some time knowledge will stretch out its hand to seize that for which it was born: it will wish to rule and take possession, and alongside it you will rule and possess.[34]

*Manly, warlike, brave. Rejecting this slimy civilization and the big-city education it prizes. Heroic and silent, scorning danger, proud, pleasure-loving, and predatory. Free. Shrewd. Generous in victory. At ease with the conquerors they have conquered.*

You may know many of these people, but I confess to knowing none. And these are only the preparatory men, the ones who will make straight the path of the superman. Even they are as rare as leprechauns.

But Nietzsche's phrase "these men will have their festivals" brings to mind what reality offers in their place. Thinkers who prepare us to live our lives without religious consolations do not often resemble Nietzsche's preparatory men. They may, however, be like the sometime Oxford don and Cornell philosophy professor, Richard Robinson, author of a careful, influential, and rather sad book, *An Atheist's Values*. Though not a preparatory man, and certainly not a superman, he was a careful writer and a good philosopher. And he left an honest account of what a mid-twentieth-century atheist thought must be done.

The first sentence of one of Robinson's insightful paragraphs might have come from Nietzsche: "As our situation is far sterner than the theist dares to think," Robinson says, "so our possible attitude toward it is far nobler than he conceives." A fine beginning. But what follows does not sound like Nietzsche at all. Nietzsche calls for festivals for the new man, but Robinson would settle for less. "Symbols" would do. Even "procedures."

> We need to create and spread symbols and procedures that will confirm our intentions without involving us in intellectual dishonesty. This need is urgent today. For we have as yet no strong ceremonies to confirm our resolves except religious ceremonies, and most of us cannot join in religious ceremonies with a good conscience. When the *Titanic* went down, people sang "Nearer, my God, to thee." When the Gloucesters were in prison in North Korea they strengthened themselves with religious ceremonies. At present we know no other way to strengthen ourselves in our most testing and tragic times ... That is why it is urgent for us to create new ceremonies ... It is not enough to formulate honest and high ideals. We must also create the ceremonies and the atmosphere that will hold them before us at all times. I have no conception of how to do this.[35]

Do we perhaps owe such festivals as Earth Day to aspirations like these? The strange urgency of Robinson's writing makes one wonder why, more than a century after Nietzsche's death, atheism is still so wanting in symbolic support. Robinson explains:

> When we contemplate the friendless position of man in the universe, as it is right sometimes to do, our attitude should be the tragic poet's affirmation of man's ideals of behaviour. Our dignity, and our finest occupation, is to maintain our own self-chosen goods as long as we can, those great goods of beauty and truth and virtue. And among the virtues it is proper to mention in this connexion above all the virtues of courage and love. There is no person in this universe to love us except ourselves; therefore let us love one another. The human race is alone; but individual men need not be alone, because we have each other. We are brothers without a father; let us all the more for that behave brotherly to each other. The finest achievement for humanity is to recognize our predicament, including our insecurity and our coming extinction, and to maintain our cheerfulness and love and decency in spite of it, to prosecute our ideals in spite of it. We have good things to contemplate and high things to do. Let us do them.[36]

You need not be an atheist to be moved at these words. Their earnest integrity demands to be acknowledged. But the post-Nietzschean atheist in Robinson's description does not bear any comparison to the Nietzschean superman. He is nowhere near as glamorous as even the heroic preparatory man. Robinson's atheist is *friendless, tragic, alone, unloved, fatherless, insecure,* and *doomed.* Not at all what Nietzsche called for. But the description of him is closely related to what Jean-François Lyotard would later call the "postmodern condition," in which "each person is thrown back upon himself," like a Nietzschean hero, while unfortunately realizing "how little that self amounts to."[37] In the latter point postmodern man resembles Robinson's atheist antihero.

More interesting still: Robinson's words – *friendless, tragic, alone, unloved, fatherless, insecure, doomed* – would do as a succinct paraphrase of Pascal's description of human wretchedness. Robinson's atheist is in fact barely discernible from Pascal's wretched man. How fitting it is therefore that Pascal intended to introduce the main argument of the *Pensées* under the title "the wretchedness of man *without God.*"[38] As Pascal liked to observe, *les extrémités se touchent.*[39]

I am not trying to prove that Pascal is right and his atheist critics wrong. Perhaps the Nietzschean superman is a possibility. Preparatory men may even now be among us, going their silent ways. But if so they must still be lying low like shy deer in the woods. They have not yet made Pascal's description of human wretchedness obsolete. Instead Robinson's description of an atheist's values seems to boil down to the same thing.

### Therapy

The evidence that human nature can be transcended is less than overwhelming. And if it can't be transcended, then it can't be cured. But what refuses to be cured can sometimes be palliated. One still might argue that Pascal's emphasis on human wretchedness was misplaced if some effective *therapy* were available to mitigate human suffering, even if it only relieved the symptoms and left our wretched nature intact.

Wretchedness is not a medical condition, so medical therapy is not the kind at issue. Even with its medical sense out of the way, however, the word 'therapy' remains ambiguous in another way. At the high end of its semantic range, it can mean the same thing as 'cure,' but that is not how I am using it. I am using it in its broader, popular sense in which it applies to that wide swath of palliative interventions that fall short of being cures. They are often classified under the euphemism of *treatments.* Although cures for human misery are unavailable, the new question is whether there exist therapies, or treatments, sufficiently powerful to make Pascal's bleak analysis of the human condition irrelevant.

To what extent can therapy make our natural wretchedness endurable? Therapy covers a multitude of treatments. Do any of them come close enough to cures to disqualify Pascal's picture of wretchedness as "an image of the human condition?"[40] To prove him wrong, a candidate therapy would have to be at least as good as, say, insulin, which does not cure diabetes but enables most diabetics to live fairly normal lives. Are any treatments for wretchedness in the same league as insulin?

To judge by the vast number of therapies on offer, you would think that there must be at least one that is effective against wretchedness. Their inexhaustible variety makes ours an ideal age in which to investigate the matter empirically. In a book called *In Therapy We Trust*, Eva Moskowitz documents the proliferation in recent decades of both the demand for and supply of therapeutic treatment. Therapy is sought out and offered with almost religious zeal, so much so that Moskowitz derisively refers to it as our "therapeutic faith."[41] "Today Americans turn to psychological cures as reflexively as they once turned to God," she says. It is our "therapeutic gospel."[42]

It is true that Philip Rieff, in his landmark study *The Triumph of the Therapeutic*, referred to therapy as "the *unreligion* of the age and its master science"[43] (my emphasis), but he is not really disagreeing with Moskowitz. By 'unreligion' Rieff appears instead to mean a substitute for religion, since the subtitle of his study is "uses of faith after Freud." Rieff and Moskowitz agree that therapy can be an ersatz faith.

An enormous priesthood serves this faith. "In the United States today," Moskowitz reminds us, writing in 2001, "there are more than 40,000 psychiatrists, 65,000 family therapists, 125,000 psychologists, 10,000 psychoanalysts, and 150,000 social workers. The varieties of therapy on offer are nearly endless."[44] A sceptical reader need only walk through one of the proliferating medical plazas found in every city to be quickly satisfied on this point.

Moskowitz speaks as if faith in therapy were peculiarly American, but the three tenets she identifies as its creed claim many believers outside the United States. First, it holds that happiness should be our supreme goal; next, that any obstacle to achieving happiness is psychological; and, finally, that all such obstacles can be removed by therapeutic means.[45] If these tenets are true, then Pascal stands refuted.

Moskowitz, however, does not think that they are true. She laments that "there is little rigorous psychological thinking in our culture.

Rather, we embrace fast, simple, and often mindless solutions."[46] "Feeling management" and "pop psychology" "blind us to underlying economic and political realities."[47] Pascal would have suggested she add physiological, metaphysical, and, especially, theological realities to her list of matters the therapy industry has not adequately considered.

A mountain of dysfunctionality remains for therapists to level. Pascal calls it wretchedness. The therapy industry offers treatments for it, but, according to Moskowitz, the treatments fail. Therapies of the kind she describes offer neither a scientific nor even a quasi-religious path to happiness. They don't lead to happiness at all, though they promise it.

On the other hand, their failure to refute Pascal does nothing to establish his account of human wretchedness. There may be better therapists with better methods than those dealt with by Moskowitz. She has in fact been criticized for focusing too much on the superficial side of today's therapeutic industry.[48]

There might also be a point of weakness in Pascal's account of wretchedness, owing to its dependence on the idea of the Fall. As has already been pointed out, moral weakness functions in Pascal's thought as both a sign of our fallen condition and a root cause of our wretchedness. Therapy might be able to make us happy after all, if it could either free us from moral weakness or block its ability to make us wretched. Could it do either thing?

The earlier discussion of Nietzsche suggested that there is no *cure* for moral weakness. But a facetious advertisement published by Roy Sorenson in 1997 in the philosophy journal *Mind* appeared to show that such a cure could be had more easily than philosophers had previously suspected. He called his idea a "breakthrough in therapeutic philosophy."[49] Anyone suffering from moral weakness was invited to deposit $1,000 with Sorenson, who undertook to refund the full amount the next time the depositor performed a morally weak act.

One thing is certain: no subscriber will ever take advantage of Sorenson's money-back guarantee. No depositor will ever request his money back, because, after making his deposit, he can never be morally weak again. Why not? Because, if he contemplates an act of moral weakness, it will remind him that he stands to recover his $1000 by performing it. At that point the act he contemplates becomes one of calculating self-interest rather than moral weakness. Too bad, though. Acts of self-interest don't qualify for the refund; only acts of moral weakness do. And these the depositor can no longer commit.

Sorenson takes well-earned satisfaction in the novelty and ingenuity of his scheme:

> Old approaches focus on punishing the weak willed. This follows the anti-quated behaviorist principle that negative reinforcement extinguishes bad behavior. The new humanitarian approach rewards incontinence – and lavishly at that. The key is to make the reward so strongly motivating that an otherwise irrational act becomes rational.

The joy of the thing, Luc Bovens comments, is that "we will be able to let our passions soar while casting off the stigma of [moral weak-ness]."[50] And, he adds, "it is good to be reminded that there are other ways to deal with the proverbial sirens in our lives than by stuffing our ears with wax or having ourselves tied to the mast."[51]

Part of the satiric fun in this "cure for incontinence" lies in calling Sorensen's method "therapy." Like modern therapy, it is not moralis-tic; like modern therapy, it takes an affirmative rather than a critical view of the passions. Sorensen's method is also like modern therapy in a third important way. The cure it offers is verbal. It heals by moralizing nature, transforming egoistical self-indulgence into something morally good.

No commercial therapy has ever been quite so successful. Therapy can't moralize nature the way sophistry can, but it tries to get the same result by naturalizing morality instead. According to the philosopher Mike Martin's recent description,

> the therapeutic trend in ethics has the tendency to approach moral matters in terms of mental health, for example by pathologizing vices (alcoholism as a disease), psychologizing virtues (self-respect as self-esteem), and libe-ralizing attitudes (sex as good, guilt as suspect).[52]

Thus, real-life therapy involves creative re-description of the world. Some naturally achievable state of physical and mental competence is deemed to be healthy, and the privation of that state (for example, in alcoholism) is seen as sick. Therapists do not call alcoholism evil, or if they do, they mean by it only that alcoholism is an obstacle to health.

The *bien pensants* recoil at the idea of applying moral categories to a condition such as alcoholism, though it is known to lead to cancer of the stomach, kidneys, and liver, as well as to anxiety, depression, violent outbursts, and suicide, and to contribute to the destruction of families and communities. Still, to view the moral, medical, psychological, social, and economic destitution of many alcoholics in ethical terms is, to a modern therapist, a throwback to the age of Pascal. If the therapist admits it is undesirable to be an alcoholic, he means no more than he would in saying it is undesirable to have cancer. The "victims" of either condition may be viewed as wretched, but only in the sense that makes them candidates for therapy.

The flip side of all that lofty forbearance is that therapy also has no place for self-respect, as the passage quoted above mentions. Self-respect is alien to the therapeutic mentality because it implies the existence of some objective scale by which moral conduct can be evaluated. You can't respect yourself without judging yourself by some standard. The therapist replaces self-respect by the subtly different ideal of *self-esteem* – the latter being a subjective condition of self-approval that can be generated and maintained in the absence of real merit or achievement.

Finally, the therapist presents himself as his client's partner. He is there to help his client achieve a feeling of general well-being, including sexual well-being, and to aid the client in deflecting any adventitious sense of guilt.

Martin has more confidence in the therapeutic outlook than have Moskowitz or Rieff. At least some therapeutic methods can be understood as a sophisticated marriage of medicine and morality, Martin argues, anchored both in virtue ethics and in pragmatism.[53] The new conception of therapy reflected in these methods can lead to ways of coping with everything from alcoholism to marital conflict to violence – ways that are not merely new, Martin says, but achieve significant results.

However, Martin is better at justifying the therapeutic trend from within its own assumptions than he is at justifying the assumptions themselves. He banks on calls for external justification dwindling in the face of a growing list of therapeutic successes. "My hope," he writes in the epilogue to his book, "is that disagreements become less about the legitimacy of the therapeutic trend and more about specific areas of promise and peril."[54] Martin is thus content to allow empirical success rather than theoretical argument to justify the therapeutic trend.

So what would Pascal think of the claim that the "therapeutic trend" can make us happy, even in the weak sense of making us subjectively content with what objectively is misery? Can therapy provide even a reasonable simulacrum of happiness?

Pascal would be the first to concede that palliative therapy is better than nothing. It would fall under his broad topic of "diversion," without which, he acknowledges, there would be little to celebrate in the present life.

> Without diversion (*divertissement*) there is no joy; with it there is no sadness. Diversion is what the happiness of the rich and famous consists in. For they have people to divert them and the power to keep the diversion going.[55]

The fact that such diversion is by its nature available only to the wealthy few is not its greatest drawback in the eyes of Pascal. He condemns it chiefly for offering a defective kind of joy – something less than happiness – even to those who can afford it. Therapeutic treatment also falls too far short of happiness, he could say, to challenge his claim that our condition is objectively wretched.

Diversion, as its Latin root suggests, involves a detour. To divert you is to escort you away from some place you cannot or should not go through. Diversion puts a fig leaf on our wretchedness; it dances us around our moral dereliction. It may distract us from disagreeable things, but it does not sever our connection to them. If joy is induced by therapy, it is joy of a spurious, sickly kind, like the laughter of someone who is feverish or mad, or the stupid contentment of the slave. People would not seek out the violent, risky, loud, and complicated activities they do, both in their occupations and in their entertainments, were they not seeking to be distracted from boredom and from the misery of their condition. The whirligig of their lives is, however, no substitute for happiness, which even they know "can be possessed only in quiet, not in tumult."[56]

Diversion is to happiness what hypnotherapy would be if it were offered to slaves as a substitute for emancipation. We seek therapy so avidly not because it gives us even the semblance of happiness but to avoid facing the fact that achieving happiness is not within our power.

Martin might reply that if Pascal is right, and therapy never confers happiness, then its ineffectiveness ought to be proverbial. Every generation has sought natural means of achieving happiness. If none has been successful down the centuries, you'd think the futility of therapeutic naturalism would already be an empirically established fact. Why has the bad news not sunk in? Why do our immemorial disappointments, unrelieved by a single success, generate nothing but therapy and more therapy?

Pascal asks himself the same question about diversion. "Such a long test, so continuous and uniform, should have convinced us we are too weak to attain the good by our own efforts," he observes. So why didn't it?

Pascal's answer is that our inductive abilities were damaged in the Fall along with our deductive ones. "We learn little from examples," he says, especially when the examples are trying to teach us something we don't want to be true. "Experience deceives us, leading us from one misfortune to the next, until death ends our journey forever."[57]

The fault lies once again with the Fall and the weakness of will it brought about. Add to these the usurping role played by the faculty of imagination after the Fall. "That proud power, enemy of reason ... has established in man a second nature ... It cannot make fools wise, but it makes them happy, to the envy of reason that can only render its friends miserable."[58]

Not that imagination makes fools *really* happy. All it provides is what Pascal was earlier calling the "joy" of diversion, something less than genuine happiness. But if to be a fool is to desire such deceptive joy, then our second or fallen nature makes fools of us all. It also gives Pascal a credible explanation of why the appetite for therapy is undiminished after millennia of disappointments. On the one hand, weakness of will limits our ability to learn from experience, when it tries to teach us inconvenient truths. On the other hand, there is the seductive charm of imagination: able to bypass reason and enlisting all its beguiling power in the service of whatever we wish to believe.

* * *

I did not invent the possibility of a continuing dialogue between Pascal and his posterity. It was implicit in the tournament of champions, the subject of Chapter One. There is also an explicit call for just such an "ongoing interchange of for and against" in one of the *Pensées*.[59] This interchange must continue, Pascal tells us, until confidence in every commonplace has been destroyed.

In calling for an exchange of that kind, Pascal, of course, follows the sceptics' lead. But for him the sceptical interchange is not an end in itself. Once our beliefs are shaken, the tide of scepticism can be allowed to ebb, and the healthy opinions of ordinary people, which

Pascal elsewhere calls "reasons of the heart," can reassert themselves. The second stage of the "continual interchange of for and against" is to acknowledge the persistence and integrity of these healthy, ordinary opinions.

It is at this stage that point and counterpoint, for and against, can achieve their highest purpose. They can bring us to see that it is not the commonplaces of common people that are vain, but we ourselves, who hold these commonplaces to be true, yet cannot on our own maintain the moral equilibrium to which we aspire. To bring us to that realization is the dialectical program of Pascalian inquiry, on which I have concentrated in this chapter. Readers who understand him as a philosopher always appreciate its power.

Dialectic is not, however, the only excellence of Pascalian inquiry. If it were, he would never have embarked upon an apology for the Christian faith. An apology does more than merely defend the fortress of belief; it moves outside it and attempts to persuade the unbeliever to come in. But can a philosopher who is neither a sceptic nor a dogmatist assemble convincing reasons for belief? That is the question to be considered in Chapter Four.

# 4 Reluctant Inquirer

## Emotions

A rare titled fragment, called "order," sketches the grand strategy of the *Pensées*. "Men despise religion," it says:

> They hate it and are afraid it is true. To cure them you have to begin by showing that the [Christian] religion is not contrary to reason. Venerable. Worthy of respect.
>
> Next make it desirable. Make them wish it were true. Lastly, show them it is true.[1]

The dominant metaphor in this fragment is that of *cure*. It concerns therapy. Not the *palliative* kind Pascal was seen to reject in the last chapter, but the kind that actually cures.

From malady to cure *non valet consequentia*; some illnesses must simply be borne. The question is only how to bear them well.[2]

However, where cures do exist there must first be ailments. The fragment just cited proposes to cure a psychological rather than a physical ailment: the unwarranted hatred and fear that religion arouses in many people. The treatment Pascal prescribes will involve three steps.

First, he will show people, to whom original sin makes fear or hatred of religion natural, that Christianity is not contrary to reason but venerable and worthy of respect. Next, he will show them that it offers them something desirable. If he can replace fear and hatred of Christianity with desire for what it offers, then their anti-Christian animus will almost be cured. All that will remain is for Pascal to show them that the claims of Christianity are indeed true.

The last step, however, is larger than its predecessors for reasons Pascal discusses in connection with philosophical failure and the doctrine of the Fall. The truth of Christianity's claims cannot easily be *shown* to unbelievers. As a result of the Fall, people are by nature blind towards religious claims, with a blindness that can only be removed by grace.[3] Thus, the strategy Pascal is outlining here can only be fully implemented with those who receive grace.

A strategy that is therapeutic in nature, calls for transforming emotions, and is dependent on grace looks like a dubious ally. To its credit, it offers a mode of inquiry that is neither sceptical nor dogmatic, and thus is not excluded by the tournament of champions. But it does not look very philosophical. The task of the next three chapters is to show why we must also consider it to be philosophy.

Start with the idea of therapy. Not all who fear or hate religion are candidates for therapy. Secular people have good reason to fear any religion that makes secularism a crime. Everyone has reason to fear religions that persecute unbelievers or exhort their followers to commit crimes. It is not a disorder when persecuted people hate the religions that persecute them.

On the other hand, some fears and hatreds are unreasonable and *are* legitimate candidates for therapy. Fear of enclosed spaces, or crowded ones, hatred of people in general or women in particular are all commonly treated as pathologies.

It is now fashionable to press the word 'phobia' into psycho-ideological service. Labels such as 'homophobia' or 'Islamophobia' are used to challenge the competence of people who, in the judgment of the person wielding the epithet, evince insufficient approval of the practices in question. The implication of the label is that the reluctance of the 'phobic' person is pathological. Pathologizing the emotions is far from being an unfamiliar practice today, though it is obviously open to abuse.

What may look odd to contemporary readers is to see the fear of Christianity pathologized. Today it is more common to put the mental health of its defenders in question. The anthropologist René Girard claims the majority of our contemporaries take for granted "that religion is a psycho-pathological phenomenon."[4] Pascal surprises us a little by inverting that analysis and applying it to irreligion.

There are some people, however, even today, who take the line of Pascal. The neologism 'Christianophobia' does exist. It even rates its own entry on *Wikipedia*. But it has far less currency than either of the other ideologically motivated 'phobias' I just mentioned and is a more recent coinage made in imitation of them. There is also the revealing fact that the diffident article on Christianophobia gets no further than its title line before alerting its readers to "Criticisms of Christianity." Neither Islamophobia nor homophobia is so reflexively self-critical.[5]

Such asymmetries are not difficult to explain. Fear of Christianity resembles other fears but has deeper historical and social implications. The West is the traditional home of Christianity. It has shaped our moral and political institutions. The secular struggle to find a post-religious identity is by its nature a struggle against Christianity. That is why many (René Girard says a majority) of the best educated and articulate citizens of the West, whether in academia or the media, regard the fear of Christianity as prudent and suspicion of it, if not hatred, as an intellectual virtue. That our publicly professed attitudes now tend to be secular in the very countries where, in Pascal's day, it was Christian, implies the existence of an operational fear of this kind.

Secularization is only one of innumerable changes that have taken place since the age of Pascal. But it's a critical one. The building of a secular society is one of the main achievements of the modern age, meriting the careful study to which it has been subject. For one recent study, the most perplexing feature of secularization is its magnitude. How can it be that, whereas in Western society around 1500 A.D. "it was virtually impossible not to believe in God," today "many of us find this not only easy, but even inescapable?"[6] One effect of that vast change of outlook is to make Pascal's strategy for overcoming Christianophobia seem naive.

Given where we now stand, and what so many of us now believe, can the hatred or fear of Christianity still be regarded as pathological? Pascal's confidence in treating it that way may look misplaced.

But there is something also to be said in its favour. The contemporary philosopher Thomas Nagel, himself an atheist, makes a point very like Pascal's in the closing chapter of his book, *The Last Word*, a chapter with the interesting title "The Fear of Religion."

Nagel acknowledges that religious institutions can sometimes provoke legitimate fear or hostility, as can superstition and religiously motivated disinformation. Emotional resistance to such things is, of course, not pathological. But neither is it related to the religious fear Nagel wishes to acknowledge.

The fear of religion he means, the kind that may be irrational, goes beyond justified hostility and reasoned rejection. "I speak from experience," Nagel writes, being strongly subject to that fear myself: I want atheism to be true and am made uneasy by the fact that some of the most intelligent and well-informed people I know are religious believers. It isn't just that I don't believe in God and, naturally, hope that I am right in my belief. It's that I hope there is no God! I don't want there to be a God; I don't want the universe to be like that.[7]

The fear Nagel is trying to isolate here is connected to other passions. It begets the hope and desire that atheism turn out true. Concerning that cluster of anti-religious emotions, Nagel holds up for scrutiny a meta-fear: the fear that his first-order emotions may lack objective justification.

Such philosophical candour makes Nagel the kind of interlocutor Pascal was looking for: a reflective exponent of atheism. Nagel's discussion of fear of religion is not prompted by self-indulgence or intellectual exhibitionism. It has a creditworthy philosophical motive. He discusses it because of his meta-fear that fear of religion, though "not a rare condition," is philosophically indefensible. It may even involve a vicious circularity. What if fear of religion begets the very naturalism and scientism by which it is normally justified? Or, in Nagel's words, what if the modern world's "cosmic authority problem" is "responsible for much of the scientism and reductionism of our time?"[8]

We know that our emotions can affect what we believe. But neither Nagel nor Pascal would say that opinions arising from emotional or other noncognitive sources are automatically disqualified. The truth or falsity of our beliefs depends not on their causes but on the quality of the arguments in their favour.[9]

If the emotions always misled us, then they would have a kind of negative reliability. Since you could always be sure they were mistaken, you could believe the opposite of what your emotions make you want to believe. They are treacherous because they only mislead us some of the time and are at their most misleading when we think them innocent. That is why, when the only thing buttressing our opinions is our emotional commitment to them, we cannot be confident of being right.

Nagel's meta-fear is that the secularism guiding so much contemporary thought, including his own, may rest more on emotion than on evidence. That is the point connecting Nagel with Pascal's project in the *Pensées*. They see the same problem from opposite sides and with opposite hopes.

Nagel represents today's version of the evolving post-Christian or secular anthropology to whose early stages Pascal's *Pensées* are addressed. But Nagel's version is still one that Pascal's strategy can address. He does not seek to abolish the emotions that are directed against religion, but to redirect them in religion's favour.

Because Nagel and Pascal are both careful philosophers, each is wary of the strengths of the other position. Nagel admits to being made uneasy by the fact that some of the most intelligent and well-informed people he knows are believers. Pascal credits atheism with the philosophical credentials Nagel fears it may lack. Atheism is rationally defensible according to Pascal in the sense that it can answer any of the standard arguments for belief with which he is familiar.[10] "We can't convince infidels," he concedes, adding, of course, "nor they us."[11]

Pascal also welcomes emotion when it comes to the aid of philosophically rigorous investigations. What he dreads is an interlocutor who doesn't care enough about religious questions to have commitments. "Negligence in an affair where people themselves are at stake, their eternal future, their all," Pascal exclaims, "irritates me more than it wins my sympathy. It astonishes and horrifies me. It is monstrous."[12]

A passionate atheist would therefore seem more reasonable to Pascal than a dispassionate one. And since he does not think atheism can be defeated by logical demonstration, he cannot treat emotional commitment to it as in any way illicit. His argument against atheism must therefore be independent of Nagel's meta-fear. Pascal will reorganize the facts that trouble Nagel and suggest an original solution to the problem they raise.

The originality of Pascal lies in what he asks us to do: we are to think of properly defended atheism not as a bad argument but as *a bad bet*. Pascal will try to show that people with Nagel's "cosmic authority problem" have invested their emotions – their desire, hope, and fear – in the wrong places. He will say that the secularist's bet is irrational, even when his arguments are not.

It is far from obvious that such a strategy makes sense, and Pascal is aware he owes his reader an explanation. If the atheist is making a bad bet, he will want to see an alternative. The alternative Pascal proposes will seem even more radical to a contemporary reader than it would have appeared to a reader of Pascal's time. Most atheists can envision circumstances in which they would make a strategic retreat to agnosticism. But Pascal will ask them to jump straight from atheism to belief without lingering in the agnostic middle. But that comes later. The first step will be, just as our fragment says, to satisfy his reader that Christianity is "not contrary to reason."

## The Burden of Proof

Showing Christianity not to be contrary to reason is easier than proving it true. However, that doesn't mean the task will be easy. In the case of something as old, wide, and deep as Christianity, it is not even obvious what it entails.

For example, it can't mean proving Christianity noncontradictory. That would be both too little and too much: too little, because most fairy tales probably have that much going for them; too much, because no one could demonstrate the consistency of anything so comprehensive as a religion. Whether or not we suspect Christianity of inner contradictions, we must recognize that it is open-ended, subject to disagreement, to development, to varieties of interpretation, and to multiple levels of meaning. Religions are too big to be subjected to formal logical scrutiny, and probably no one thinks they can be.

Pascal's aim is rather to establish Christianity as a body of thought, which a skilled and careful thinker can adopt, and within which he can express himself without sacrificing the intellectual integrity expected of a philosopher. This is what I take him to have in mind in the order fragment when he calls Christianity "venerable" and "worthy of respect."

To *try* to inhabit this system of belief is what Pascal means by betting on it. No reasonable person would bet on something he believed was contrary to reason. So the first step Pascal must take is to establish that Christianity is not so. What burden, then, does he have to assume?

The only one he does assume is that of refuting well-known criticisms of the Christian faith. At every perceived weak point in the anti-Christian's position, Pascal launches his assault: "Those who have difficulty believing look for a pretext in ..."; "It is quite ridiculous to be scandalized by ..."; "The hypothesis that ... is completely absurd ..."; and so on.[13] So successful is this strategy in Pascal's eyes that he can't resist expressing his satisfaction with it: "Truly it is delightful," he says, "for a religion to have such unreasonable enemies. Their points of opposition are so innocuous that they serve instead to establish its truth."[14]

But critical readers are bound to suspect this strategy of being insufficient. Our granting that there can be no consistency proof for a religion, they will say, does not entitle Pascal to claim the high ground. Why should he assume that, as long as his faith is not demonstrably incoherent, it is consonant with reason? Doesn't he need to justify this assumption?

Pascal doesn't think so. Or rather, he thinks, as Roman Catholic apologists always have, that the Church possesses unassailable doctrines, which may be defended but are not in need of philosophical proof.[15] Authority has its principal power in theology, Pascal says, "because there [authority] is inseparable from truth."[16]

Such an attitude may sound complacent, but there are surprisingly good arguments in its favour. Saint Thomas supplies some of the best of them at the outset of the *Summa Theologica*. There is a natural hierarchy of the sciences, he asserts, and the position a science occupies in the hierarchy helps determine what burden of proof it is required to assume. A science such as physics, for example, would not try to prove its first principles to someone who put them all in question. How could it? To prove them, it would be forced to appeal to those same principles. And that would mean arguing in a circle. A suitable reply to such a critic would have to come from a science further up in the hierarchy. Likely the science required would be metaphysics.

What would happen, then, if the critic were stubborn and also put the principles of metaphysics in question? It would depend, says Thomas, on how he did so. If the critic conceded some metaphysical principles and denied others, the metaphysician could try to establish the disputed ones by appeal to the ones not in dispute. But if the critic admits none of the principles of metaphysics, then, Thomas thinks, it is not possible to argue with him (*non potest cum eo disputare*).

Thomas is not implying that such a critic would be unanswerable. Far from it. It's just that a metaphysician would not be able to *rebut* the critic's argument without arguing in a circle. Not that circularity is necessarily a bad thing either. If metaphysics is sound, then the arguments offered to the anti-metaphysician may also be sound. It's just that they will be circular and, therefore, to this stubborn and misguided critic, unpersuasive. Thomas thinks the metaphysician would be better advised to scrutinize the reasons (*rationes*) of such a critic and find a way to refute (*solvere*) them. That is not impossible, because a critic who rejects all of metaphysics is himself doing metaphysics, though unknowingly, and hence, inevitably, doing it badly.

Even in an age suspicious of hierarchies, scientific and otherwise, it does not seem outrageous to hold that metaphysics occupies a privileged position with respect to the sciences and, therefore also with respect to its critics. For example, although Thomas Nagel offers no argument in favour of a hierarchy of the sciences, he accords a privileged position to metaphysics when defending realism in *The Last Word*.

I shall call Aquinas's position the *fortress argument*. It holds that metaphysics does not have to establish its credentials in the eyes of a critic who questions everything about it, because the nature of such criticism is to forestall any answer. Socrates mocks a person who asks to be instructed about the number twelve, but with the proviso that his instructor not come to him with any nonsense about its being equal to seven plus five or ten plus two. The fortress doctrine likewise exempts the metaphysician from dealing with critics of this kind. He only need defend his discipline from specific allegations of error or contradiction.

Now Thomas thinks Sacred Doctrine occupies an even stronger fortress. It is entitled to a place of privilege because it has no superior (*non habet superiorem*) in the hierarchy of science!

> If the critic (*adversarius*) should believe none of [its] doctrines, which are in fact divinely revealed, then there will be no way left to prove the articles of the Faith by arguments (*rationes*). But it is still possible to refute arguments against the Faith, should he adduce any.

Thomas's confidence in the unassailability of Sacred Doctrine rests on an argument that remains a centrepiece of Catholic apologetics. "Since," he says,

> the Faith leans upon infallible truth [i.e., what is divinely revealed], and it is impossible to demonstrate the contrary of what is true, it is obvious that the "proofs" (*probationes*) adduced against the Faith are not demonstrations, but refutable arguments.[17]

Pascal took a similar view. He mocked the way in which modern thinkers dare to advance novelties in theology, where everything new is false, and resist them in physics, where progress arises only through innovation. "I leave it to persons of judgement," Pascal says, "to recognize the importance of this abuse that perverts so unjustly *the order of the sciences*" (my emphasis).[18]

However, the fortress argument has never been more elegantly stated than it was by Cardinal Newman in a lecture written for the School of Science at Dublin College, and first published as part of his book *On the Idea of the University* (1852):

> I say, then, he who believes Revelation with that absolute faith which is the prerogative of a Catholic, is not the nervous creature who startles at

every sudden sound, and is fluttered by every strange or novel appearance which meets his eyes. He has no sort of apprehension, he laughs at the idea, that anything can be discovered by any other scientific method, which can contradict any one of the dogmas of his religion. He knows full well there is no science whatever, but, in the course of its extension, runs the risk of infringing, without any meaning of offence on its own part, the path of other sciences: and he knows also that, if there be any one science which, from its sovereign and unassailable position can calmly bear such unintentional collisions on the part of the children of earth, it is Theology. He is sure, and nothing shall make him doubt, that, if anything seems to be proved by astronomer, or geologist, or chronologist, or antiquarian, or ethnologist, in contradiction to the dogmas of faith, that point will eventually turn out, first, *not* to be proved, or, secondly, not *contradictory*, or thirdly, not contradictory to anything *really revealed*, but to something which has been confused with revelation.[19]

If there is a Roman Catholic apologetic tradition in existence long before Pascal and long after him, it should not be surprising to find that he works within it. Especially when it is justified not only by its antiquity but also by its cogency.

And yet there is one way in which Pascal's adherence to tradition *is* surprising. It contrasts with the position adopted by the most celebrated philosopher of the same period, also French and Catholic, René Descartes. Despite being famous for several biting criticisms of Descartes, Pascal is in a surprising number of ways a Cartesian.[20] Why, then, did he not follow when Descartes forsook the security of the fortress argument and based his apologetic thinking on a freestanding, a priori, purely rational argument for the existence of God?

## Descartes

When it came to Sacred Doctrine Descartes thought Catholics ought to shoulder a heavier burden of proof than the fortress argument concedes. They shouldn't base their belief in God's existence on revelation. Instead they should construct an a priori proof of God's existence of the kind Thomas Aquinas thought to be impossible. Descartes adopts this position in full knowledge of the fortress argument, to which he nods before setting it aside. "It is absolutely true," he writes,

that one must believe in God's existence because it is taught in Sacred Scripture, and, conversely, that Scriptures are to be believed because we have them from God. This is because faith is a gift from God, and he who gives grace to believe everything else can also give it so that we may believe he exists. Nevertheless this reasoning cannot be offered to unbelievers (*infidelibus*), because they may judge it to be circular.[21]

Descartes addresses this point directly to the Jesuits, his former teachers. Notwithstanding the tension between the fortress argument and Descartes's proposal, he had two reasons to think the Jesuits might be receptive to what he proposed. In 1513, in the eighth session of the Fifth Lateran Council, Pope Leo X had enjoined philosophers to "attempt with all their strength to make evident to their students the truth of the Christian Religion and to refute the quite refutable arguments to the contrary."[22] The Jesuits, created to be the vanguard of the counter-reformation, had incorporated that injunction into their own statement of pedagogical principles, the *Ratio Studiorum*.[23]

Second, there was the fact that, through their missions in China and in North America, Jesuits were in contact with unbelievers who might indeed find the tight connections Christians take for granted between Scripture and God impenetrably circular. The missionary would have to make a way for unbelievers to break into that circle by deriving one of its terms (God) from things the potential converts already believed. For these reasons Descartes hoped his attempts to prove the existence of God without appeal to revelation would win his former teachers' support.

Contrary to what many of his readers think, Pascal does not deny that a priori proofs are possible. Belief can come about through reason as well as through custom or inspiration, he admits.[24] But we learn from his sister that he mistrusted rational proofs on two counts. Not that they are worthless (*méprisables*) if they are well constructed. But even when well constructed, or perhaps especially then, formal arguments do not reflect the way people ordinarily reason. Not everyone is capable of following logical demonstrations, and even those who are only retain the impression of their force while they have the argument before them. An hour later they begin to wonder whether they have not fallen prey to some fallacy.[25]

Even if Pascal's concern had been the missionary context, with its need for strategies of encountering radical cultural differences, he might still have thought that formal proofs of the existence of God were the wrong instrument. But the audience Pascal wished to reach with his apology could not have been more different from the one facing Jesuit missionaries. Pascal wrote for people often called *libertines*.

He called them doubters and know-it-alls.[26] They belonged to the most privileged strata of French society. We might think of them as the first post-Christians. Their outlook was, or at least prefigured, the one we now call secular.

It is true that Pascal engages other religions (mainly Islam, Judaism and what he calls "the religion of China"), but they are encountered not in their own right but only as competitors of Catholic Christianity. Pascal's main target is readers with a cultural understanding of Christianity. The *Pensées* is aimed less at winning new adherents from other religions than at winning lapsed or lapsing Christians back. About other religions Pascal is content to show that they do not constitute positions of strength from which damaging criticisms of Christianity could be derived.

Purely defensive apologetics, offered from within the doctrinal fortress occupied by the Catholic apologetic tradition, are what is required for meeting any attack from the outside. The burden of proof lies with the critic of religion to show where the contradictions of Christianity lie.

Pascal acknowledges that the Christian faith is replete with what he calls "contrarieties."[27] It is important that they be acknowledged, but equally important that they not be confused with contradictions. Pascal attempts to reconcile them, and by that means to understand "the true [religion]."[28] Richard Parish nicely remarks that "the coexistence of such apparently contradictory truths in a dogmatic synthesis" is what defines orthodoxy for Pascal.[29] That is how the Faith appears to a dialectically astute insider. As its defender, Pascal's task is to show that alleged *contradictions* are not part of Christian doctrine, or, if they are, not contradictory.

Unlike Descartes, Pascal was deeply concerned with defending the fortress. However, he did not permit the fortress to become his prison. The larger ambition he cherished for his apology was to meet lapsed believers outside the fortress and offer them reasons for reconsidering belief.

That is where a greater difficulty lies. What kind of arguments can Pascal have at his disposal, when he admits from the outset that there are no useful demonstrations of the Faith? There are indeed substantial sequences of fragments with titles such as "Proofs of Moses," "Proofs of Jesus," "Prophecies," and "Miracles," which Pascal gathered and intended to use as empirical evidence of the truth of Christianity. But not all of them have equal weight. The preface to the Port Royal (1670) edition of the *Pensées* represents Pascal's apologetic strategy as heavily weighted towards prophecy.

> M. Pascal attempted to prove the truth of [Christianity] from the prophecies [of the Old Testament]. He went into much more detail concerning them than he did on other subjects. Because he had done a great deal of work on prophecies, and had his own highly developed opinions about them, he explained them in a most intelligible way. With remarkable dexterity he laid out both their meaning and their fulfilment, expounding them with complete clarity and power.[30]

The difficulty is that few apologists today (let alone philosophers) would want to rest their case on such contestable evidence. Most would regard it as a recipe for failure. Nor would Pascal's chances of apologetic success be much enhanced by a second indicator of the truth of Christianity, to which he attaches great significance – Christianity's success in explaining human beings to themselves. Anthropology belongs necessarily to the field of religion, Pascal contends, because there is no secular path to self-knowledge. "God," Pascal says,

> has hidden that prize so high, or rather so deep, that we can never reach it. Hence it is not by the proud activity of our reason but through simple submission that we can truly come to know ourselves.[31]

Religion provides the theoretical means to "recognize our nature's grandeur as well as its meagreness, and the reason for each." Secular anthropologies fail to account for one aspect or the other. "What but the Christian religion," Pascal asks, "has accomplished [both]?"[32]

A reader may be more or less sympathetic to Pascal's project, more or less inclined to think that Christianity has said the last word on anthropology. But few Christian apologists (and fewer philosophers) would think it anything but quixotic to assail the position of careful secular critics of Christianity, armed only with one's conviction about the superiority of Christian anthropology and the evidence for the Faith provided by such phenomena as miracles and prophecy. These weapons may be useful in defending the Faith against those who attack it from outside, but what power could they retain outside the fortress, where argument is conducted on secular rather than religious principles?

These reservations are all justified, but in the event Pascal is able to elude their force. He recognizes that the anthropological and prophetic arguments are not the right ones with which to launch his attack. People's minds are initially too brittle, he thinks, to receive these arguments. They must first be made suppler. That is why Pascal begins with *emotional therapy*, as he promised to do in the order fragment with which this chapter began.

The goal in the order fragment is to "show them that [Christianity] is true." But the first step in that direction is to heal the emotions.

## The Fragment *"Infini Rien"* (IR)

The emotion therapy Pascal proposed for lapsed Christians is strikingly presented in a fragment famous as "the wager" but actually called by Pascal "Infinity nothing" (*"Infini rien,"* henceforth IR). The main part of this longish and much-discussed fragment sketches a kind of dialogue in which Pascal attempts to persuade a generic unbeliever to live his life as if Christianity were true. This unbeliever, who is committed to reason, discovers in the course of the dialogue that his religious scepticism is not as reasonable as he had imagined, but only something that mimics reason. He comes to see that his rejection of religion was in fact *caused* in him by his passions. He is shown that, to change his way of thinking, he needs to weaken the passions that misdirect him and put other more reasonable passions in their place. Pascal proposes a therapy to help him make that transition.

The vast library of secondary literature devoted to IR could occupy an avid reader for years. It has made IR the most famous of Pascal's thoughts and, ironically, the least understood. This paradox needs to be explained.

In IR Pascal says unbelievers should simply behave as if they believed in Christianity, taking holy water, having masses said, and so on. No definitive account has been given about why Pascal proposed such an improbable form of conduct. Despite the oceans of ink that have flowed over it, and, in part, because of it, no one really knows what Pascal meant when he said acting this way "will make you believe by natural means, and will make you stupid."

The cure Pascal ends up proposing for unbelief is nothing if not puzzling. Can belief be produced on demand? Can it be acquired by pretending to have it? And, most bizarre of all, what advantage does Pascal think there is in becoming stupid? There are no definitive answers to these questions, and the text of IR is a minefield into which no scholar casually strays.

On the other hand, it is also not easy to avoid it. Though the *Pensées* resist any attempt to impose a definitive order on it, systematic discussions of Pascal are rarely able to avoid significant engagement with IR.[33] The present study will be no exception.

IR contains Pascal's most elaborate treatment for the disorder of unbelief. There he excavates the emotional foundations of unbelief, and shows how, in certain circumstances, those foundations can be rebuilt.

I say these things are to be found in IR, but looking for anything there is a scholarly adventure at several different levels. Just navigating the fragment is the first problem. Its length makes it difficult to refer to exact passages in a way that allows a reader to find them with ease. I have fixed that by providing my own translation of IR in Appendix B and dividing it into small sections, each with an identifying reference. The French original, divided in the same way, is supplied in Appendix A.

Those who read IR in its original French should know that there are some minor differences between the Lafuma and Sellier editions. In the Lafuma version, it runs to just over 1,650 words, covering pages 550a to 551b and appears as L418; in Sellier, it is the slightly longer fragment S680 and covers pages 457 to 467. The two versions have minor differences in wording and order, and Sellier includes some text in S680 that Lafuma assigns to other fragments. However, the part I will be examining is included in both, and their differences are not significant. Except when otherwise noted, I shall be following the Lafuma text as reproduced in Appendix A.

Much larger differences will puzzle those who compare English translations. If you are not already familiar with IR, you will find it easiest to give Appendix A or B a careful reading before beginning my commentary. On the other hand, if your interest in Pascal the philosopher does not go to the length of wanting to master the devilishly complicated IR, you can simply skip the remainder of this chapter and pick up the story in Chapter Five. If you do so, however, there are four controversial points you will have to grant me.

1. Unbelief is founded not upon reason but upon the emotions, especially fear.
2. That fear is misplaced. If unchecked, it will lead us to continue living in a manner that will destroy our happiness, both in this life and in the life to come.

3. However, the fear of Christianity can, in some cases, be cured.
4. If you take the cure, you will learn first to focus on the good to be obtained from Christian belief, and later to value that goodness so highly that your former fear of it will subside and be transformed into desire that the Christian religion be true.

Before considering how Pascal defends these strange claims, there are a few more caveats to put before the undaunted reader, for the difficulties associated with IR have only begun to be told.

**Scholarship Sprawl**

I mentioned earlier that IR has been spoiled by too much scholarly attention. Just as desirable places to live often become less desirable as people flock there, so literary texts can become more and more opaque the more scholars try to clarify their meaning.[34] Like dense and featureless suburbs surrounding a charming town, endless tracts of scholarship prevent rather than facilitate access to a text. Of this maxim IR is a paradigmatic example.

Take the manuscript of IR to begin with. So many thorny editorial problems have been raised about it that one can wonder whether any exact argument or arguments can be attributed to it or whether the order in which they were meant to appear can ever be recovered. In his commentary on IR, Georges Brunet introduces the manuscript problem in these lively terms:

> A draft diabolically scribbled, barely legible in places, mangled, without order, heaped with erasures, corrections, and revisions; an amalgam of mathematical arguments, psychological observations and mystical effusions. That is how the celebrated fragment we normally call "the Wager of Pascal" appears before we begin to study it.[35]

The photographic reproduction of the manuscript pages in Brunet's commentary bears out his description. This means that ordered and relatively intelligible edited versions of IR, such as those of Lafuma and Sellier, on which the present study will be based, are editorial artefacts resting on centuries of Pascal scholarship, whose verdicts, even though assumed for present purposes, cannot be taken as final. As Ian Hacking comments, "every blot of ink or raindrops on [the manuscript pages] has been given minute analysis."[36] Concerns about the manuscript, if allowed to do so, could delay the study of the arguments or usurp it altogether.

But study of IR is menaced not only from below but also from above. If manuscript uncertainties deny us an established text, a significant part of the secondary literature has emancipated itself from text-based scholarship altogether. I am not referring here to the tendency second-ary literature always has to become itself a subject of tertiary literature. That, of course, happens in the case of IR. But IR presents unique chal-lenges at the level of secondary literature itself. IR is both unfinished and unconventional. Its ideas are like kites. Once scholars begin to run with them, they soon soar out of contact with the text.

The best example is the novel argument at the heart of IR, which applies the then new mathematical notion of probability to a philo-sophical question. Scholars assure us that it is unprecedented.[37] Pascal's innovative approach has been celebrated since the first edition of the *Pensées*. The downside of IR's originality, however, is that it awakens appetites for mathematical depth and technical precision that the argu-ments as stated are less and less able to satisfy.

In his own time Pascal argued boldly, and in conformity with the best understanding of probabilistic reasoning then available, that belief in the existence of God is a *better bet* than belief in his nonexistence. Philosophers were understandably intrigued by Pascal's boldness and originality. So they have been trying ever since to test and explain his meaning by applying to IR methods of statistical reasoning, decision theory, and the logic of probability in the mature forms these disciplines have acquired since Pascal's time. These scholars honour Pascal in the only way scholars can – by taking his arguments seriously. And they bring out implications that are instructive. At the same time, however, they promote IR to a glory it cannot sustain. Pascal's wager recedes far-ther and farther from view in the magnificent, but anachronistic, mir-rors scholars hold up to it.

For example, the last half-century of study cannot be said to have brought us closer to understanding whether the wager argument is sound, or even valid. Ian Hacking (1972) pronounced all three of the *separate* wager arguments he claimed to discover in IR to be valid, though unpersuasive. Jeff Jordan (2006) discovered a fourth argument there, which he said to be both valid and persuasive. But Alan Hájek (2003) ends an article critical of the logic of IR, and including a magiste-rial survey of the relevant secondary literature, on a less encouraging note. "It seems," Hájek writes, that Pascal's Wager and all the reformulations of it that I have considered face a serious problem. Moreover, I believe that it is a problem that runs deep, not one that will go away with some clever tinkering. For I see no prospects for characterizing a notion of the utility of salvation that is reflexive under addition *without* being reflexive under multiplication by positive, finite probabilities. Yet it seems that nothing less will salvage Pascal's reasoning. (emphasis in original)

Hájek goes on to argue that, regardless of how we take Pascal to respond to this problem, difficulties will arise to ensure that "any future version of the argument will succumb to this dilemma."[38]

The reference to "future versions" of the argument is what I would like the reader to notice. Pascal's text is no longer thought capable of answering the questions we raise about it. And it is true that there is nothing in IR by which to determine whether "the utility of salvation is reflexive under addition but not under multiplication by positive finite probabilities." If such matters are ever resolved, it will therefore have to be, as Hájek says, through "future versions" of IR.

The obvious difficulty, however, is that Pascal will not have written any of these future versions. Many of the questions raised by IR scholarship are of intrinsic interest, but they have caused a great part of the secondary literature to become airborne in this way, leaving the textual launching pad as an insignificant dot far below.

All these caveats are meant only to warn the inexperienced reader of Pascal that the text of IR is a middle realm threatened by manuscript scruples from below and up-to-date logical studies from above. The matters to which I wish to draw attention fall right in the middle, between the two extremes, and if I appear to be treading carefully there, it is because I am. I will be confining myself to what Pascal actually says about the wager, and therefore hoping not to be in conflict with any correct projection of his words into more sophisticated logical or statistical settings.

## Commentary

The first thing to notice for present purposes is that Pascal's talk of wagering is *metaphorical*. He introduces it near the beginning of IR with the words, "A game is being played at the limit of [an infinite] distance in which either heads or tails will be the outcome." I shall have more to say about these words below, but here I just draw attention to their metaphorical character. Pascal does not believe, or intend us to believe, that any such game is literally being played in the unlocatable place of which he speaks.

Metaphors organize our thoughts about things *other than* themselves. They resemble piped-in music in shopping centres in that they achieve their purposes best when they are not consciously observed. The wager metaphor is meant to organize our thoughts about our lives, getting us to focus on aspects of belief formation that are *like* wagering. To the extent that the metaphor makes us think about wagering itself, it fails as a metaphor. Georges Brunet aptly refers to IR's "mathematical veneer that shatters when touched."[39]

## Life, Life*, Life∞

The next thing to consider is that the IR fragment is not in the last analysis about betting. It really concerns what we ought to do with our lives. 'Lives' in what sense, you may well ask, because the word 'life' takes on several different meanings, which it will be useful to distinguish right from the beginning. When it appears with no superscript, 'life' will mean what we usually understand by that word before we wax philosophical – namely, biological human existence between conception and death. But in Pascal's thinking, this biological idea of life is not bedrock. It is always an abstraction from life as it is actually lived. Real life comes in two species.

'Life*' will refer to life as Pascal thinks it became after original sin.[40] Life is life* for us today, though our ancestors, Adam and Eve, knew a life different from any available since Eden. Our first parents knew what I will call 'life∞.' Life∞ is life as God intended it to be, as it was before the Fall, as it may begin to become again in a state of grace, and as it will be in its fullness in the afterlife, at least for believers. The infinity symbol is chosen here to capture the expression "infinitely happy life" used by Pascal in IR.

Life* is a life of degradation; life∞ is one of exaltation. Each is available to be lived. Two truths stand "firm and certain" in the eyes of faith:

> One is that man, whether as originally created or in a state of grace, is raised above all nature, made like God and a participant in God's divinity. The other truth is that in the state of corruption and sin man falls away from this state (*est déchu*) and becomes like the beasts.[41]

The first truth describes life$^\infty$; the second, life*. No other lives are available to be lived.

## Preface of IR: *Geworfenheit*

The IR fragment begins with words that remind some readers of the Heideggerian notion of 'thrownness' or *'Geworfenheit.'* [In what follows, passages from IR will be italicized to set them apart from other quoted passages. They are also provided with a reference letter that will enable them to be found quickly in Appendix A or B.]

> a. *Our soul is flung (jetée) into a body where it finds number, time, dimensions. Our soul reasons about this and calls it nature, necessity, and can believe in nothing else.*

Such is the pathos of life*: we come to our senses and find ourselves housed in a body in a world of three dimensions, surrounded by an indeterminate number of living and lifeless beings, moving together instinctively through the steps of an infinitely complex dance to the music of time. We speculate about our situation endlessly but grasp it only in part, because the structure we seek to know is the same one that constitutes the minds with which we seek to know it. These limitations and interdependences can only be transcended if what Pascal calls *grace* intervenes, and life$^\infty$ enlarges our vision.

## Preface of IR: Infinity and Nothingness

> b. *Unity joined to infinity adds nothing to it ... The finite disappears (s'anéantit) before the infinite. That is how our spirit is before God.*

Pascal does not say we are nothing. We are a unit. But in comparison to God, we are *like* nothing. We do not augment God's grandeur any more than a unit augments an infinite magnitude. Pascal retains the medieval view that God is the natural measure, next to whom we are as nothing. The Protagorean and modern idea that man is the measure does not tempt Pascal. "The most your lights can accomplish," he writes, "is to bring you to the point at which you recognize that it is not within yourselves that you will find either truth or goodness."[42]

To compare God to an infinite number is also metaphorical. God is not literally a number. Nor is he literally the infinite space, to which he is also compared. He only resembles such things because, like them, he has no limits. They differ from God, however, in being really made up of units (like numerical infinities) or of extension (like spatial ones). Pascal would agree with Thomas Aquinas and the Catholic tradition generally that we are not equipped to understand the nature of God, except by such partial analogies.[43]

### Preface of IR: God's Existence

d. *We know his existence by faith.* (550b)

There is a medieval dictum that we can know *what* something is (*quid sit*) and still be in doubt as to *whether* such a thing exists (*an sit*).[44] If someone describes to you the crested robin, which resembles the familiar robin except for its conspicuous blue crest, you will know exactly what he is talking about. But you won't be certain whether such a thing exists unless you have actually observed a crested robin. To my knowledge, no one ever has. Concerning any contingent being *quid sit* and *an sit* seem to be related in the same way: you can know the first while remaining uncertain about the second.

But Pascal, like Descartes before him, is interested by odd cases in which *an sit* and *quid sit* are related in the opposite way: the cases where "we can know the existence of something, but *not* know its nature." Descartes thinks the *cogito* enables us to know our own existence before we know what kind of thing we are,[45] but for Pascal it is God whose existence is known first. We know God's existence *by faith*, he says in the words just quoted. And we know it only by faith. Neither the senses nor reason furnish any pathway to God:

c. *We know neither the existence nor the nature of God, because he has neither extension nor limits.*

The first part of passage c looks as if it contradicts passage d. If we know God's existence by faith (d), then why does Pascal say we don't know it (c)? However, there is no real contradiction. The two passages refer to different ways of knowing – knowledge by faith and knowledge by reason or experience. Only by faith do we have knowledge of the existence of God, but it gives us no information about what he is like. This is one of several ways in which God is hidden from us, God's hiddenness being another important doctrine in the thought of Pascal.

Passages a to d are the preliminary details about life* that Pascal wants us to have in hand as he pushes us to consider what to do with our lives: We are each thrown into life*, and so discover ourselves to be one among other time-bound individuals of our own kind and of different kinds. We are agents, yet always acted upon. But neither acting nor being acted upon provides any certainty about the meaning of our lives. Faith points to the existence of a limitless or infinite being, next to whom we are like nonentities, but faith tells us no more than that this being exists.

## The Body of IR

From this point forward, IR resembles a dialogue between Pascal and an unbeliever whose particular condition of unbelief become clearer as the dialogue unfolds. I shall number each speech by a separate lowercase letter in bold type. Unfortunately, the speeches are not attributed to speakers as they are in a Platonic dialogue, with the result that one of IR's many puzzles is to know to which speaker some of them belong. I will use a bold capital letter indicating the speaker to whom I attribute each one: **P** for Pascal; **I** for the interlocutor; **P/I** in one place where Pascal seems to put words in the interlocutor's mouth. In longer speeches, where I need to interject comments, I shall number their parts **P1**, **P2**, and so on. Whenever the trees begin to obscure the forest, the reader should consult appendices A and B to see the passages under discussion in their proper setting.

Different stages of IR make sufficiently different logical points that they are sometimes construed as constituting separate wager arguments. As already mentioned, Ian Hacking identifies three such arguments which he says are related in the following way:

> Pascal's procedure in the thought "infini rien" is to offer (a) an argument from dominance. Then, if its premises be rejected, to offer (b) an argument from expectation. Then, if the second lot of premises be rejected, to offer (c) an argument from dominating expectation.

Hacking seems to me to be right as far as he goes, but he doesn't go far. There is so much more to IR than the three arguments Hacking discusses. Taken together they make up less than 20 percent of the fragment. But it will also be obvious from what Hacking says of a, b, and c that they can just as well be treated as three moves in the larger conversation between Pascal and his interlocutor. That is the traditional way of understanding them and the way I shall adopt here. On this interpretation, IR is a conversation in which Pascal makes a sustained attempt to persuade the interlocutor to change the course of his life. The three separate arguments Hacking identifies are episodes in that larger conversation.

## Naturalism

Before the interlocutor is allowed to speak, Pascal lays down an important rule of engagement:

> **aP1** *Let us now speak according to natural lights.*

The word 'now' indicates the preliminaries are over. 'Natural lights' means Pascal will not attempt to establish any point by appeal to revelation, transcendence, or supernatural beings. Today we would call the posture he is adopting 'naturalistic.' He adopts naturalism not as a reflection of his own belief but as a temporary concession to the presumed outlook of his interlocutor, with whom nothing can be taken for granted about God. aP1 also implies an agreement not to admit as evidence in IR anything that can only be known by faith. aP1 does not exclude appeals to reason, however, which is no doubt why Pascal repeats his claim that reason teaches us nothing about God:

> **aP2** *If there is a God he is infinitely incomprehensible, because having neither parts nor limits he has no connection with us. We are therefore incapable of knowing either what he is or whether he is.*

You may wonder whether Pascal has already painted himself into a corner. Methodological naturalism is fine. It's exactly the step Descartes took (and advocated to the Jesuits) in proving the existence of God. But that was because Descartes knew he could appeal to reason and so force his interlocutors to acknowledge the existence of God, even if they were unwilling to do so. But if Pascal can appeal neither to reason nor to faith, how can he lay claim even to the bare concept of God, which he must take for granted if the conversation is to continue?

Luckily, things are not as bad as they look. It is possible to have semantic competence even where there is no knowledge either by faith or by description. Take the word 'infinity,' for example. People in the

Middle Ages had the semantic competence necessary to use the word, even when they had little understanding of its mathematical properties. Non-mathematicians today use it in much the same way. There is no way to experience infinity. If basic semantic competence could not be taken for granted in a learner, there would be nothing on which to build, and no one would ever acquire the mathematician's more sophisticated concept. Something similar is true of the concept of God. Pascal only needs to appeal to his interlocutor's semantic competence in order to launch the argument of IR.

The limits Pascal places on reason may seem to be handicaps, but in fact they are essential to the argument of IR. If either the existence of God or his nature were knowable by reason, Christian belief would immediately become inconsistent. The explicit limitation of reason is, therefore, a sign of the integrity of Pascal's argument:

> **aP3** *Who can blame Christians for not being able to give a reason for their belief, when they profess a religion for which no reason can be given? ... Their want of proof is just what absolves them of a want of sense.*

The ancient theologian Tertullian famously said that he believed in Christian doctrine *because* it was impossible. Pascal defends something almost as shocking when he says that the Catholic faith is coherent *because* it has no rational warrant. It is not a throwaway line but the pivot on which the rest of the fragment turns. It forces the unbelieving interlocutor to ask a profound question: How could it ever be sensible for him to commit himself to a system of belief that may be logically consistent but is unsupported by reason? Pascal appears to put the whole body of Catholic doctrine up for discussion and then to defend it by admitting its lack of proof. Such a tactic may frustrate rationalistic criticism, but surely it must be fatal to Pascal's apologetic ambitions. Could any reasonable person be persuaded to adopt a faith so thin that it cannot even be attacked? The interlocutor makes exactly this point. Pascal's opening gambit (aP3) "may excuse those who offer their faith as unprovable, and exempt them from blame when they bring it forward without proof," he concedes:

> **bI** *but [aP3] does not excuse anyone who accepts it.*

The interlocutor's point is plausible, and its censure falls on more than just prospective converts. Since everyone who now accepts the

Christian faith must have done so for the first time at some earlier date, bI applies to every Christian believer. Anyone who at any time has come to believe Christian doctrine must have done so during a lapse of due epistemic diligence. Either that, or Pascal must show that there are conditions under which a reasonable unbeliever might accept the Christian faith.

It needs to be emphasized here that IR is talking about *Christian* faith, not just some generic religiosity or featureless theism. Explicit reference to Christians is made in aP3, to Scripture in Mp, and to holy water and masses in Op6. For that reason I do not follow Jeff Jordan's claim that Pascal employed the wager "as an ecumenical argument in support of theism generally," an argument he says would have done just as well for Judaism or Islam as for Christianity.[46]

It is true that the logical point at issue – whether we are ever justified in holding beliefs for which reason gives no warrant – has applications beyond Christianity. But they also go beyond all religion and apply to belief formation on any subject. The point of bI, however, plainly is to ask whether it can ever be reasonable for unbelievers to adopt a particular body of beliefs – Roman Catholic ones. It is in answer to that question that Pascal believes he can apply some of his recent and exploratory insights into games of chance:

> **cP1** *Let us examine that point. Put it this way: God either exists or he doesn't. But which way do we lean? Reason is no help. An infinite chaos separates us from God. A game is being played at the limit of that distance in which either heads or tails is going to be the outcome. What will you wager?*

Once again I must draw attention to the banal fact that wagering is introduced as a metaphor. There is not really a game being played with a coin. The analogy would still be imperfect even if there were such a game, because this one is not really "being played." The game is already over. The toss of this imaginary coin took place at a moment that is logically in advance of time. Either heads or tails is already facing up and always has been. It is just that we don't know which it is. We are betting therefore on a merely subjective uncertainty.

The question is whether God exists or not. Two options about which (Pascal repeats)

> **cP2** *reason will not lead you one way or the other; reason undermines neither.*

The idea is not new to IR, but the wording is important. cP2 makes a concession to the interlocutor with one hand while taking something away from him with the other. In conceding that reason will not lead you either way, Pascal shows that he takes agnosticism and even atheism seriously. He acknowledges the logical coherence and intellectual defensibility of the entire range of unbelief. But when he says that reason undermines neither belief nor unbelief, he refuses the interlocutor's rebuke of those who accept Christian faith without any reason. If the interlocutor were right, reason would at least tell us what not to choose in this case, but by cP2 it doesn't even do that. "Therefore," Pascal says to the interlocutor:

cP3 *don't condemn those who have chosen, since you know nothing about it.*

The dialectical energy at this point of IR is very high. The thrust and parry is elegant and swift. This last rejoinder is slick, but it does not persuade the interlocutor, who sees an opportunity for escape that Pascal has not yet closed off. Sometimes it is not what you choose that is blameworthy, the interlocutor thinks, but the act of choosing itself. It is epistemically blameworthy, the interlocutor asserts, to adopt any position for which evidence is wanting. "I will blame [Christians]," he says,

dI *for having made not this choice but any choice. For although the one who takes heads and the one who takes tails are equally blameworthy (*en pareille faute*), both are to blame. The right thing is not to wager.*

## Rationalism

By rejecting the proposed wager in this way, the interlocutor declares himself to be a rationalist according to my use of the term. He thinks that all actions can and should be undertaken only when reason justifies them. In the present case, then, where reason is silent, the interlocutor infers that some third option must exist. It must be possible, he thinks, *not to bet.*

Pascal does not agree. Rationalism has led the interlocutor astray. His supposed third option is simply a mirage, an artefact of rationalism itself. A rationalist looks theoretically at the ever-branching road of life and imagines that at every fork the traveller can take branch A, or branch B, or neither. But in real life, where momentum carries us irresistibly forward, travellers who do not seize the moment and turn their steps into path B will be swept onward in A. The option of not choosing is simply not there.

Pascal thinks we are not only hurled into life but also hurled along it. The decision whether to believe in the existence of God is made at a fork in life's road. A junction is approaching. You will either depart from your present course by an act of will or be swept past the junction, following the same course as before. Thus, "wagering is not voluntary," Pascal says,

**eP1** *You are embarked (embarqué).*

eP1 excludes the option of not betting, but Pascal packs more than that into the idea of our being "embarked." Part of what he means cannot be made explicit without violating the rule of naturalism (aP1) to which IR is bound. It concerns a famous doctrine, coming originally from Augustine, concerning the relation between faith and understanding. To see what Pascal intends in IR, but cannot say there, we can turn to another fragment in which he writes:

> If we should never act except to obtain what is certain, then one should do nothing because of religion, for it is uncertain. But how many things do we undertake for uncertain ends – ocean voyages, battles ... When we work for tomorrow or for the uncertain we are acting reasonably (*avec raison*), for according to the rule of division (*la règle des parties*), which has been demonstrated, working for the uncertain is what we ought to do.[47]

The exciting idea here is that, in religious contexts preeminently, but also in many others, it is not only not fallacious to act without reason's approval; it can be "what we ought to do." But one thing leads to another. If we want to understand the *reason* Pascal gives for leaving reason out of account, we need to know something about the "rule of division" to which he appeals. It is the same rule he will use to justify the wager to the interlocutor in IR.[48] But in the fragment just quoted, Pascal is interested in the close connection of that rule to the context of faith – especially, but not exclusively, religious faith. He thinks this "rule of division" demonstrates that it can be reasonable to act by faith in cases where reason offers no guidance.

Part of what Pascal is asserting here is the old Augustinian idea of "faith seeking understanding."[49] Pascal thinks he has better reason for asserting it than even Augustine did. He has better reason because he

(Pascal) can prove it. "Saint Augustine," he says in the same fragment, "saw that we work for uncertain outcomes on the sea and in battle etc., but he did not see the rule of division that shows we ought to do so."[50]

What rule exactly Pascal has in mind and how it vindicates Augustine are difficult questions to answer. It is not the whole of his *règle des partis* that comes into play here. That rule resolves the complex question of how to divide equitably the money already staked in a game of chance, should that game break off for any reason before a winner has been declared. What is crucial for the IR fragment is not Pascal's mathematical solution to this question but an insight from it concerning the proper way of *calculating expected value*.[51] I'll call it CEV.

A simple statement of CEV appears near the end of *The Art of Thinking*, a text in logic written by Pascal's close friends Antoine Arnauld and Pierre Nicole. It occurs in a section concerning "the judgement we ought to make of future accidents." Since their discussion of CEV is thought to have been inspired, if not dictated, by Pascal,[52] it will be useful to cite it here because it gets at precisely the thought that is the motor of the wager argument in IR. As the authors of *The Art of Thinking* state it, the upshot of CEV is as follows:

> In order to judge what to do, whether to try for a benefit or to avoid an evil, it is not sufficient merely to consider the benefit or the evil by itself. You must also consider the probability of its coming to pass or not.[53]

The authors of the *Port Royal Logic* criticize the unreasonable person whose behaviour is determined by unfounded hopes or fears, and they go on to say that their principal aim with this rule is to encourage reasonable hopes and fears.[54] It would be foolish for an office worker, for example, to insist on wearing a helmet during working hours for fear of what would happen if the roof collapsed. It is also foolish to sell your house to buy lottery tickets, guided only by the thought of how rich you will be if you win. The fear in the first case and the hope in the second are ill considered for the same reason: they take into account only the feared or desired end, not the likelihood that the chosen means are necessary to avoid that end or sufficient to bring it about.

Pascal thinks the CEV rule proves Augustine right in thinking that we are sometimes justified in acting on faith. That is the first thing he has to make the interlocutor see. But Pascal also thinks the situation in which the interlocutor finds himself in IR is a case in point. He has to bet because he is "embarked." How does that follow?

Once again we find Pascal pushing against the limits of the wager metaphor. Wagering normally means putting your money where your mouth is, betting on something you believe is going to happen. As a rueful Lord Byron observed,

> most men (till by losing rendered sager)
> Will back *their own opinions* by a wager.

But the interlocutor of IR is asked to wager *against* his own opinion and in favour of Pascal's. Moreover, Pascal is asking him to bet on an outcome that is not recommended by reason. Reason gives you no grounds for expecting either outcome, yet you are told you *must* commit yourself to the one you would not initially have wished for.

The wager metaphor is no longer running things at this point. Here, the ruling metaphor is that of being 'embarked.' Pascal loads that word with all the strangeness of this novel situation.

The nautical metaphor etymologically present in *embarqué* is not exploited. It was already dead in seventeenth-century French,[55] as it is in the English equivalent 'embarked.' But in both languages, the cognate expressions retain their metaphorical association with a *journey begun*.

The picture of someone "embarked" recalls the *"âme jetée"* with which IR began. Life* originated for us when our soul was hurled into a body. Our consciousness dates from that event but, of course, was not present in it. For as long as we have been conscious of ourselves, we have never been anything but *embarked*.

In using that word, Pascal draws on the powerful literary archetype of *life's way*. Before we can become aware of ourselves in life, long before we appreciate the human condition in sufficient depth to form the concept of life*, we are already "in the middle of life's way," where Dante places himself in the opening words of the *Divine Comedy*. Or to vary the literary example, the embarked protagonist of John Bunyan's *Pilgrim's Progress* find himself born (thrown) into the City of Destruction, at the antipodes of the Celestial City. The whole of the "straight and narrow way" the pilgrim will have to climb, with all its lurking dangers, separates him from heaven. Yet only if he ventures up that steep, daunting road can life* be transformed into life∞.

As soon as rumours of life∞ reach our ears, our lives become problematic to us in a way they never could have been before. Life* can no longer be innocently continued. The road of life forks before us. A question arises for us that never previously was a question: Will our future be more of life* or will it be turned towards life~? Pascal's interlocutor has just come to recognize that these options are before him, and Pascal tries to persuade him that there are no others. He must either choose the straight and narrow way leading to life~, or else continue his aimless wandering through what Bunyan calls the City of Destruction and what I have called life*. It is urgent that the interlocutor choose, because he is embarked. An instant from now, life's momentum will sweep him past the fork at which he finds himself. Pascal's next move brings us back to calculating expected value:

> **eP2** *Which will you take then? Look, since you have to choose, let's look for what is least in your interest.*

If we put eP2's point positively, the interlocutor is urged to focus his attention exclusively on what is *most* in his interest. But that seems to be the very thing CEV advises against. To understand Pascal's subtlety here, we have to see why looking only at the payoff in this case is really an instance of CEV rather than a breach of it.

Recall that the point of CEV was that we should consider not only the payoff some action may possibly bring but also the likelihood of its doing so. Pascal appears to have forgotten the second clause in eP2. But he hasn't. It's just that, when it comes to the existence of God, the probability of either outcome is incalculable. Reason proves nothing either way. (See aP2 above.) Now because we cannot calculate the probability of God's existence, the reader has *only* the first clause of CEV (i.e., the payoff) to consider.

Pascal has not made the gross error of forgetting his own principle here, but he may have made a more subtle error. He has been criticized for assuming without proof that unbelievers must assign some positive probability to God's existence.[56] If God's existence had no probability at all, these critics say, then it would not be one of the options on which the interlocutor could bet. However, Pascal's principle that reason tells us nothing about the existence of God ought to save him from this objection. No unbeliever could say the probability of God's existence was zero, for that would make God's nonexistence a truth of reason, which, by aP2, it cannot be.

The assignment of probability to God's existence is a thorny detail in the argument of IR, but it is no more than a detail. The important point is that reason does not show us what to do when the possibility of pursuing life$^\infty$ presents itself. Therefore, if we had only the rule of CEV to go by, we would be entitled either to do nothing or to pursue the course that appears to offer us the greatest benefit. Because we are embarked upon life*, however, doing nothing is not an option. Momentum will carry us past the point of choosing, unless we *now* choose to search for life$^\infty$.[57] If life$^\infty$ offers a better payoff, the only reasonable response is to pursue it.

Pascal treats our ignorance concerning God's existence as if it were a singularity. But it isn't. N.N. Taleb, in a fascinating book about the impact of improbable events, draws inspiration from this very moment of IR and grasps its broader importance. "The idea behind Pascal's wager," he writes,

> has fundamental applications outside of theology. It stands the entire notion of knowledge on its head. It eliminates the need for us to understand the probabilities of a rare event (there are fundamental limits to our knowledge of these); rather, we can focus on the payoff and benefits of an event if it takes place.[58]

But Taleb is not the only one to extend the application of Pascal's point. David Hume applies the same analysis to our ignorance of the future, and draws from it a similar lesson. Because our actions are always directed towards the future, and reason provides no guide to it, we are free to choose whatever action we think might bring about the future we would desire. Reason's job is only to find means adapted to our ends. Or as Hume famously puts it, "reason is and ought only to be the slave of the passions."[59]

Pascal is more cautious than Hume and arguably more judicious. He gives the passions a leading role only in the restricted context of belief in the existence of God. And even there the charter of the passions is not absolute. Reason is not simply passion's slave, because, as the later stages of IR will attempt to establish, the passions need to be schooled before reason can be justified in serving them. We must not simply pursue and flee the objects of our hopes and fears. We must wait until reason makes these passions reasonable.

Believers and unbelievers literally have different kinds of minds, according to Pascal. Each is open to one kind of evidence and closed to another. The mind of an unbeliever is governed by concupiscence; that of a believer by grace. What seems to be evidence to believers may not register with unbelievers, or may even seem to them to count as evidence against the believer's position. "Not the prophecies," Pascal explains,

> not the proofs of our religion, not even the miracles are of such a nature as to be called absolutely convincing. But they are sufficiently so that belief is not irrational (*sans raison*). There is enough evidence and enough obscurity that some are enlightened and others confused. But the evidence favouring belief is at least equal to the evidence for the contrary, so that reason cannot determine anyone against it. The only reason not to follow the evidence in favour of belief, therefore, must be concupiscence and malice of heart. That is how it comes about that there is enough reason to condemn unbelievers, though too little to convince them, and hence that those who follow the evidence seem to do so by grace rather than reason, and those who shun it seem to act not from reason but concupiscence.[60]

The claims of this passage tally well with those of Pascal's essay on "The Art of Persuasion." Concupiscence influences not just the unbeliever's assessment of evidence, but even what will count as evidence for him. That is why Pascal would agree with Hume that reason is in fact the slave of the passions. But because the concupiscent mind is a fallen mind, Pascal would not agree with Hume that the passions *ought* to be in control. Not, at least, until they have been reformed.

The authors of the *Port Royal Logic* who set out Pascal's rule for reasonable conduct (CEV) also follow him in connecting it to emotional therapy. Its purpose, they say, "is to make us more reasonable in our hopes and our fears."[61]

At this point in IR, however, Pascal is still not ready to begin reordering his interlocutor's emotions. First, he reminds him of his situation:

**eP3** *You have two things to lose: the true and the good; and two things to draw on: your reason and your will, your knowledge and your beatitude. Your nature seeks to avoid two things: error and misery.*

The interlocutor's situation can be represented in a simple chart:

| To Draw On | To Avoid | To Lose |
| --- | --- | --- |
| a. Reason (knowledge) | Error | Truth |
| b. Will (beatitude) | Wretchedness | The good |

The chart is a straightforward expression of CEV as it would apply to any situation in which we face a choice and an uncertain outcome. We must consider the good/evil that is promised (line b) as well as what reason/knowledge tells us about the likelihood of attaining it and the consequences of not doing so (line a). In the interlocutor's case, however, unusual conditions apply. First, he has no way of determining the likelihood of attaining the good or avoiding wretchedness. Hence, Pascal says, the first line of the chart (line a), does not apply. Second, he has to choose.

**eP4** *Because you must choose, your reason is not wounded any more in choosing one side than the other. One point is thus disposed of* (vidé).

The interlocutor's position is unusual in this way: because the first line of the chart has been found inapplicable, he is now rationally justified in acting the way foolish people act. Or to put the point more carefully, the act that would normally be foolish is not foolish under present conditions. The interlocutor need only consider line b, the payoff in goodness that is promised him. The wagerer need only think of what he has to gain: *beatitude*. Hence, Pascal prods him with the question:

**fP/I** *But what of your beatitude* (béatitude)?

Beatitude is better than happiness. It is a state of fulfilled existence that is found only with life$^\infty$. Thomas Aquinas defines beatitude as "total satisfaction of the will" arising through the attainment of a perfect good.[62] Philosophers often reserve the word to denote this blissful state and contrast it with 'happiness,' which normally and etymologically means a contingent state of well-being associated with good fortune.[63]

In French, *béatitude* contrasts with *bonheur* in a similar way. So the unbeliever in dialogue with Pascal is left to consider only the question of how to procure beatitude. Should he bet God exists, and live accordingly, or not?

**gP1** *Let us weigh the gain and the loss if you choose "heads," that God exists. Let us appraise the two cases: if you win, you win everything, and if you lose, you lose nothing. Wager then without hesitation.*

What does Pascal mean by winning "everything"? Life$^\infty$ is what we stand to gain. It is everything in the sense that it is unending, and within it we are promised the maximum fulfilment of which our finite nature is capable – that is, beatitude. Beatitude is everything in that nothing added to it would increase its excellence. To possess any greater good we would need a greater capacity for goodness than human beings have. A drinking glass cannot hold the ocean, but it is full when it is full. It can make no use of the water it would take to fill a larger vessel.

It is also not clear why Pascal says the wagerer stands to lose nothing. If you really had to "bet your life," as has sometimes been said of Pascal's wager, then you would be threatened with annihilation if you lost. Losing, you would lose *everything*.

But Pascal takes for granted that life goes on regardless of how we bet. We are standing not in front of the abyss but in the middle of life's way, at a fork in the road. Life* lies behind and also stretches before us. It is the path along which we are impelled. Life$^\infty$, an alternative future, branches away from this path, and we can follow it if we summon up our will to do so. If we choose to follow that alternate branch, we will lose only life*, the life into which we were born.

As was already seen in Chapter Two, life* is in fact the source of all our wretchedness, though the unbeliever may not recognize that at the time of making the wager. But behind the veil, as things really are, what he stands to lose is even less than nothing, only a life of merely negative value. He is in an analogous position to someone who does not know he is terminally ill "risking" his present state of health for a chance to win perfect wellness. Though he doesn't know it, he is placing less than nothing at risk.

Pascal does not try to intimidate the wagerer by discussing the wretchedness that God may supernaturally attach to the afterlife of anyone who does not wager for his existence, though of course Christian doctrine commits him to believing in such wretchedness. On the other hand, there is also a sense in which losing life* *is* losing something. There is bound to be a certain amount of inconvenience attached to giving up life*. To say that losing it costs you nothing is like saying that you would lose nothing by exchanging the shack you live in for a mansion, or your worn out clothes for a luxurious suit. In saying such losses are nothing, you overlook the small inconvenience of change.

The unbeliever cannot prove that life* is the only life possible, or that the promises of life$^\infty$ are illusory. He sees his options narrowing quickly to the one Pascal is prodding him to.

## Many Gods?

Many critics of Pascal think there is a huge escape hatch still available to the interlocutor at this point, and that Pascal has no means of sealing it off. Critics have asked again and again what would happen if there were more than one *god* making rival demands on unbelievers, each god, let us suppose, asserting his uniqueness as unequivocally as the Judeo-Christian Yahweh does?[64] Versions of this criticism, as Jeff Jordan points out, are "legion."[65]

If the rival gods make incompatible demands on the unbeliever while offering identical infinite rewards to those who meet their demands, then an equally compelling wager argument could be constructed for each competing god. Which shows, according to Jordan, that Pascal's decision matrix, based on the existence or nonexistence of a particular god, is flawed, "because the states it employs are not jointly exhaustive of the possibilities."[66]

Jordan shows that this objection can be answered, provided we interpret IR as advocating a kind of generic theism, like that defended in William James's famous essay, "The Will to Believe."[67] This solution solves the problem as Jordan sees it, but there are two reasons why it ought nevertheless to be rejected.

First, it is textually indefensible as an account of Pascal. William James presented his generic understanding of religion as an improvement on Pascal's attempt "to force us into Christianity by reasoning as if our concern with truth resembled our concern with the stakes in a game of chance."[68] James was right about the Christian setting of Pascal's wager fragment, which I documented earlier in this chapter, and Jordan is therefore wrong to treat it as dispensable. Pascal is not trying to turn the interlocutor of IR into what is nowadays called "a spiritual person." The aim is to convert him to Catholic Christianity.

In the second place, even if it were textually defensible, Jordan's retreat to generic religion doesn't solve the problem. It makes Pascal's binary decision matrix applicable to more cases, but not to all. It only handles cases where *belief* in a god is the proposed key for eternal felicity. But let some crackpot offer ceaseless ecstasy to those who are freeze-dried at a high point in their lives and you will have a competitor to all religious positions. The binary decision matrix will prove inadequate once again. Now the wagerer must choose among belief, unbelief, and freeze-drying. And the existence of that third option reinstitutes a fourth, which Pascal's version was able to exclude: the option of doing nothing.

Going generic is therefore no solution to the "many gods" objection. We might as well stick to the textually grounded view in which the interlocutor is asked to wager on the Roman Catholic faith. The cost of following Pascal is also low, because the many gods objection is a spurious one, and surprisingly easy to defeat.

To put the matter provocatively, the "legion" of objectors notwithstanding, there never was a many gods problem to begin with. Pascal is talking about *God*, as Christians understand him, and uniqueness belongs to him essentially. The Christian concept of God is by definition monotheistic. Not only does the Christian God proclaim himself unique, he has qualities that prove him to be so. He is, after all, omnipotent. A second omnipotent God would be as incompatible with the first as an immovable object with an unstoppable force. For logical reasons, there cannot be more than one omnipotent God. Therefore, there is, literally speaking, no many gods problem.

What can and actually do exist are rival *descriptions* of how you must act if you wish to please the only God there is. Yet here again the challenge to Pascal is not as serious as sometimes imagined. There are not arbitrarily many of these descriptions, as some of Pascal's critics assume. If someone just concocts for argument's sake some "perverse master" deity, who rewards all and only those who do not believe in God, he is not offering a description that could possibly pertain to God.[69] And anyone who mistook the perverse master deity for a serious religious option would likely have other intellectual handicaps as well, such as difficulty understanding jokes.

I'm not trying to pass off flippancy as argument but pointing to the weakness of flippant descriptions of God. There are more than enough *serious* rival descriptions of what we must do to please God to put Pascal's decision matrix right back in jeopardy. Judaism or Islam will suffice for that. Both describe the duties believers owe to God in ways that are incompatible with Christianity, because both deny the divinity of Jesus Christ. Perhaps there are other serious monotheistic religions that make further incompatible claims, but two are more than enough to make the point.

Judaism, Christianity, and Islam really exist. They all have adherents, some of whom, at least, are acquainted with the demands of one or more of the others. Call these people "informed adherents." If there were any merit in the many gods objection, then the informed adherents of all three religions would be irrational, for, according to that argument, they must have become believers under circumstances that offered no conclusive reason for belief.

Pascal rejects the many gods argument, at least as applied to Christian believers. While recognizing the existence of many God descriptions, he denies that they have any significance for the wager argument. To understand his thinking, we must step outside of IR for a moment.

First, Pascal thinks the one God, on whose existence he invites us to wager, is the source of *all* the competing descriptions of what he demands. For Pascal, that is, the plurality of religions is merely one of God's many disguises. *Vere tu es deus absconditus*, Pascal is fond of saying: truly, you are the hidden God. "If there had only been one religion," Pascal writes, "God would have been evident."[70] One of the attributes, therefore, of the God about whom we are to wager, is that he causes there to be descriptions of himself that are incompatible with Christianity.

Not that all the competing descriptions are of equal value. Suppose there were an animal we knew to exist only by its spoor, an animal no one had ever observed. It certainly would not follow that every description offered of it would be equally worthy of belief. Neither is every description offered of the hidden God. One main purpose of the *Pensées* is to show that Christianity offers a more credible account of what God wants of us than is given by other religions.

Christianity has always taken a plurality of God descriptions for granted. It originated, after all, in a polytheistic world, in which every description of the divine was to some degree in competition with every other. On Saint Paul's visit to first-century Athens, he discovered, among the innumerable altars of that very religious city, one that was almost neurotic in its inclusiveness. It was marked, "to the unknown god." When the opportunity of preaching to the Athenians arose, Paul began his sermon by commending their religiosity, and then exploited their neurosis. "Him whom you worship unawares," Paul said, referring to the unknown God, "I here proclaim."[71] Christians have been saying the same thing to serious rival religions ever since. And with good reason, Pascal thinks, not because they have any apodictic proof of Christianity but because the evidence is in its favour.

One part of that evidence lies in the miracles with which Christian credentials were initially established.[72] Fulfilled prophecies are a further indicator in Christianity's favour. Pascal calls them "abiding miracles."[73] He cites them in a remarkable fragment in which he also addresses explicitly the many gods objection. "I see a number of religions," Pascal says:

> saying contrary things, and hence all false but one. Each wants to be believed on its own authority and threatens unbelievers. That is not enough to make me believe, however. Anyone can say that. Anyone can claim to be a prophet. But in Christianity I find prophecies, and they are what not just anyone can produce.[74]

Those who think Pascal failed to notice the many gods objection must have overlooked this passage. His simple answer is that Christianity is supported by evidence other religions lack.

The appeal to evidence may work well against the many gods objection, but you may wonder whether it doesn't contradict the stipulation at the beginning of IR that reason does not rule either way on God's existence (IR, point c)? However, I think Pascal's point here is just subtle, not self-contradictory. Consider this analogy: reason doesn't tell us whether the Sasquatch exists, but our uncertainty about its existence does not imply that every Sasquatch description has equal evidence in its favour.[75]

Furthermore, even if Pascal were wrong about the predominant evidence in favour of Christianity, it would not affect his argument against the many gods objection. There is an important aspect of belief formation to which the objection pays insufficient attention, and which is sufficient to defeat it. Our response to what God demands of us does not depend only on the description offered by a given religion. It also depends on what part of that description we are acquainted with, and on our mental receptivity at the moment we encounter it. The receiver has as much to do with the message received as the transmitter does. Some descriptions may be too demanding for us, or too simple, at the time we encounter them. Sometimes we are unprepared to listen; at others we hearken to mumbo jumbo with a too-credent ear. That is why we may find ourselves wagering on different religions at different times of our lives, or on the same religion more than once. Yet on each occasion the decision matrix will be exactly the one Pascal presents. We will be deciding for or against conforming to the will of God, as a given God description depicts it. And the many gods objection will be of no account.

In the controlled climate of the classroom, professors of comparative religion might contrive a situation in which students are made to wager on many religions at once and find it can't be done for the very reasons Jordan sets forth. But religious smorgasbords do not exist in ordinary life. Like culinary ones, they must be created artificially. The normal thing is to encounter the claims of God somewhere in the middle of life*'s way. Different wagers may be proposed to us in different circumstances by different serious religions, or by the same serious religion on different segments of our way. On each serious occasion we have to bet. If we wager on more than one religion during our lives, at most one of them will describe God correctly. Nothing about the wager excludes the possibility that we may choose a wrong religion or reject the right one. If that were not possible, then there would be no infidels and no apostates. But neither can anything rule out our having multiple opportunities to choose.

All serious religions insist that their summons to belief is the most serious moment of our lives. If we are serious people, deep will call to deep, and we will begin to *search*. Once a search is begun in earnest, Pascal thinks, the seeker is already close to port. "You would not be looking for me," he has God say in a later fragment, "if you had not already found me."[76] God is the natural end point of every search, even if not every searcher finds him. Pascal, of course, means God as he is, and believes that to be as the Catholic Church describes him.

In IR Pascal points the interlocutor immediately towards the religious destination at which, in any case, his search would end, provided it were conducted under ideal conditions and for a sufficient length of time. Searching would end in Christian belief, because eventually the seeker would encounter the greater (though not overwhelming) weight of evidence in favour of Christianity, and encounter it at a time when he was receptive to its power. To experience that serendipity is, in religious terms, to receive grace, and seekers who receive it always become believers.

## Endgame

So the many gods objection is a red herring. The interlocutor of IR may have wagered before, and new wagers may confront him after the one he faces today, but here and now he must choose between exactly the two alternatives Pascal has put before him. By this stage of the argument he knows he has to bet. So all that remains for him to consider is which outcome would be best for him, if he bets on it. Once again, Pascal sets this out formally (gP1):

| Bet | To Win | To Lose | Stake |
|---|---|---|---|
| God exists | Everything $= $ life $\infty$ of $\infty$ happiness | Nothing $= $ life* | Life* |

Pascal indicates his own satisfaction with this way of describing the interlocutor's real situation by exclaiming:

**gP2** *That is wonderful!*[77]

The interlocutor, however, is only partly convinced. He accepts the logic of Pascal's description without succumbing to its charm:

**hI** *Yes, I have to bet, but perhaps I am betting too much.*

Only infinite happiness is to be considered; on that point the interlocutor agrees. But he is still not persuaded that life* is such a small thing to lose. He holds back.

From a logical point of view, the interlocutor's hesitation is absurd. Anything that falls short of life$^\infty$ is worthless in comparison. Existentially, however, the hesitant interlocutor has a strong justification. Life* is the only life he knows. Moreover, Pascal's own theories tell us that the interlocutor will view his situation with the concupiscent eyes of life*. Situated as he is, in the middle of life*'s way, the full splendour of life$^\infty$ is beyond his grasp. Even to get a glimpse of life$^\infty$ is a gift of grace, and we cannot assume that the interlocutor has received it. To normal concupiscent minds, the realities of life$^\infty$ are hidden. "All things are veils that cover God," Pascal tells Mlle de Roannez.[78]

In his exhortation to the wagerer, Pascal calls life$^\infty$ "everything," but neither *definiens* nor *definiendum* will be other than sound and fury in the interlocutor's ears. He can no more comprehend how small life*'s comparative value is than he can appreciate the greatness of life$^\infty$. Furthermore, life* feels safe because it is familiar.

Even to Pascal, talk of life$^\infty$ conveys no particular meaning. He admits that, while we know of the existence of an infinite, "we are ignorant of its nature." The meaning of infinity was an acknowledged puzzle in seventeenth-century metaphysics. Spinoza, writing in 1663, just a little after Pascal's death, remarks that the "question about infinity has always seemed to everyone to be most difficult, indeed inexplicable."[79]

· The word 'everything' is just as bad. It is a word that only has meaning when a domain of reference is specified. If you ask to see everything on my desk, or everything on my hard disk, I have a pretty good idea of what you want me to show you. But ask to see absolutely *everything*, and I don't know where to begin. Pascal specifies no domain for the *everything* represented by life$^\infty$, and probably none could be specified. Therefore, we can attach little meaning to life$^\infty$. We understand it best as a term of reverence, implying a goodness surpassing any we can imagine. The only warrant for thinking such a life to be possible is that it is endorsed by Scripture and the Church, though such supports are inadmissible in the context of IR. Admissible or not, however, Pascal has dialectical, though not demonstrative, arguments, based on miracles, prophecy, and other considerations, showing these supports can bear weight. The reason they are inadmissible here is that they would not be persuasive to an unbeliever who considers them with a concupiscent mind.

So there is an undeniable, but not fatal, vagueness to the notion of life$^\infty$. Unless, as one critic claims, the notion is worse than merely vague. According to this objection, Pascal's use of the notion of "infinite utility" makes the calculation of probabilities impossible.[80]

Oddly enough, the acknowledged vagueness of life$^\infty$ may save Pascal from this objection. No precise error can be attributed to him. IR is not talking about infinite utilities in any mathematical sense, though the wager metaphor suggests such a sense to mathematically sophisticated readers. The real subject of IR, however, is unfathomably great blessedness, or a life of perfect fulfilment. Life$^\infty$ is a quality rather than a quantity, though Pascal does not always clearly distinguish the two.

Still, even making every concession to Pascal's own vocabulary, and construing the wager in the way most favourable to the argument's success, one easily sees how the inducement life$^\infty$ offers in favour of belief may not be sufficient for the unbeliever. Because of his concupiscent mind, he may shrink from forsaking the palpable reality of life* for the uncertain delights of life$^\infty$. Pascal leaves his readers groping at this point. The argument slips a little out of focus. Pascal's answer does not meet the interlocutor's main objection:

**iP1** *Let's see. Since there is equal chance of winning or losing, if you had only two lives (to win) against one (to lose) you could wager, but what if there were three?*

Pascal's point is mathematically sound. If you had two lives to win and one to lose, and equal chances of winning or losing, the expected value would be ½(2) + ½(0), which is 1.[81] Making this bet would neither improve nor worsen your current situation. You could either bet or not, as you saw fit, just as Pascal says. But if you stood to win three or more lives, Pascal will argue, you should gladly risk one to do so.

**iP2** *You would have to bet (because you have no choice) and you would be imprudent when you are forced to play not to bet your life (vie) to win three in a game where the odds of losing and winning are equal.*

It is easy to anticipate that Pascal's next step will ramp up the possible gain to the infinite level he associates with life$^\infty$:

**iP3** *But there is an eternity of happy life. And that being so, even if there were an infinite number of possible outcomes (hasards) of which only one was in your favour, you would still be right to bet (gager) one to get two, and you would be making a mistake if, when obliged to play, you refused to stake one life against three in a game where only one of an infinite number of outcomes is in your favour, if there was an infinity of infinitely happy life to win.*

There are a number of logical problems with the reasoning here which I will not attempt to untangle.[82] But there is also a textual difficulty that cannot be passed over. iP3 immediately follows iP2 in the text of IR as we have it, but the thought expressed in the two passages is not in perfect continuity. To continue the thought of iP2, iP3 ought to be offering the wagerer not an "infinity of *life*" but an "infinite number of *lives*." The argument should be moving from two lives, to three to an infinite number of them. The shift from lives to life (in the singular) shows that the qualitative notion of life$^\infty$, at which Pascal is really aiming, has displaced the quantitative notion of a series of lives, which he uses merely to continue the wager metaphor. This is the point at which the idea of wagering ceases to be a vehicle for the argument and becomes almost an obstacle to it.

The wagerer is not betting his life in order to win a quantity of others like it, though that is how Pascal talks up to the end of iP2. Instead the wagerer is being asked to bet his life* in order to win something qualitatively different, namely life$^\infty$. Pascal's probabilistic rendering of the argument in iP2 may be a rhetorical tour de force, but it only gets off the ground by misrepresenting the real nature of the bet. The real question faced by the wagerer is whether to prefer life$^\infty$ to life*, when they have no common measure.

The quantitative picture of iP2 will never suffice to make the point of iP3. As we have already seen, the life* put at risk in the wager is in reality not a good thing or even a neutral one. It is bad through and through. Life* is not a source of happiness but of misery. To "win" two or more of life* is like winning a second or third sentence in prison, or another week of flu, or bonus sessions in the torture chamber. Neutral lives, merely biological ones, are not available in Pascal's world, either to be lived or won. The situation depicted in iP2 is therefore not the one the wagerer really faces, and its logical problems do not affect the great existential question Pascal wishes to set before his reader.

There is another way in which iP2 misrepresents the wagerer's real situation. Where it is merely false to suggest that extending life* would constitute a greater good to the person who "won" the extension, it would be monstrous to imply that an infinite number of consecutive lives* would be the same thing as life$^\infty$. Life$^\infty$ is to life* a qualitatively superior mode of being. An infinite prolongation of life* would literally be Hell.

Pascal develops the contrast between the two forms of life more clearly in another place, where he invites us to consider

> whether it is not indubitable that the only good in this life [i.e., life*] is the hope of another [i.e., life$^\infty$], that one is only happy to the degree one approaches to that other life, and that, since there will be no further sorrows (*malheurs*) for those who are assured of eternity, there is also no joy (*bonheur*) awaiting those who have no inkling of it.[83]

The shaky transition from iP2 to iP3 brings to mind the tentative character of the edited IR fragment and the choppy manuscript on which it rests. We simply don't know what Pascal might have done with the argument of iP2 in a polished version of IR. As it stands, the transition from iP2 to iP3 is accomplished in one inconclusive lurch from quantity to quality. The qualitative conclusion is meant to piggyback in some way on the quantitative premises, and yet it is manifestly unable to do so. That would be a fatal objection to the argument of IR, were it not that Pascal can defeat the interlocutor's professed attachment to life* by other means. His reformulation of the wagerer's present choice shows how:

iP4 *in this case there is an infinity of infinitely happy life* [i.e., life*] *to win, one chance of winning against finite chances of losing, and what you risk is finite* [i.e., life*].

Unfortunately, as Pascal attempts to amplify the point of iP4 he lapses from his normal standard of clarity. As a result, the translation I am offering next is somewhat speculative and the sceptical reader should compare it to Appendix A.

iP5 *Wherever the infinite is present, but the risks of loss are not infinite as against the likelihood of winning, there is no place for opinion* (parti). *There is nothing to deliberate* (balancer) *about; you have to risk everything you've got. And thus, when you're forced to play, you'd be crazy to keep your life* [= life*] *instead of risking it for an infinite gain* [i.e., for life*], *an outcome no less likely to occur than a loss which amounts to nothing* [because all you risk is life*].

## An Objection

The wager argument ends here, with the implicit conclusion that the interlocutor should wager for God's existence. But he still hesitates on two counts. First, he seeks reassurance that Pascal's argument is not a fallacious one. He wonders in particular whether there might not be an "infinite distance" between what he certainly risks and the infinite good he hopes to gain, such that those two infinities cancel one another and render the bet a bad one, or at least a doubtful one. The details of this murky objection are not important for present concerns. Pascal is able to reassure the interlocutor that the wager to which he is being invited is an overwhelmingly good bet:

jP1 *[O]ur proposition has infinite force when the odds of losing or winning are the same, and there is infinity to be won.*

If the odds are fifty-fifty and you have to bet, each bet is equally reasonable. But if betting one way promises you immeasurable good at no cost, and the other way promises you nothing, then you must of course bet on the immeasurable good. "That is demonstrative," Pascal declares.

**jP2** *And if there is any truth men are capable of grasping, that is it.*

What exactly is Pascal claiming to have demonstrated? Neither the truth of Christianity nor the existence of God.[84] His argument resembles the ones that used to be called *practical syllogisms*, whose conclusions were not a proposition for contemplation but an action to be undertaken. Pascal's syllogism takes the form of an argument about wagering, but, as I have stressed, it exploits the idea of wagering only metaphorically. The argument's conclusion is not literally that the wagerer should bet on God. Its literal meaning is that everyone should live his life as if God, as conceived by the Catholic tradition, exists. Here is how the practical syllogism runs when the metaphorical role of the wager is removed:

1. Life* is what we will live unless we choose to live otherwise.

    Lemma 1: Life* appears to those living it as a mixture of happiness and unhappiness followed by death.
    Lemma 2: The value of a completed life* is at best nothing.

2. There are good reasons for believing that there is a life of infinite goodness (life$^\infty$) which can be obtained, if we choose to live as if God, as understood by the Catholic Church, exists.

    Lemma 3: There are also good reasons for doubting whether there is any such thing as life$^\infty$ (or God).

3. A probabilistic model (supported by the mathematical consensus of Pascal's age) says that where 1 and 2 and the three lemmata obtain, it is reasonable to live as if God existed.

    ∴ We ought to live as if God existed.

## Hesitation

The interlocutor accepts the syllogism as a whole. "I confess, I admit it," he says. But something still troubles him:

**kI** *is there no way of knowing the outcome of the game* (le dessous du jeu)*?*

The *game* is the metaphorical one with which the corpus of the wager fragment begins, *the game being played at the limit of an infinite distance,*

*in which either heads or tails is going to be the outcome* (cP1). The interlocutor wants to know whether there is not some way to know its outcome
in advance. What would disturb him in the syllogistic formulation
would be lemma 3. Is there no way to lift the veil of ignorance lemma 3
imposes, behind which he is supposed to wager?

Pascal's answer is as unexpected as it is brief. We expect him to say
there is no way to lift the veil. Reason is no help (cP1), and we are not
allowed to appeal to faith (aP1). Yet he unceremoniously breaks the
naturalistic rule established at aP1, and unbroken up to this point, and
says that we *can* know the outcome of the game, provided we enlist the
help of what he calls

    **mP1** *Scripture and the rest.*

Pascal must mean that the Bible, taken as a revealed text, along with
doctrinal matters infallibly decided by the Roman Catholic Church
("the rest"), would resolve the interlocutor's doubts. Which, of course,
they would, if he only believed them. But the interlocutor does not
believe them at this point, and the rule of IR was to make no appeal to
such matters.

Perhaps Pascal would have omitted the reference to *Scripture and the
rest* in a final draft of IR. But not necessarily. Although recommending supernatural aids violates IR's naturalistic rule, it does not, strictly
speaking, violate IR's overall logic. That logic is dialectical and remains
inviolate, because the interlocutor in his reply rejects Pascal's attempt to
stray beyond the rules. Moreover, the mention of *Scripture and the rest*
serves the valuable rhetorical purpose of allowing the interlocutor to
reveal his fatalistic attitude towards his own unbelief. "My hands are
tied and my tongue is mute," he says,

    **nI** *I am forced to wager and yet not free to do so. I am not released from betting,
and yet am so made that I cannot believe. What do you expect me to do?*[85]

To this objection Pascal makes a complex reply, to which, yet again,
libraries of secondary literature are devoted. From this point on, the
text of IR twists and turns so often that what precedes it looks straightforward. I shall take it in short instalments and try to reveal the underlying logic in my commentary.

In the first place, Pascal responds to the personal psychological
turn the interlocutor gave the argument when he said, "I am so made
that ..." Pascal sharpens and psychologizes the interlocutor's analysis.

The interlocutor is paralyzed, Pascal says, not by fate but by disordered passions.

oP1 *[R]ecognize at least that your inability to believe arises from your passions.*

The connection Pascal wishes to establish between the interlocutor's passions and his inability to believe is not an arbitrary one. It is one strand in the web of Pascalian psychology. Pascal connects it both to his notion of the fallen concupiscent will and to his analysis of philosophical failure, with its dependence on the fallen intellect. Against the background of his psychology, and given the earlier steps of the argument of IR, there can be no other cause of the interlocutor's paralysis than the passions:

oP2 *since reason draws you toward wagering and yet you cannot do it.*

In life\*, as we saw in Chapter Two, people often fail to detect the passions' role in undermining reason. They pass quickly and unconsciously from wanting to believe some proposition to asserting it as a certainty, as if they had come to hold it through the exercise of reason. In the technical terminology discussed in Chapter Two, they *confabulate*.

Pascalian confabulators fail to notice the gap between what the passions lean to and what can legitimately be asserted. Even when the gap is large, it can be indetectable to fallen minds. Pascal increases the level of magnification to make it obvious.

oP2 forces the interlocutor to acknowledge that reason is drawing him *away* from what the passions desire. Pascal doesn't say which passions are involved, nor does it matter. Whichever are in play, they incline him towards life\*, and the interlocutor finds himself unable to resist their blandishments. This situation is delicate for Pascal, because he is committed to saying that there is no natural remedy for the grip the passions have on us. Or, to put it more accurately, the natural remedies that are proposed are failures.

There is a fragment where he explains how they fail:

The civil war of reason against the passions led peacemakers into opposing camps. Some tried to renounce the passions and become gods; the rest to renounce reason and become brutish animals ... Neither camp was successful. Reason gives no peace to those who abandon themselves to the passions. It carries on denouncing their baseness and injustice. In those who try to give up the passions, on the other hand, they remain as lively as ever."[86]

The interlocutor has just awakened to this civil war of reason and passions in his own life. He cannot follow reason because his passion is too strong. But Pascal will not let him get away with following his passion. Where, then, is the middle way between the demands of reason and the persuasiveness of passion? Pascal thinks it lies in weakening the interlocutor's passions. A passion weakened now may be mastered later. Thus, he suggests the interlocutor should:

oP3 *try to convince [himself] ... by weakening [his] passions.*

**Therapy**

Fragment L12/S46, with which this chapter began, foretold a therapeutic stage in Pascal's apologetic strategy. It begins here. The interlocutor accepts Pascal's point that his emotions are blocking the best course of action. For the first time he wishes to find a way around them. "You want to cure yourself of unbelief (*infidélité*)," Pascal says, describing the interlocutor's new, open frame of mind,

oP4 *and you ask about remedies.*

In response, Pascal points to empirical evidence that remedies exist:

oP5 *Learn from those who were bound like you and who now wager all they have. They are people who are familiar with the way you wish to travel, and are cured of the illness from which you seek to be healed.*

The strangeness of the remedies Pascal is about to propose lies in the dual nature they need to have. In the first place, the emotions that dominate life* cannot be tamed by natural means. On the other hand, a natural remedy is the only kind the interlocutor is prepared to accept. So which kind of remedy is it to be, natural and ineffective or supernatural and inadmissible? Pascal believes he has a remedy that squares the circle: a natural remedy with supernatural effects:

oP6 *follow the method by which [those who have already become believers] began. They accomplished it by doing everything as if they believed, taking holy water, having masses said, and so on. This will make you believe by natural means,*

*Natural means*, then, to a supernatural end! Another bold, ingenious twist in this tortuous argument! But the course of IR never did run smooth. Pascal ends the sentence just quoted with a dark phrase, which I will cite first in the original French. Taking holy water and so on will make you believe, he says,

oP7 *et vous abêtira*.

## *Abêtir*

About the verb *abêtir*, used by Pascal only in this place, much too much has been written. I wish I could avoid adding my own pebble to the heap, but this unusual term holds the key to the therapy Pascal proposes in IR.

There are two things *abêtir* could mean. One comes from its ordinary use, the second from its etymology. The difficulty is that neither appears to make sense in this context. Both need to be buttressed by extended, and therefore tenuous, explanations. *Abêtir* would normally mean "to make one stupid"; but it could also mean "to make one like an animal."

Since it is hard to see why Pascal would think either stupidity or animality to be advantageous to a person struggling to find religious belief, some scholars have concluded that *abêtir* must have been a slip of the pen, and Pascal meant something else. That thought has led them on exercises of vast erudition and ingenuity, as delightful to read as they are unlikely to be true.[87]

We'll never be certain what Pascal meant to say. But the best scholarly practice is to stick with the text we are given, until defending it proves impossible. I will therefore consider two different lines of argument in defence of *abêtir*.

Could *abêtir* have been used with its usual meaning in this context? Could Pascal have meant that the payoff for imitating a life of religious devotion is to become *stupid*? That is how I translated it in Appendix B, which has Pascal saying that: "[Taking holy water etc.] will make you believe and make you stupid." I think that is the right translation, but as a concession to the appearances against it, and to the opinion of most commentators (also against it) I shall call it the "stupid interpretation."

It is certainly strange for a religious apologist to recommend stupidity to a potential convert. It's the kind of comment we would expect from Christopher Hitchens, or Richard Dawkins, or some other professional atheist, rather than from a Christian apologist. In a context meant to encourage an interlocutor to embark on a religious life, how could Pascal imagine that becoming stupid will be one of the inducements?

Considerations like these have prompted scholars to look further afield, working back from *abêtir* to the root word, *bête*, which is not just a French adjective meaning "stupid" but also a noun meaning "animal." The latter meaning makes possible a new interpretation of oP7. Pascal can be understood to say not that betting on God's existence will make us stupid but that it will make us animal-like instead.

That inducement is still far from a ringing endorsement of devout religious practice. But the attraction of this interpretation becomes clearer when its animalism is connected to the philosophy of Descartes. If Pascal's *bête* is the Cartesian *animal-machine*, then he could be saying that to cause the *machine of the body* to engage in belief behaviour will produce real belief in its associated mind. With these connections established, the beast can be used to conjure away the strange word *abêtir*, and thereafter discreetly substitute the more acceptable word *machine*.

This interpretation is well enough established among Pascal scholars that Roger Ariew, in his recent translation of the *Pensées*, renders oP6 and oP7 as, "This will make you believe naturally *and mechanically*" (my italics).[88] A footnote accompanying Ariew's translation connects the Cartesian "beast or machine" with Pascal's *abêtir*.

The main evidence for this interpretation is the advantages it has over the other one. I have found no univocal assertion in Pascal that the body is a machine, though there are fragments representing his apologetic project as involving mechanism, and these could be tied in to IR. If the unbeliever is reluctant to begin searching for God, Pascal says in one such fragment, the right reply would be "the machine."[89] Such texts cannot carry the day, however. Not only are they themselves ambiguous, but there are also other texts telling us that, unlike Descartes, Pascal thought that reasoning was mechanical.[90]

A further difficulty lies in connecting machines and Cartesian animals. In one fragment Pascal finds two points on which to contrast animals with his calculating machine. The machine comes closer to thinking than they do, but it lacks will, which they possess.[91] He could hardly be further from Descartes, who thinks neither that machines reason nor that animals will.

It is also unclear that the remedy Pascal prescribes to the interlocutor of IR, "taking holy water, having masses said, and so on" is mainly a bodily regimen. Taking holy water involves the body, but having masses said does not seem to. The "beastly interpretation" (as I shall call it) of *abêtir* is therefore on no firmer textual ground than the "stupid interpretation."

A psychological insight is presupposed in oP6 to which both interpretations can lay equal claim. It is plausible in itself, and independent of Descartes's theory of bodies or of animals. OP6 presupposes a behavioural law (call it BL) to the effect that:

> If you do not now believe X, then, by acting as if you did believe it, you can ultimately come to believe it.

BL is plausible enough for some contemporary psychologists to endorse it,[92] and it is certain that Pascal believes something like it. "Custom is our nature," he writes. "To grow accustomed to the faith is to believe it."[93] In another place he says, "Exterior penances dispose us toward interior ones as humiliations do to humility."[94]

Pascal also imagines an interlocutor saying to him that if he (the interlocutor) had only had faith, he would have given up the pursuit of pleasure. To which Pascal sees himself responding, "if you abandoned your pleasures, you would soon have faith."[95]

If BL is true, then, actions can generate belief. But that can be true whether or not the body is a machine, and whether or not beasts are. It would be convenient, then, for the beastly interpretation, if it could just make do with BL and quietly drop all reference to the Cartesian beast. Unfortunately, though, it can't. It needs that particular beast to explain away Pascal's strange word, *abêtir*.

The beastly interpretation has further shortcomings. First, even supposing Pascal subscribes to BL, it is not sufficient on its own to give him the conclusion he wants in IR. No doubt many beliefs can be acquired simply by pretending to have them, but the ones needed in IR – Christian beliefs – are not among them. At least, not according to Pascal. A Jesuit might think they were, but on this point Pascal follows the Jansenists. Like all Catholics, Jansenists believe we need grace in order to form saving Christian beliefs. However, Jansenist Catholics do not believe God gives sufficient grace to everyone.[96] Therefore, since grace is necessary to form Christian beliefs, and not everyone has it, there is no necessary connection between imitating the behaviour of a believer and acquiring the corresponding belief. Where grace is absent, BL does not hold. A theologically enhanced version of BL will

be necessary. I will call it TL. TL is derived from BL by adding the italicized theological provisos:

> **TL**: If you do not now believe in the truth of *Christianity* then, *through God's grace*, you can come to believe it by acting as if you do.

Grace is indispensable. Without it, the false goods of life* always
lead us astray. "Man is a subject full of error that is natural to him,
and ineradicable, except by grace," Pascal writes in another fragment,
which continues: "The passions of the soul trouble him and create
false impressions in him."[97] Therefore, if Pascal is invoking any law in
IR, it would have to be TL, the theologically boosted variant of BL, in
which grace is acknowledged as necessary for belief. But if the connection of the Cartesian animal-machine with BL was tenuous, with TL it
is null.

Things only get worse for the beastly interpretation. If it were correct,
the word order in oP6 and oP7 would be wrong. Pascal should not be
saying,

> [holy water etc.] will make you believe and make you like an animal,

But instead,

> [holy water etc.] will make you like an animal and make you believe.

The beastly interpretation supposes a lawlike connection to exist
between bodily behaviour and belief. Bodily behaviour is supposed to
*cause* belief. Why, then, would Pascal put the effect (belief) before the
cause (being like an animal)? Why didn't he say instead that behav-
ing like an animal will cause you to believe? The textually responsible
answer to that question is that he didn't say so because it wasn't what
he meant.

The beastly interpretation has a lot to answer for if you consider all its
shortcomings together. There is the merely etymological relation of *bête*
to *abêtir*, the lack of connection between Cartesian mechanism and the
indispensable theological law (TL), and the fact that, on this account,
Pascal inverts the relation of cause and effect. These objections make
a good case for reconsidering the stupid interpretation of *abêtir* – that
is, the interpretation in which *abêtir* has its normal meaning of making
someone stupid.

The objection to this interpretation lies in the difficulty we all have in imagining how being stupid could be advantageous. But once the weaknesses of the beastly interpretation have been taken into account, we have a reason to take its rival seriously, and the objections to it look less imposing.

Recall that Pascal introduced the rule of calculating expected value to remedy a certain kind of stupidity. People act stupidly, this rule says, when they pursue the prize they want without calculating how probable it is that they will win the prize through performing the actions they contemplate. Reasonable people are required by CEV to consider *both* the prize *and* the probability of obtaining it. By considering both matters together they avoid acting stupidly.

As we have already seen, however, the interlocutor in IR is in a unique situation with respect to CEV. All he knows of the probability of God's existence is that it is greater than zero.[98] In normal cases, such knowledge would be insufficient to justify a bet. He would suspend his judgment. However, in this case, by hypothesis of IR, he cannot suspend his judgement – he is "embarked" (eP1). The interlocutor therefore has no choice but to bet. Relative to these exceptional circumstances, both requirements of CEV *have been satisfied*. The probability assessment counts as having been made (though only vacuously), because there were no probability data to be considered. To outward appearances, then, the interlocutor, when he wagers, acts as stupid people do, pursuing the prize without regard to the probability of achieving it by the chosen means. *This* may be the stupidity Pascal intends when he says that betting in favour of God's existence "will make you believe, and will make you stupid."

In absolute terms, the stupid interpretation of *abêtir* is, like its rival, somewhat strained. Pascal does not refer directly to CEV at this point in his argument (oP6 and oP7). Moreover, if he is applying CEV, he overstates his case. He should only have said that betting on God "will make you *look* stupid." You won't really be stupid. After all, you did satisfy the requirements of CEV, even though you will not appear to have done so to casual observers of your actions. In the context of IR, however, you have made the advantageous, and therefore the wise, wager.

Notwithstanding this objection, the stupid interpretation is still more attractive than its rival. First, even if not explicitly evoked in oP6 and oP7, CEV is the guiding principle of the wager metaphor itself, as already mentioned above. And the stupid interpretation of *abêtir* has four further advantages. It takes the verb in its ordinary meaning, connects it with the ongoing argument about CEV, and does not require us to alter the word order of IR. In the fourth place, BL and TL, the laws about belief formation, fit better here than they do with the beastly interpretation. BL can be treated merely as a psychological commonplace, unconnected to the Cartesian beast; (TL) can explain how the interlocutor, if he were given grace, would see the "stupidity" Pascal is advocating as therapeutic wisdom.

## Fear of Religion Revisited

The stupid interpretation has yet another virtue. Because the interlocutor cannot be assumed to have grace at this point in IR, it enables us to understand his reaction when he hears that he will become stupid.

**pI** But that is what I fear,

he exclaims.

Who does not fear becoming stupid? Since the interlocutor at this point may lack grace, and have disordered passions (see nP1), the step to which Pascal is urging him naturally appears stupid to him. So the question becomes: How will Pascal persuade him that the commended course of action is not *really* stupid?

It should come as no surprise that the emotion causing the interlocutor to hold back is *fear*. The fragment L12/S46 with which we began, and the discussion of Thomas Nagel's "fear of religion" that followed, have prepared us to understand that. What now needs clarification is the precise nature of the interlocutor's fear, which Pascal's religious therapy will try to remove.

Though the goods of life* may be illusory and its evils many and real, someone in the interlocutor's position will nevertheless find it difficult to bet against it. Life* has formed the horizon and interpretive matrix of his life thus far. So it is natural for him to fear that forsaking life* will diminish the quality of his life. It was perceptive of Pascal to see so deeply into a secular psychology which, if Charles Taylor (2007) is correct, was still centuries away from maturity.

Taking account of the interlocutor's insecurity helps us make better sense of Pascal's reply. We need help because the text is once again cryptic, probably defective, and subject to multiple interpretations. I have filled it out below with what I think is implied and left the unadorned original in Appendixes A and B. Specialists can form their own judgment. Pascal is addressing the interlocutor's claim to fear the stupidity Pascal recommends: "But why?" Pascal asks,

> **qP1** *What have you got to lose? But to show you that [the reasoning of IR] leads to [adopting a Christian lifestyle], it is [enough to note that the Christian lifestyle leads to] the weakening of the passions which are your great obstacles, etc.*[99]

qP1 is breathtakingly undiplomatic. The interlocutor has just said that becoming stupid is exactly what he fears. After such an admission, it is less than polite to ask, as Pascal does, what he's got to lose. Such, however, are the infelicities of rough drafts. Of course Pascal does not mean that the interlocutor is already so stupid that he has nothing to fear. Instead he is trying to make the interlocutor see that wagering on God's existence could not possibly worsen his condition, and therefore is not *really* stupid after all. Pascal reminds him that however precious life* may seem, it promises nothing in comparison to the good of life∞, and that the enabling assumption behind life* – that there is no God – is no more likely to be true than is the opposite assumption implicit in life∞. Thus, the interlocutor cannot make his position worse by betting on life∞. That is why he has nothing to fear.

That is the point of qP1. At this stage of the argument, however, it is not really new. The interlocutor has already come that far. qP1 does nothing to undermine the interlocutor's present hesitation. He knows life∞ to be theoretically preferable to life*. But to him that is pie in the sky. His present hesitation has existential causes. Ultimately it derives from the ordinary weakness of human reason when it has to contend with the imagination. "Put the greatest philosopher in the world on a plank more than wide enough to hold him," Pascal says,

> and even if his reason convinces him it's safe, if there is an abyss below, his imagination will take over. Some philosophers can't so much as endure the thought without sweating and growing pale.[100]

In IR Pascal invites the interlocutor to step out onto the plank of *choice*. Objectively the choice is clear, but beneath him yawns the abyss of subjective uncertainty. That is why telling the interlocutor he has nothing to lose, though true, does not advance the argument. He understands it, but imagination takes over and he grows afraid.

Pascal's second point in qP1 is also true, and equally ineffectual. "The Christian lifestyle leads to the weakening of the passions which are your great obstacles," he tells the interlocutor. Making the right bet will indeed weaken the passions that now paralyze the interlocutor, but saying so does not touch the real ground of his hesitation. The interlocutor does not hesitate because he thinks Pascal's medicine will not work. It is the working of the medicine he partly fears. The interlocutor is not persuaded that life* is a sickness, or, if it is, that he wants to be cured of it.

At this point the text of IR throws another unanticipated curveball. In both the Lafuma and the Sellier editions, this last speech of Pascal's is followed by the note "End of this discourse," though the same discourse carries on after it. Predictably the commentators go into overdrive.[101]

The commentators rightly point out that the discourse doesn't end where the text says it does. What Pascal should have written at this juncture was "Dramatic turn in this discourse." Though Pascal goes right on speaking after the mysterious announcement of the end, he adopts a brand new tactic, as if he had just that moment understood his interlocutor's real concern. Pascal gives up trying to diminish the interlocutor's fear and tries to build up an opposing passion instead. He will try to awaken in the interlocutor a powerful *desire* for life∞. This is the precise point at which Pascal takes the second step of the grand strategy outlined in fragment L15/S46, with which this chapter began. Here Pascal will "make [Christianity] desirable. Make them wish it were true."

Pascal's new beginning takes the form of a new question:

**qP2** What harm will it do you to take this bet?

It's only a rhetorical question. Pascal immediately supplies an answer that puts the emphasis not on what the interlocutor has to lose in rejecting life∞ but on what he has to gain even in life*:

**qP3** *You will be faithful, honest, humble, grateful, beneficent, a sincere friend, authentic ... It is true you will not be involved in poisoned pleasures, in glory, in voluptuousness, but will you not have other joys? I tell you, you will profit in this life and with every step you take on this path you will see such certainty of gain, and so much nothingness in what you put at risk, that you will know at*

*last that you wagered for something certain and infinite, which cost you nothing.*
(my emphasis)

Pascal breaks the logjam by appealing to advantages the wagerer will experience *in this life*. The interlocutor's last reservations are overcome:

rI Oh these words carry me away, they delight me,

he exclaims.

The great transformation aimed at throughout IR comes so abruptly to completion, the promised emotional therapy succeeds so suddenly, that the reader is likely to either underestimate what has happened or suspect a trick. The negative emotion of fear, which hitherto has made the interlocutor cling to life*, is overcome by a new constructive, forward-looking *desire* – one that turns the interlocutor towards religious faith, making him desire life$^\infty$. But where has this new desire come from? Pascal is still subject to the rule of naturalism established in aP1. Has he really gotten the interlocutor to embrace life$^\infty$ without breaking that rule?

I believe he has. Pascal has cured the interlocutor's fear of religion without appealing to anything more than fallen human concupiscence, the desire for personal gain associated with life*. He wins the interlocutor over by persuading him through concupiscence to embrace the *lifestyle* of life$^\infty$. The interlocutor can pursue the lifestyle for the intrinsic benefits it confers without having the beliefs that would justify it metaphysically. An instrumental justification is sufficient for getting started.

Pascal showed the interlocutor that he will even "profit in this life" if he lives by the principles of life$^\infty$. Behave in life* as you would in life$^\infty$ and it will give you a more excellent life. What is more, TL guarantees it will also bring you to the antechamber of authentic religious belief.

The last paragraphs of IR show that rightly ordered desire can conquer fear. The interlocutor's appetite for a faith he does not yet possess is awakened by the argument of IR. He finds his new condition attractive and uplifting.

Pascal has led the interlocutor through two of the three principal steps outlined by the strategic fragment with which this chapter began. The unbeliever who once feared Christianity now desires it to be true, and is taking steps to induce in himself the belief that it is true.

Yet his journey has only begun, for his desire that Christianity be true is at this point still a concupiscent one. To complete the course, according to fragment L12/S46, he must come to see that the Christian religion really *is* true. He must become a convert, and that can only happen with the help of grace.

It is impossible to say whether the remaining step is large or small. There is no quantitative measure for a step involving qualitative changes in the inquirer and in which divine intervention is involved. It resembles a *metabasis eis allo genos* of the kind the ancients believed could not be accomplished. If it cannot be accomplished, or can only be accomplished by inexplicable intervention in the form of grace, then it looks as if Pascal's apologetic strategy cannot be understood as philosophical after all. That would be a sad outcome to the struggles we have just been through. But the next chapter will propose a happier one.

# 5 Burdens of Proof

Two of the three steps outlined in fragment L12/S46 have been taken. The wagerer has been cured of his fear of religion and has come to a point where he desires Catholic teachings to be true. What remains is for him to be convinced of the truth of the Christian faith, a process normally called *conversion*.

Yet converting and convincing have quite different connotations. Convincing someone of the truth of anything looks like a job for philosophy. Converting someone does not. Philosophy's methods are naturalistic, that is, free of supernatural causes. They are also transparent in the sense that each step an inquirer takes is taken because of evidence pointing in that direction. Conversion, on the other hand, presupposes divine grace. Converts are supposed to rise above the concupiscent nature with which they are born and acquire Christian virtues, something that is impossible without supernatural assistance.

That is where a lot of the difficulty lies for a philosophical reading of Pascal. Philosophers do not see how reflective inquiry can lead by naturalistic and transparent steps to religious conversion.

Pascal, of course, does not hold that all conversions are based on reasoned inquiry. Religious faith often comes to people as a gift, and is no less valid when it does.[1] But such converts are not the ones who become inquirers, nor was the *Pensées* written with them in mind. Pascal's concern is with people like the wagerer, who demand to have reasons for what they believe.

Having reasons, for Pascal, does not mean having proofs. We have already seen that Pascal left no place for proofs in religious conversion. In disjoining reasons from proofs, however, Pascal once again arouses the suspicion of philosophers. In an essay titled *What Happens After Pascal's Wager*, Daniel Garber puts the bits of Pascal's story that are likely to trouble a philosopher in italics:

> Pascal's God doesn't ask for a blind faith: it is a faith supported by reasons. But these reasons can only be appreciated *after I am in a particular state of mind: only after I am committed to him, in a way, after I have already dedicated myself to the search for God, only after God has moved my heart*. Before I have faith, reason and experience are impotent, they are unable to give me real knowledge. But *after* the spiritual transformation, I am in a position to recognize the validity of the arguments for God's existence, the miracles and the prophecies, the experience of nature itself. Only after the conversion can the believer appreciate the *rational* grounds of his or her faith.[2]

Later in the same essay[3] Garber identifies three points in Pascal's account of which he thinks philosophers will be wary.

First, if the inquirer is trying to find reasons for believing something he wants to be true, isn't that wishful thinking? Why should such a quest result in truth rather than *self-deception*?

Second, since the main engine for arriving at Christian beliefs seems to be the *noncognitive* regimen of religious ritual, even if the beliefs it produces in the inquirer turn out to be highly rational, mustn't the method by which he acquired them generate second-order suspicion of these new first-order certainties?

And, finally, it is a contingent matter that a Christian wager argument was put to this inquirer. A similarly structured argument could have been made in a different religious flavour, and the inquirer might now be a Jew or a Muslim or something else rather than a Christian. Garber acknowledges that many of our beliefs have contingent causes in this way, but nevertheless finds it troubling when religious ones do.[4]

### Is Pascal's Method of Inquiry Incoherent?

These are fair questions. If they turn out to be unanswerable, then the path to conversion cannot be made philosophically transparent, and the line of argument begun in the tournament of champions and continued in IR will collapse under the weight of its own contradictory or otherwise unfulfillable assumptions. The innovative apologetic strategy of the *Pensées* will reveal itself to have been a failure.

Such a result would, of course, be disappointing. It would put out of reach Pascal's ambition to find a form of philosophical inquiry that is neither sceptical nor dogmatic, yet is capable of addressing the legitimate and perennial questions of religion.

That such a mode of inquiry exists cannot be taken for granted. Not only must Garber's questions be answered, but the suspicion underlying them must also be dispelled. That suspicion can be expressed in the form of a dilemma: A Pascalian inquirer at some point arrives at a fork in life's road. One prong in that fork (one horn of the dilemma) leads to conversion: the inquirer decides to pursue life$^\infty$. But for the inquirer to make that decision presupposes a philosophically ungroundable intervention of God, a miraculous receipt of grace, for which there can be no natural explanation. The other prong (or horn) sees the inquirer continue along the path of life*. He continues to be reflective and philosophical but makes no conversion. Thus, no matter which path he chooses, so the dilemma concludes, the inquirer cannot end up as both a Christian and a philosopher.

Some have thought that Pascal willingly impales himself on the first of this dilemma's horns. According to them, Pascal's inquirer moves resolutely towards conversion, leaving philosophy behind. That is the view of Pascal I am putting in question. The alternative I propose is that Pascal finds plenty of room between the horns of this dilemma to pull both faith and philosophy (in its post-tournament sense) to safety.

People overlook the gap between the dilemma's horns because they think that, whenever God is involved, nothing happens by natural means. That inference needs to be examined with care. I'll call it "the God problem."

Another version of what is essentially the same objection puts the weight on Pascal's claims about the spiritual impotence induced in us by the Fall, and the *miracle* that is therefore required for conversion. If a miracle is required, people think, then Pascalian converts end up with goods they haven't paid for in philosophical cash. I'll call this version "the miracle problem."[5]

The God problem, the miracle problem, and the Garber questions are not easy to answer. Worse still, they are not the only difficulties facing a philosophical understanding of conversion.

## Fallen Nature

Our fallen nature creates further obstacles to conversion. Because of the Fall, the inquirer begins the process of conversion with a sinful, concupiscent character.[6] As long as he remains graceless, he will be both concupiscent and blind.[7] Concupiscence is not only wrong-headed but also "self-determining."[8] It causes people to stray from good behaviour, even if they manage to exhibit it for a certain time. In the Augustinian terms favoured by Jansenists, concupiscent persons focus their interest on creatures and neglect the creator. But "whatever incites us to attach ourselves to creatures is bad, because it hinders us either from serving God, if we know him, or from searching for him, if we do not. Yet we are full of concupiscence and therefore full of evil."[9]

The finitude of our powers, the brevity of our days, the misguidedness of concupiscent desires, all incline even earnest inquirers such as the wagerer has now become to fail in their search. A searcher not centred on the mediator, Jesus Christ, Pascal says, will easily mistake the thin, unsatisfying glimmer of deism for the light he is seeking. Or, worse still, his search may end in gloomy atheism instead. Two outcomes, Pascal adds, that Christianity abhors almost equally.[10] A concupiscent inquirer therefore remains "a subject full of error that is natural to him and that cannot be eradicated without grace."[11]

### Grace

The help the inquirer will need from God in order to convert is what theologians call *grace*. Grace is understood to be a supernatural gift and a necessary condition for conversion.[12] But how could any process that depends on grace simultaneously be naturalistic and philosophically transparent?

Pascal's strict Jansenist conception of grace only compounds the problem. Jansenists agree with orthodox Catholics that grace is never given on the basis of merit, but they depart from orthodoxy in holding that grace is not offered to all people.[13] So we can't take for granted that the inquirer we are discussing will receive it. On the other hand, conversion cannot occur without grace. Therefore, we need to take grace for granted to examine whether his conversion takes place by philosophically transparent steps. Are we perhaps stuck already?

Even if that problem can be resolved, however, the Jansenist conception of grace is unorthodox in another awkward way. Not only do they believe God stingier with grace than Catholics are supposed to think, Jansenists also believe that grace, once given, is irresistible. Pascal calls this irresistible grace *efficacious* (as opposed to merely *sufficient*). Those who have it cannot fail to persevere in their faith, he says, and those who lack it also lack any power to obtain it.[14] This is what makes the God problem look intractable.

The Jansenist account of grace also exacerbates the miracle problem. Efficacious grace will forestall philosophical inquiry if, like magic, it produces instantaneous conversion in the inquirer. The path towards conversion will contract into a single inscrutable moment, and the transparent process of inquiry that was supposed to lead there will be superfluous.

There would, of course, be no problem, if it were possible for the inquirer to convert without the help of grace. However, that way lies the Pelagian heresy, and nothing is further from Pascal's mind.[15] Man's fallen nature, and our many shortcomings that derive from it, make conversion without grace impossible. If a philosophical account of conversion is to make sense, it will have to be compatible with a strong Jansenist understanding of grace.

## Supernatural Blindness

Concupiscence blinds us to evidence favourable to conversion. Yet there is a worse kind of blindness to fear. In Pascal's harsh Jansenist universe, there is also supernatural blindness brought about by God, a species of anti-grace that is a punishment for sin.

"You know nothing about how God works," Pascal writes, "unless you take it as an axiom (*principe*) that he blinds some people and enlightens others."[16] Infidelity and incredulity are sometimes punished by blindness, as they were in those Jews who failed to recognize the divinity of Jesus Christ.[17] There is also evidence of supernatural blinding, Pascal says, in fanatical opponents of Christianity, who fiercely oppose a faith that seems to shape their own notion of the good.[18]

Jesus himself is forthright about not always being forthright. One reason he gives for teaching in parables is to conceal his teachings from certain listeners, "lest at any time they should see with their eyes and hear with their ears, and should understand with their heart, and should be converted, and I should heal them."[19] And whether or not Jesus spoke in parables, both what he said and how he said it, according to Pascal, were calculated "to leave evil people in their blindness."[20]

God is particularly likely to blind the wise and learned,[21] who are prone to intellectual pride. Such blindness therefore poses a heightened threat to the rationalistic inquirer we know the wagerer to be at the end of IR. As long as he remains blind to religious realities, no one can tell whether his blindness is merely a residue of his fallen nature, about to disappear, or an irrevocable divine imposition.[22] There is just enough light for the elect to see, Pascal says, and enough darkness to humble them. Correspondingly, "there is enough darkness to blind the reprobates, and enough light to damn them and remove their excuses."[23]

The distinction between natural and supernatural blindness reflects what John McDade calls two *caesurae*, or divisions, "in the Pascalian narrative ... the first derived from concupiscence (we cannot see properly) ... and the second deriving from the partial light cast by divine grace and election (God does not want to enlighten all)."[24]

## The Hiddenness of God

Important though these two *caesurae* are, they explain only visible things we fail to notice. A further source of blindness arises from what is not even available to be seen. Pascal has much to say about the "hiddenness of God." He believes God normally conceals himself from human view, and that, while he does so, the natural world appears to be all there is. Before explaining why Pascal holds this peculiar belief, let us consider the effect it has on his conception of nature.

The doctrine that God intentionally conceals himself takes for granted, but also transforms, the traditional scholastic distinction between primary and secondary causes. According to that distinction, God, the primary cause, is responsible first for the creation of every existing thing, and thereafter for maintaining all of creation in existence. But his creatures are not just puppets. God elevates them to the status of *secondary causes*, by endowing each creature with causal powers characteristic of its natural kind. The result is that most events have "natural" explanations. Natural events occur because secondary causes exercise their characteristic powers to bring them about. If the vase fell over, it is not because God did it. It happened because the cat tried to squeeze by and pushed the vase off the shelf.

It is true that the cat, the vase, and the shelf are only able to participate in this event because God maintains them in existence throughout the period in which the event occurs. But, because God is at all times preserving the entire universe in being, his sustaining role needn't be mentioned when we are looking for a natural explanation of what occurred.

Not mentioning God in ordinary cases allows us to acknowledge God's special role in extraordinary events called *miracles*. Miracles are supernatural occurrences in which secondary causality is suspended or overridden, and the primary cause directly intervenes to change the course of ordinary events. The broken vase, for example, has no secondary power to reassemble itself. Neither would all the king's horses and all the king's men be able to restore it to its unbroken condition. God, however, could intervene to cause such a restoration to take place. If he did, it would be a miracle.

. This distinction between primary and secondary causality allowed scholastic philosophers to distinguish natural from supernatural events, and so to develop a doctrine of naturalism that was consistent with the existence of miracles. This conception of naturalism had a profound influence on early modern philosophy and the new science as well.[25] Few of the new scientists rejected miracles, but they all banished miracles from science. The new science was thus committed to what could be called *methodological naturalism*.

That commitment makes Pascal's doctrine of the hiddenness of God problematic. If God makes it impossible for us to detect him, then our methodological naturalism will easily slide into *metaphysical* naturalism, a fancy term for atheism.

Descartes managed to resist this slide, but then he was a committed Catholic. "Without doing injustice to the miracle of creation," he wrote in the *Discourse on Method*, "one may believe that [if God merely established the laws of nature, and lent his ordinary concurrence to their normal operations] that alone would suffice, given sufficient time, for all things that are purely material to develop into what they are at present." Descartes is saying that the material universe as we know it could have evolved by natural processes, though, as a matter of fact, it was divinely created.

His point is that, notwithstanding the reality of divine creation, we ought to conduct scientific research as if the false evolutionary theory were true. Why? Because "the nature of things is much easier to conceive, when we see them being born bit by bit in [the evolutionary] way, than when we consider them as ready-made."[26] Science values naturalism for its ability to furnish us with explanations we can understand and apply. But science is not metaphysically naturalistic.

Insofar as he divorces explanation from truth, Descartes takes an instrumental view of scientific explanation. Pascal appears to agree with him.[27] But what is advantageous from a methodological point of view may be religiously dangerous. If God is somehow hiding himself within the natural world, if nature is his mask, then the methodological advantage of naturalism becomes a snare to minds unenlightened by grace. Someone less theologically astute than Descartes could mistake methodological naturalism, which is just a rule of the game of science, for the metaphysical limits of reality. This is what today's "new atheists" appear to do when they adopt naturalism as their ideology.[28] Pascal's inquirer might come to resemble the perhaps apocryphal Soviet cosmonaut, who is supposed to have reported triumphantly that he had been to space and found no trace of God.

You may wonder why God should be hiding, or what use anyone could make of such a doctrine. But the doctrine has religious significance that Pascal explains lucidly enough in his correspondence with a young woman to whom he was providing spiritual guidance.[29] We do not have the letter to which Pascal was replying, but in it she must have asked him about the famous miracle of the Holy Thorn that had taken place at Port Royal, in which Pascal's niece was suddenly cured of a serious disease of the eye.[30] Pascal explains to his correspondent how rare it is for God to reveal himself so openly. His normal practice involves not bold self-disclosure, Pascal says, but concealment. Or, rather, it is a mixture of both. He reveals himself to a few while remaining concealed from the many. God's hiddenness and partial self-revelations are in fact the motor of salvation history, as Pascal explains to his correspondent.[31]

God's earliest self-revelation is in nature, Pascal's letter continues, but nature, as we just learned, is also a form of concealment. Indeed, that disguise sets the bar of discovery so high that only a handful of the wisest pagans were able to see over it. Pascal is thinking of pagan philosophers like Plato and Aristotle, whom Christians long believed to have anticipated their own monotheism.[32] The pagans' success in penetrating God's disguise shows why naturalism, despite its methodological advantages, is metaphysically a mistake. Metaphysical and ideological naturalists have simply been fooled by appearances.

Later, at an opportune place and time, Pascal says, God chose to reveal himself in a fuller way through Scripture. This time only the Jewish people were permitted to penetrate the disguise.

The next historical stage of God's self-revelation is his incarnation in Jesus Christ. In this disguise he disclosed himself only to those who became Christians.

His ultimate revelation is the strangest of all. Christ conceals himself in the Church's Eucharistic celebration. In this form only Catholics are able to detect him. The Eucharist is a great singularity, lately called a luminous mystery, representing, in the words of John Betjeman, the fact "that God was Man in Palestine // and lives to-day in Bread and Wine."

Each stage of God's progressive revelation is a disguise penetrable only by grace. If God is deliberately hiding himself at each stage, it becomes all the more difficult to see how an inquirer with only philosophically transparent reasons as his guide could avoid slipping into atheism.

## Acquiring Christian Virtues

Concupiscence, the lack of grace, supernaturally induced blindness, and the hiddenness of God are all obstacles the inquirer must somehow overcome on his way to conversion. Yet each of them seems to require religious rather than philosophical means to address it. They are the principal difficulties arising from the inquirer's natural weaknesses.

But in the course of his conversion the inquirer must also acquire new dispositions that express themselves in the Christian virtues of faith, hope, and charity. It is far from obvious that this required change of character could arise out of naturalistic, philosophically transparent inquiry.

### Hope

The hardest virtue to deal with is *hope*. In French there are two words for hope, which are in many contexts interchangeable. However, one of these words (*espoir*) is more concrete, suggesting an object towards which our hope is directed. The wager argument transformed the interlocutor of IR into an inquirer by giving him hope of this kind. He hopes Christianity is true in the sense that he appreciates the advantages of life° and is prepared to investigate the possibility that they can really be obtained.

The other kind of hope (*espérance*) is more abstract and suggests an attitude of hopefulness, rather than its object. *Espérance* is also the word for the second of the Christian virtues. It involves hopefulness about our state in this life and hopeful expectations of the life to come. To attribute *espoir* to an inquirer does not go beyond what naturalism allows. But how can he get from there to the Christian virtue of *espérance*?

At the outset of his search, the inquirer cannot be assumed to have *espérance*, but he is not for that reason hopeless. Pascal sees hopelessness as the bottom rung of the fallen human condition. It is the attribute of those who are without Jesus Christ,[33] which technically the inquirer may still be. But it is also associated with atheism,[34] to which the inquirer is no longer inclined, with the pathological fear of religion, which, as we saw in Chapter Four, the inquirer has overcome, and with a state of mind whose manifestations are boredom, melancholy, sadness, grief, and bitterness.[35] Hopelessness is a state into which the inquirer could still fall. Anyone can. But the path of inquiry to which he has just committed himself is already taking him in the opposite direction.

At this point the inquirer is in transition. It is as if he had jumped from one ledge but not yet reached the one above. He hopes to find God. And that, according to Pascal, is inconsistent with despair.[36] But it is not all the hope that can be hoped for. It is not *espérance*. The Catholic understanding of *espérance* is a rich one. The philosopher Henri Brémond explains it as follows:

> For us Catholics hope (*espérance*) is all we need. We cling to the "promises" [of the Church]; we are certain they will be efficacious, provided we do not place obstacles in their way. We are certain it depends on us to make sure they are fulfilled in our own lives, with the help of *grace* that will never fail.[37]

But Jansenist Catholics, as Brémond goes on to explain, are less upbeat about *espérance*. They have too much doubt about their own condition. As Brémond says,

> [The Jansenist] does not know whether Jesus Christ died for him or not; he does not know whether he will be granted *grace* or not; whether it will be possible or impossible for him to keep the commandments.[38]

If that is Pascal's view, then there is no way the inquirer could have Christian *espérance* at the outset of his inquiry. The most he could begin with is hope (in the sense of *espoir*) that grace will be granted, that he will at some future time be able to keep the commandments, and that he will be among the beneficiaries of Christ's sacrifice.

## Living Faith and Charity

Not only does the inquirer lack Christian hope. He has not yet achieved the first of the Christian virtues either. He lacks faith, at least in the theologically relevant sense of *fides formata* or *living faith*. Living faith is understood by the Roman Catholic Church as faith accompanied by good works. That is to say, it is always informed by charity, the third of the infused Christian virtues,[39] which the inquirer once again must not be supposed to have at the outset of his inquiry.

* * *

If Pascalian inquiry is to be a philosophical undertaking, then there must be naturalistic and philosophically transparent means by which an inquirer can overcome his blindness, detect the hidden God, and acquire Christian virtues. Yet if he shakes off the concupiscent motivation that gets inquiry started, it will lose its naturalistic and transparent character.

## The Three Orders

To reconcile all these points will not be easy. The task is also hampered by the fact that the main fragments of the *Pensées* dealing with human spiritual development are among the most obscure.

It would be nice, therefore, if we could simply avoid them. However, as Hugh Davidson remarks, they, more than any others, are "the key to [Pascal's] universe of discourse."[40] And because spiritual growth is precisely what must be shown to be reason-based, transparent, and naturalistic in character, the only way to get past these fragments is to go through them. The most important of them deals with what are called "the three orders."[41]

Once again, as with the IR fragment in Chapter Four, there may be some readers who prefer to skip the detailed examination that will be necessary to make sense of the fragments relating to the three orders. Such readers can safely go on to the next section ("Is Pascal a Mystic"), provided they concede the point that overcoming one's fallen nature and acquiring Christian virtues does not entail leaving one's concupiscence entirely behind. That is what I shall try to establish in examining the three orders. To those with scholarly curiosity about Pascal, however, revisiting these puzzling fragments may have its own points of interest.

No attempt will be made to do justice to all the complexities of the main three orders fragment, but even the parsimonious treatment I intend is too complex to be briefly concluded. Since I will have to refer to it frequently in the next few pages, for brevity's sake, I will call the fragment TO.[42]

TO is somewhere between a draft and a finished text. It lacks clarity, but it does show some signs of rhetorical polish. Though scarcely a page in length, TO is Pascal's longest discussion of the mysterious things he calls "orders." Its clearest achievement is to alert the reader to one motif in Pascal's mature thought, a motif that recurs throughout the *Pensées* and beyond, almost like a musical theme, under different names, and in enigmatic variations.[43] There are fragments where only two of the orders are discussed, but they must be read in the light of other fragments, particularly TO, if their full meaning is to be appreciated.

To understand TO therefore involves a hermeneutic circle: TO helps us recognize a diverse family of fragmentary discussions of the same theme; they in turn help us fill in some of the blanks in TO. The wider we cast our net, the fuller the understanding of Pascal's three orders we will be able to achieve.

The net I shall cast will not be as extensive as a full treatment would demand.[44] The interest here is selective. We need to understand how the three orders constitute the framework for self-betterment within which the philosophical credentials of Pascalian conversions must be assessed.

In TO the three orders are called *the order of bodies, the order of minds* (esprits), and *the order of charity*. It's a mysterious list. In which of the many senses of the word 'orders' could bodies, minds, and charity represent three of them? They look more like three heterogeneous kinds of things. But if that's all they are, why only three? Couldn't milkshakes, fractions, and laughter make three more?

The first thing TO tells us about the three orders is that they are themselves hierarchically ordered: Bodies form their base, and they are crowned with charity. Minds are in the middle. When the three orders are considered from an intellectual point of view, bodies are conspicuously at the bottom; when considered from a religious point of view, charity is conspicuously on top. Minds maintain the middle either way.

But what are they orders *of*? It's hard to see what these relationships amount to when we don't know what the *relata* are supposed to include. What, for example, can Pascal mean by the order of bodies? Surely it would make no sense to try to rank Cartesian units of extension, or the material objects of common sense, on a scale of values with minds and charity.

The order of bodies would have to involve more than just extended material things if the comparison is to make any sense. And more is indeed involved. The order of bodies includes the physical properties of bodies, their relationships with other bodies, as well as their importance as tokens of political and economic power. There is even a religious dimension to bodies, which is reflected in Pascal's use of the religious term 'carnality' to characterize them. These added meanings make Pascal's concept of bodies *thick*. If only they made it clear!

Fragment TO never does get very clear. But as we encounter the idea of the three orders across a selection of fragments and other writings, it begins at least to grow familiar, which is the poor cousin of clarity. Before beginning to familiarize ourselves with it, and, if we are lucky, to understand it a little better, the higher orders should be briefly introduced.

The gap separating the order of bodies from its successor is *infinite*, we are told in TO. Infinitely above bodies, then, is the order of minds. Minds, like bodies, are to be thickly understood. Thinking things are not the only inhabitants of the second order. It also contains the activity of thinking and the achievements of the intellect, understood as items of value.

The third and highest order, at an "infinitely more infinite" remove from the first two, is the order of charity, presumably having to do with loving God and neighbour and performing charitable acts.

Though TO never gets around to clarifying what is meant by "orders," it twice goes over the cognitive and normative hierarchies they form. The second version runs as follows:

> All bodies, the firmament, the stars, the earth and its kingdoms are not worth the least of minds. For a mind knows all that, and also knows itself, whereas bodies know nothing.
>
> All bodies together and all minds together and everything they produce are not worth the least act of charity. Charity is of an infinitely higher order.

One thing I take Pascal to mean by his three orders, though at least one important scholar disagrees,[45] is that they are *three ways of putting things in order*, and especially of arranging our lives. Philippe Sellier characterizes them well as involving "existential choices every man must make."[46] In a related fragment, written earlier than the one we are discussing, Pascal actually refers to three "orders of things," though here he labels them differently as "flesh" (*chair*) in place of bodies, "mind" (same as in TO), and "will," in place of charity.[47] I will return to this fragment, which contains an important clue to the meaning of TO.

In yet another fragment Pascal speaks of the top two orders, mind and charity (here also called "heart"), as *ordering* things of some kind, possibly ideas or propositions, each in its own distinctive way. Mind orders them by way of demonstration, while charity arranges them in a way Pascal calls "digressive," and attributes to Christ, Saint Paul, Augustine, and the Scriptures.[48]

The details need not concern us. The point is that the three orders are three ways of ordering things, while at the same time they are hierarchically ordered with respect to one another.

What things do they put in order? Quite a hodgepodge it turns out, but the most important for present purposes, which all three have in common, is *people*. All three orders are in fact made up of people.[49] They correspond to patterns of relationship among people, and people belong to one order or another depending on the ordering principle that predominates in their lives.

Thinking of the orders as three classes of people captures some of what Pascal wants to say about them. Think of them as a lower, middle, and upper class. The boundaries Pascal fixes to these three classes, their inclusions or exclusions, do not coincide with those of the same names in modern social science, but they resemble social classes both in their function and in their connotations. They organize human beings in a hierarchy, according to their perceived excellence.

Pascal's lower class is preoccupied with bodies. It is made up of people whose focus, for different reasons, is on bodily things. They may pursue bodies as objects of pleasure, or covet them as possessions, or arrange them as expressions of their own political, economic, or military power. To be preoccupied with bodies can be culpable from a religious point of view. When it is, Pascal calls it carnal (*charnel*) and associates it with spiritual blindness.[50]

Still, this class contains a surprising range of people, many of whom are admirable, or at least widely admired. It includes philosophical Epicureans, for example, whose refined ideas of pleasure put them at the high end of this class.[51] It also includes people of coarser appetites who could be called epicurean only in a colloquial and pejorative sense.

The strange thing is that the lower class in Pascal's reckoning contains a great number of those we normally think of as belonging to high society, including everyone whose main preoccupation is what could be called the political, economic, or military arrangement of bodies. In TO, Pascal mentions "kings, rich people, and captains" as inhabitants of the order of bodies.

Why so many eminent people belong to the lower class becomes clearer in one of Pascal's posthumously published educational writings, bearing the title "Three Discourses on the Condition of Great Ones." It turns out that eminence in the order of bodies is normally, but, as we later learn, not necessarily, connected to concupiscence. In the third of the discourses, Pascal tells the young nobleman to whom it is addressed that to be a great lord "is to be master of a number of objects of the concupiscence of men." Pascal then describes the young lord himself as "a king of concupiscence ... that is to say, of the possession of things that the cupidity of men desires."[52]

It seems Pascal could afford to be so frank with the young man he tutored. It is more surprising that he dared make the same point in a letter to Christina, Queen of Sweden.[53] At the heart of this letter is an undiplomatic, almost impudent, comparison between political leaders and intellectuals, which the queen could only read as meaning between herself and him.

It is a Jekyll and Hyde letter, however. Pascal envelopes the invidious comparison in a cascade of sycophancy at which even courtiers of his age would surely have blushed. He ends his uneven remarks by professing to be "one whose supreme wish is to be avowed, of your Majesty, the very humble, the very obedient, and very faithful servant, Blaise Pascal."

There is much of historical and sociological interest, and not a little unintended humour, in this letter, but for present purposes only the comparison is important. It does two things. First, it reveals Pascal's opinion that political authority is normally exercised only over people's bodies. Christina is told that her command and authority over her people is of that kind. Next, it introduces Pascal's middle order, the order of minds, and the subtler kind of authority only minds can exercise. Without mentioning himself explicitly, Pascal implies that he belongs to that higher order, the knowing ones, who rule by persuasion, and whose authority derives from merit rather than birth:

> We see the same variations [of quality] among minds (*génies*) as we find among the nobility. And the power of kings over their subjects, as it seems to me, is but an image of the power great minds (*esprits*) wield over inferior ones. Superior minds exercise the right of persuasion, which in their milieu corresponds to the right of command in political government. The intellectual form of sovereignty seems to me to belong to an order as far above the political as minds are above bodies. The order of minds is also more just (*équitable*), because superiority of this kind cannot be bestowed or retained except by merit, whereas the political kind can be held by birth or fortune.[54]

Persuasiveness and merit are not the only ways in which Pascal thinks himself and other intellectuals superior to political leaders, though they are the only ones he mentions in the letter. In TO, however, he speaks of an asymmetry of awareness between minds and bodies, which once again proves the superiority of minds. Thinkers are fully aware of what motivates denizens of the order of bodies, though its glamour (éclat) does not excite them. Carnal beings, on the other hand, who command people's bodies, or are slaves of their own bodies, or both, go about their business unaware of the order of minds. They neither recognize intellectual achievement nor appreciate its grandeur.

What about the third order? Pascal has been reprimanded for never mentioning it in the letter to Christina.[55] But in TO he tells us that members of this highest order also "have their sovereignty and lustre":

> They feel no need for carnal or intellectual greatness, which would serve no purpose. It would neither enhance nor diminish their lives. The saints cannot be recognized either by [those who belong to the order of] bodies or by curious minds. But they are regarded by God and the angels. For them God is sufficient.

The "great exemplar" of this order would of course be Jesus Christ,[56] though it would be unusual to call him a saint. The word 'saint' in this context needs to be treated with care. In the Roman Catholic faith, some exemplary Christians are canonized as saints. But the word is also used in a wider sense to include the community of all believers, as when the Apostles' Creed refers to the "communion of saints."

Every believer is meant to aim at the degree of holiness achieved by saints in the narrow sense. We should beware, Pascal insists, of "that false idea that makes us reject the example of saints as disproportionate to our state."[57] However, there is no suggestion that most believers will ever merit canonization. Canonized sainthood is simply what ordinary believers must aim at if they hope to get near enough even to qualify as saints in the weaker sense.

Except when otherwise specified, I shall use the word 'saints' to mean the broader class of Christians. Saints in this sense are the same thing as the *elect*. They are a small community, housing within itself the still smaller community of the canonized. The greatest obligation of saints is to exhibit *agapē* love, the love of God and neighbour, which Christ exemplified and in which charity consists.

The three orders, when each is understood in the way just outlined, seem to identify three classes of people. The lower class is made up of leaders and the led. Thinkers form the middle class. The upper class is composed of saints.

The order of charity and the middle order of minds have cognitive advantages over the order of bodies. They are able to recognize the concupiscent will to dominate and possess that motivates the lower order. But they are not mastered by *that* concupiscence. That is what makes them "infinitely" superior to those below them. However, the gap between the middle order and the order of charity is in some unexplained way *even more infinite*. The charitable order recognizes the mind's concupiscent ambition to know as well as the cognitive and moral limitations of that ambition when it is not directed by charity. Such is the dual hierarchy of the three orders.

The reader may already have figured out that the three classes of people corresponding to the three orders are not mutually exclusive. Dual citizens crop up everywhere, and, as we shall see, they create a problem.

For example, there can be *carnal thinkers*. Epicurus, the paradigmatic philosopher of the body in Pascal's eyes, would be such a man. But it is also possible to be both a thinker and a saint, even in the narrow sense. Men like Saint Augustine and Saint Thomas were both, as Pascal in his last years strove to be, and as he hopes the inquirer will become, at least in the broader sense of sainthood, by following the regimen prescribed for him at the end of IR.

But what about the first and third orders, the carnal and the charitable? Can there be any dual citizens there? "Surely not," would be the instinctive reply. Saints are of course embodied, but they are not carnal. Pascal distinguishes at one point between what he calls "carnal Christians," who believe they can be saved by sacraments alone, and "true Christians," who know they must exercise the virtue of charity.[58] No one is simultaneously carnal and charitable in those senses.

Furthermore, when Pascal describes cupidity (a synonym of concupiscence) and charity as "two principles that divide the wills of men,"[59] he could easily be understood to mean that they divide men into the concupiscent and the charitable. Concupiscent men could not be charitable ones, and therefore the order of bodies and the order of charity could contain no common members. That interpretation would be reinforced by Pascal's assertion that "nothing is more contrary to charity than cupidity is."[60]

What Pascal says in the next breath, however, puts any such neat separation in question. For he adds: "and nothing is more similar." Pascal is well aware both of the difficulty of separating the charitable and concupiscent in real life and of the difficulty his reader will have in thinking of them together. Laurent Thirouin calls the step Pascal is about to take "an unheard-of reversal."[61]

We are not speaking now about words and their definitions. Charity and concupiscence are as different in their definitions as logical contraries must be. Each is by definition something the other is not. But charity and concupiscence are not only conceptual abstractions. They are also ways of life, typical of what I have called Pascal's upper and lower classes. It does not require much experience of life to know that flesh and blood people rarely fit neatly in the moral categories we prepare for them. Saints are not disembodied any more than sinners are, and in ordinary life, as was pointed out above, Pascal thinks it is impossible to know for certain which is which. Though God has made an exact partition between saints and sinners, it will only be detectable to us after God has rendered his final judgment. To us, saints and sinners will always be difficult to tell apart. "It is not that cupidity cannot coexist with faith in God," Pascal reminds us.[62] In simpler terms, he is reminding us that even the elect may sin.

These observations put Pascal in conformity with common sense, but they raise questions about the process of acquiring Christian virtues and God's role in it. If grace, when given, saves us from cupidity, how can cupidity and charity coexist in the same person?

In the same fragment, Pascal adds that even carnal people can be charitable, because charity can coexist "with the goods of the earth." This point is also obvious in ordinary experience. Saint Louis was none other than King Louis IX of France.[63] Temporal rulers and wealthy people may dispose charitably of the bodily things under their command. But such people are charter members of the order of bodies. And so the lower and upper classes once more overlap.

The difficulty is to know what becomes of the hierarchy of the orders, with their downward and upward asymmetries, if they turn out to have members in common. One person cannot simultaneously be higher and lower than himself. What Pascal is trying to establish with the three orders suddenly grows obscure again.

Fortunately, one of the fragments already touched on sheds some light on this problem. For quick reference, I'll call it C.[64] C presents what it calls three orders just as TO did, and the middle order, *the order of minds*, keeps the same name in C. The first big difference between C and TO lies in the names C gives to the top and bottom orders. The lower order acquires the religiously loaded name of *flesh (chair)* instead of bodies. More significantly for present concerns, the uppermost order in C is not called charity but *will (volonté)*.

Pascal's choice of names in C is illuminating. But, before attempting to explain it, another of C's peculiarities should be noted. The three orders with their new names get paired in fragment C with a shadow hierarchy consisting of three types of *concupiscence*. These concupiscent doubles are given biblical names. From low to high, they are *the concupiscence of the flesh, the concupiscence of the eyes*, and *pride*.[65]

If C existed in a vacuum, it would be impossible to decide whether Pascal was saying these three concupiscences *were* the three orders he talks about in C or whether they represented concupiscent counterparts of those three orders. The latter is what I take him to mean. Why?

I will not duplicate the work of Jean Mesnard (1988) in tracing these three concupiscences through the fragments of the *Pensées*, but will cut directly to his results.[66] The concupiscence corresponding to the first order is for Pascal the same thing as the will to power, or, as Mesnard puts it, the "need to possess and to dominate." Corresponding to the second order we find concupiscent *curiosity*, in which self-seeking or barren investigations displace the proper exercise of the mind. Paired with the third order is concupiscent pride, the attitude that causes us to put ourselves in God's place, acting out of a false sense of autonomy and refusing to acknowledge our need for mercy or grace.

C is illuminating because it calls the highest order *will* and its concupiscent counterpart *pride*. We know that will, for Pascal, can take the form of either cupidity or charity. But only when will means charity will pride be its concupiscent counterpart. This line of thought suggests a way of understanding the significance of the three orders.

Earlier we noted how, for Pascal, cupidity and charity "divide the wills of men."[67] We tried interpreting it to mean that cupidity and charity divide people into two distinct classes. But that interpretation could not be sustained. The classes of the carnal and the charitable turned out not to be discrete. Fragment C suggests a better way to interpret the division. What cupidity and charity represent are not two distinct species of will but two opposed directions in which any human will can go.

Cupidity is the will's most dangerous temptation, a gravitational force abetted by pride, drawing us downward into self-indulgence. Charity, on the other hand, is the will's highest *telos*, a centrifugal force, lent us by grace, freeing us for a life characterized by union of our will with the will of God. Cupidity is the form the will assumes naturally after the Fall. It is "depraved" and "disordered" wherever it is active.[68] Self-love, which motivates it, is a deformed image of charity. Nevertheless, fragment C allows for people of flesh and blood to be simultaneously affected by both forces.

Separating the three orders from the three concupiscences helps clarify the problem of multiple citizenships. Nothing prevents someone from exercising all three types of charity at once, or from being simultaneously a member of all three orders. The hierarchy to which these orders belong is one of ends. Bodies can be ordered charitably for the sake of minds, and minds for the sake of God. To the extent that we are members of any of the three orders we are not members of their concupiscent counterparts. But our adherence to one series or the other is, as we will see below, a matter of the habits we acquire.

Fragment C's greatest contribution is to connect the three orders and the three concupiscences to the orientation of the will. It suggests that even an inquirer who ended up as a saint would not need for that reason to have left the three concupiscences altogether behind. That is why Pascal can urge the young prince whom he is instructing to "despise concupiscence and its kingdom, and aspire to the realm of charity."[69] The ruler is invited to look at the stinginess, brutality, debauchery, and ultimately the stupidity that characterize concupiscent lives. But his bare concupiscent desire to live well can suffice to make him look higher.

What exact transformation Pascal expects the young ruler to undergo is, alas, left unclear. "Others will tell you how to find the way," he says; "it is enough for me to have deflected you from a brutal life."[70] But in the light of the wider discussion of the three orders that has gone before we can see at least in outline how the Pascalian inquirer must go. "At this point," writes Hugh Davidson,

> the two meanings of *ordre* – as succession and as hierarchy of domains – converge. In a real sense the two lines of analysis turn into one. The indifferent or hostile *honnête homme*, to be jarred into a sense of the opposed

tendencies in his and man's nature, who is pulled away from his amuse-
ments and changed into a *chercheur,* and who seeks first the advice of the
philosophers, only to see his problems become fixed and impossible to
solve, then can plausibly turn to a survey of religions that would lead him
to a sympathetic inquiry into the meaning of the Scriptures.[71]

This seems right. The inquirer must move from hostility to inquiry,
and through philosophy to Scripture. "What is such a man doing,"
Davidson then asks, "if not moving up the ladder defined by the three
orders?" Moving up is exactly what is supposed to happen, but questions about how it is to be accomplished remain.

### Is Pascal a Mystic?

Fragment C prescribes an upward path from concupiscence to union of
our will with the will of God. This, and the fact that there are three main
steps in the path, reminds some readers of Christian mysticism. Pascal
has been compared to mystics like St John of the Cross.[72]

There are indeed some striking similarities between the three orders
of Pascal and the three stages of mystical development as St John understood them. In Laura Garcia's elegant summary, St John teaches that,

> what we need in order to be united with God is to be empty of ourselves.
> When we are filled with our own desires and preferences, our own plans
> for our lives, God cannot fill us with Himself. Union with God is primarily
> a union of wills, so entering into His life means coming to will what He
> wills, in preference to what we ourselves will. Because of original sin and
> our own personal sins, we tend to seek ourselves and to find our good in
> creatures rather than God, so the process of unification is also a process
> of purification. We must be detached from creatures in order to be fully
> united to God.[73]

There is nothing in this general description with which Pascal would
disagree. Though written to describe the teaching of St John of the Cross,
it could serve just as well as a description of the religious assumptions
of Pascal.

Parallels can also be drawn between the ascending stages as the
two thinkers understand them. The first stage in the mystical ascent
to union with God, according to St John, is a renunciation of sensual
knowledge called "the dark night of the senses." Pascal would agree, as

he would agree with the renunciations St John thinks this dark night to entail. In Garcia's summary:

> Through the voluntary mortification of one's appetites and the willing acceptance of suffering and trials, one is enabled to achieve a measure of self-control and the ability to forego pleasures that would lead one away from God or that are incompatible with His will.[74]

Suffering, trials, mortification of the appetites, and so on would all be involved in Pascal's recommendation to the wagerer that he "do everything as if he believed."[75]

The agreement we find between St John and Pascal up to this point is clear, but not surprising. The "dark night of the senses" may be St John's term, but the idea was a commonplace of mystical thinking by the seventeenth century. Even the unmystical Descartes made it his own. His *Meditations*, in their title as well as their method, imply an ascent from reliance on the senses to a meditative equilibrium in the mind.[76]

Freeing oneself from the senses is an exercise to be carried out only once in a lifetime, according to Descartes, as a means of achieving self-knowledge and knowledge of God.[77] Pascal's view is quite different. Pascal speaks of an ongoing "war between the senses and reason," a war in which reason never triumphs once and for all.[78] Nevertheless, because thinking is our nature (we are "thinking reeds"), we must engage in unremitting war against the senses, the passions, and whatever else attaches us to the order of bodies.[79] For Pascal, this relentless struggle with concupiscence defines the religious dimension of life.

Pascal may be less sanguine about our ability to overcome the senses than either Descartes or St John, but he can at least recognize St John's "dark night of the senses" as the (unachievable) goal by which to measure our progress. Comparison between the two thinkers begins to break down, however, at the second stage of mystical ascent, the one St John famously called "the dark night of the soul." Garcia tells us,

> it involves a detachment not just from our appetites but from our cognitive faculties of understanding, memory, and imagination. The object of faith, which is God Himself, so far exceeds the human mind that we cannot arrive at much knowledge of Him by way of our natural powers.[80]

According to St John, it is only in the obscurity of these two "dark nights," where even the intellect is in darkness, that God acts to fuse the entirely passive human will with his own, and so brings about "the third and final stage of the ascent to God." Garcia describes the end point of the mystical ascent as

> the passive purification of the soul by God's actions within it. Through this fire of purgation, the soul's appetites and faculties, unable to derive satisfaction in any other object, are withdrawn from everything and concentrated simply upon God.[81]

St John's second and third steps lack any cognitive dimension. Reason is occluded. God acts, uniting our will to his, but the human mind remains passive.

If Pascal took a similar view, then charitable minds would not be able to exhibit the kind of wisdom (*sagesse*) we have seen him attribute to them. They could not be simultaneously the highest cognitive order, as Pascal thinks, and lacking any cognitive dimension, as they are according to St John. Why, then, have some scholars thought Pascal and St John to be saying the same thing?

It may be because they have not distinguished reason from rationalism. For example, the theologian Hans Urs von Balthasar writes: "[B]oth John of the Cross and Pascal stress, albeit in different ways, the aspect of the experience of faith ... in the believing person, and, for both authors, [it] stands in outright opposition to the light of reason."[82]

Von Balthasar is partly right. There is outright opposition between faith and *one* of reason's manifestations, the one Pascal calls the *esprit de géométrie*. The geometric mind espouses dogmatic rationalism of the kind Pascal discredits in the tournament of champions, the kind that seeks to demonstrate everything by appeal to clear definitions, first principles, and orderly demonstration. Reason in this form is the rationalism that crowds out faith. But in that form it is also unreasonable.

Reasonable reason is more closely connected with what Pascal calls an *esprit de finesse*. In this form the mind grasps by intuition (*sentiment*) in a single glance (*d'un seul regard*) matters that are too basic, or too subtle, to be demonstrated, though they are highly reasonable.[83] Between *finesse* and faith there is no conflict. Therefore, the opposition between faith and reason, which von Balthasar believes he finds in Pascal, is not "outright," as he says, but partial.

The path of inquiry that interests Pascal is too cognitive to be mystical.[84] But if we are not dealing with mysticism here, then there remains the unsolved problem of how the inquirer can be converted by naturalistic and philosophically transparent means. How can he work up from his concupiscent beginning in the order of bodies and become a member of the order of charity? The complexity of the question having at last been fully acknowledged, it is now time to try to answer it.

### Nature and Grace

Let us begin with the problem posed by grace. It is a requirement for the kind of spiritual progress the inquirer is expected to make. Only by its means can he overcome his fallen nature, his natural blindness, and any supernatural blindness God may have caused in him at an earlier stage of his life. But if it is a supernatural gift of God, how can it be consistent with naturalism?

Even to raise the matter of grace may seem to beg a fundamental question. Grace, as Pascal understands it, isn't offered to everyone. So we can't just assume the inquirer we are interested in receives it. On the other hand, without that assumption, how can we begin to investigate whether receiving grace is compatible with a naturalistic and philosophically transparent process of conversion?

However, logic and theology can be reconciled more easily than this objection implies – without contradiction, question begging, or theological error. If the inquirer we are considering were drawn at random from the pool of all mankind, we could assume nothing about his chance of receiving grace. That is Jansenist doctrine, and our discussion need not put it in question. But to make him interesting for further study, it is essential that *our* inquirer at some point be a recipient of grace. We must therefore draw him not from the pool of all mankind but from the smaller class of people who receive grace.

There are such persons. Not even the dourest Jansenist denies it. We commit neither a fallacy nor a theological error, therefore, in assuming that the inquirer *we* are discussing is one of those people. To assume he receives grace says nothing about how he will come to his Christian beliefs any more than assuming a certain patient will recover from some disease explains the means by which his recovery will be effected.

The Puritan writer John Bunyan faced the same problem in writing his classic allegory of the Christian life, *Pilgrim's Progress*, and he solved it in the same way. From the outset of Bunyan's tale, the protagonist is called "Christian," even though we learn that he began life with the name "Graceless." If he had been destined to remain graceless, however, he could not have been the subject of Bunyan's tale. Neither could he be of Pascal's.

If Pascal were a garden-variety Catholic, the way would now be clear to move on to another question. Knowing the inquirer will receive grace, we could consider what, in his freedom, he will do with it. However, Jansenists always find a way of complicating things. The Jansenist doctrine of efficacious (or irresistible) grace seems to bring us back to what I earlier called the miracle problem. Doesn't the introduction of efficacious grace mean that conversion will occur instantaneously, as if by magic, so that there will be no role for philosophy to play in it?

Such a show-closing contraction of the convert's path is, however, not strictly entailed even by the doctrine of efficacious grace. According to Pascal, election makes no humanly discernible change in the person of the elect. Even in our own case, Pascal thinks, we cannot be sure of having received grace. We can only judge from people's behaviour whether they are acting *as if* they had received grace, and we have no more to go on when we examine ourselves. At any stage of life, our only option is to treat ourselves and others as if we were all candidates for efficacious grace, and none of us a certain recipient.

> Everyone in the world is obliged to believe, but in a form of belief mingled with fear, not accompanied by certainty, that he belongs to the small number of the elect, and never to judge other men while they are alive on earth, however wicked or impious they may be, not to be among the number of those predestined [to receive grace]. The discernment of the elect from the damned must be left in the impenetrable secrecy of God.[85]

Grace should not be thought of as bringing about magical changes in mundane affairs. To receive grace is to be like the biblical character, Abel, whose sacrifice was acceptable to God. Not to receive grace is to be like Abel's brother, Cain, whose sacrifice was rejected. A human observer would not have been able to tell from looking at their sacrifices which one would be acceptable.

Think of grace as a necessary condition of conversion rather than the means by which conversion occurs. Efficacious grace is like an open door, perfectly consistent with our having philosophically transparent reasons for passing through it. When grace is absent, that door is closed.

The provision of efficacious grace nevertheless has some consequences. It means there are three kinds of people. Pascal calls them "the ones who never come to believe, others that come to believe but do not persevere, dying in mortal sin, and a group who both come to believe and persevere in charity until their death."[86]

The inquirer we are interested in has to be one of the third group, the ones who receive the grace to persevere and who therefore belong to the elect. With that assumption made, we can finally begin to examine the means by which his conversion comes about.

God allows himself to be *found* by those who search for him, Pascal says.[87] But God does not dictate the terms in which our search must be conducted. What, then, could prevent Pascal's inquirer from finding reasons to believe? Nothing could prevent it, as it seems to me, provided there is some way to acquire Christian virtues without quenching the concupiscent desire for life∞ that motivates an inquirer's search.

## Acquiring Christian Virtues

Let us begin as before with the virtue of hope (*espérance*). When the inquirer embarks on his search at the conclusion of IR, he has no more to work with than a concupiscent interest in the payoff associated with life∞. He has hope only in the weak, objective sense of *espoir*. The Christian virtue he is aiming at (*espérance*) belongs to qualitatively different territory. It is an inner attitude of confident expectation that he is indeed a recipient of divine grace and that God's promises will be fulfilled.

Henri Brémond said the Jansenism of Pascal's time did not admit such confident expectations. But Brémond goes on to conjecture that Pascal might not have shared their opinion. Instead he might have anticipated a view Jansenists of a second generation would espouse, one closer to the orthodox Catholic understanding of hope. It would allow for a kind of confidence which,

> taken in its fullest expression, consists in regarding oneself as among the elect, and therefore in hoping (*espérer*) to receive all the blessings (*faveurs*) God showers on those who belong to his happy flock.[88]

The difficulty with Brémond's suggestion is that Pascal explicitly disavows such confidence. More than once he treats it as a snare. Witness a comment he makes about the sacrament of confession:

One man told me that he experienced great joy and confidence on leaving the confessional. Another said he remained fearful. I thought that of the two of them one good man could be made, and that each was deficient in lacking the state of mind the other had.[89]

Again, in his first essay on grace, Pascal says that our hope of being among the elect should be mixed not with confidence but with fear.[90]

It is not that attaining the infused virtue of hope, *espérance*, is impossible, according to Pascal. That would be absurd. If no one had *espérance*, there would be no Christians. But Pascal leans towards minimalism. The view Brémond toys with attributing to him is too confident. Christian hope is a delicate flower, Pascal thinks, hard to coax into bloom, harder still to keep alive. Like a delicate flower, it trembles. Fear is its constant companion.[91]

Not even the Christian elect experience *espérance* as steady, confident expectation. The most anyone can experience is *episodic hope*. It comes in isolated bursts of confidence, fearfully maintained in a chaotic stream of often contrary experience. Rarely does confidence approach certitude; never does it justify complacency.[92]

It is hard to find the right balance between confidence and fear. Their interplay provides dramatic tension in Pascal's thought, notably so in a fragment of great authority usually called "the Memorial."[93] This fragment commemorates the tumultuous "dénouement" of what is called Pascal's "second conversion."[94] On the night of 23 November 1654, his religious struggles came to a head in a passionate encounter with "the God of Abraham, Isaac and Jacob." The event was so precious to Pascal (but also so elusive) that he kept an ecstatic account of it sewn into the lining of his overcoat. And yet the Memorial was at the same time so personal that even his friends and family learned of its existence only after his death, when they found its hiding place.

The Memorial is deeply religious and intimately personal, but I shall comment on neither of those aspects. So what is left? Its other striking feature is its undulating structure, rising, as it does, towards confidence, and declining again towards fear.

The initial encounter with God is so forceful it infuses even the diffident Pascal with more than mere confidence:

Certitude, certitude, feeling, joy, peace.

He continues on this elevated plane for several lines, punctuating this first portion of the meditation with another outburst:

Joy, joy, joy, tears of joy.

Then, abruptly, in a line which may be deeply autobiographical,[95] confidence evaporates and is replaced with anxiety:

I have separated myself from him.

Anxiety in turn begets the wish that separation from God may not be permanent. Pascal wishes very strongly to be found among the elect. That wish is no sooner expressed, however, than self-accusation again overwhelms it:

I have separated myself from him, fled him, crucified him.

Accusation brings back the wish for union, but now it takes the form of fear-tempered hope, the kind Pascal thinks appropriate for a believer:

Let me never be separated from him.

This wish is hopeful, because it implies that Pascal has already achieved a genuine union with God, which is "the plenitude of the Absolute."[96] But still Pascal fearfully acknowledges the possibility of another separation, even while hoping it will not befall him. The words, "Let me never" recognize how fragile union with God must be, always threatened by separation. One condition for continuing union is rigorous self-denial:

Total submission to Jesus Christ and to my [spiritual] director.

Gouhier sees the Memorial in the first instance as an ascetic text rather than a mystical one.[97] Total submission. Fervent commitment to self-denial.

Every line of the Memorial is heartfelt and passionate. But can Pascal guarantee the performance of the ascetic regimen he envisages? If he has separated himself from God in the past, and acknowledges it in the present, how can he be certain he will not do so again in the future? A relentless struggle between confidence and fear propels the reader forward in quest of resolution, and none is found until the couplet with which the fragment closes, whose last line is a quotation from Psalm 118:[98]

> An eternity of joy for a single day's exercise on earth.
> I shall not forget your word.

Take the quotation first, "I shall not forget your word." It is a performative tautology: Pascal is *reciting* the word he means never to forget. The commitment to remember it is one he will keep.[99] But remembering God's word is not the same as putting it into practice, especially when practice involves the relentless self-denial Pascal associated with conversion.

The last line therefore cannot be understood perfectly without its predecessor, a line in which he exhorts himself to "a single day's exercise." Even a single day of rigorous asceticism would be difficult for anyone and impossible for many, but Pascal does not mean literally a single day. The 'exercise' will have to be practised over the rest of his life. It is a single day only when its duration is compared with the eternity of joy to follow.

Still, life's little day can be long in human terms, and so full of unpredictable reversals that no promise of fidelity, however heartfelt and passionate at the time of its making, is certain of being kept. The possibility of falling short is inherent in all we promise, and indwells every *exercise*.

Therefore, from time to time, there will be lapses, like the periods of separation to which Pascal confesses in the Memorial. There will be times in which God is rejected, or, in Pascal's most striking image, in which Christ is crucified. No one can be confident of having grace. "[People of] every condition, even the martyrs, must be fearful according to the Scriptures," Pascal writes.[100]

Although any punishment allotted to such lapses would be deserved, God is also merciful, at least to some, and we must always assume reconciliation to be possible. "Let us do penance," Pascal says, "to see if perhaps [God] will take pity on us."[101] Doing penance and hoping are thus part of the exercise Pascal envisages. That is why they were enjoined upon the inquirer in the IR fragment.

Everything in Pascal's thinking converges on this weighty idea of searching or inquiry. Simple hope (*espoir*) makes search desirable. And even if the inquirer achieves the Christian virtue of hope, it is not a milestone he soars by on some victorious upward journey. *Espérance* is not a milestone but an *exercise*. And he must perform it in victory and in defeat. In that exercise, hope tempers fear and fear hope. The search for God unfolds in a pattern of glimpses and losses.

Pascal does not deny that there is progress: "the feeble search we make for God, when he first gives us the wish to disengage from our worldly commitments, is quite different from the way we search for him after he has cut these ties; at that point we run toward him in the path of his commandments."[102] Progress indeed, but running involves momentum and direction rather than certainty.

Repeated glimpses do, however, begin to shape the expectations of the inquirer, and so to form his mind. Pascal has not yet told us what the inquirer is glimpsing. So far he has told us only that in these glimpses hope is encouraged and strengthened. But hope never turns into direct vision. Pascal would agree with St Paul: "Hope that is seen is not hope."[103] There is no certainty. *Deus absconditus*.

Pascal does not think God's hiddenness a bad thing. Hope seen and grasped securely would lead to complacency, which is undesirable in itself. If it could be achieved, complacent hope would also stifle the growth of the other Christian virtues, faith and charity. But hope of the tentative and yet recurrent kind Pascal describes has incalculable instrumental value in fostering the other virtues.

Charity for one. Pascal writes against "those who out of confidence in God's mercy become slack in the performance of good works." Self-satisfied people underestimate how indebted they are to God. Pascal's vivid sense of human unworthiness makes confident Christianity look absurd. Realistic Christians, he thinks, will weigh their unpayable debt against the possibility of divine mercy. "It is because there is a merciful God that we ought to make every kind of effort."[104] The nearer we come to *espérance*, the more we will perform acts of charity, because we will have the right mixture of hope for mercy with fear of punishment.

Works of charity, in turn, are expressions of living faith, according to orthodox Catholic doctrine.[105] Those who, with faith, look for God in nature, find him, where before they found only darkness and shadows.[106]

But faith cannot be acquired once and for all any more than hope can. One of Pascal's apologetic ambitions in the *Pensées* is "to make faith live once more in people in whom it has been extinguished."[107] If faith were a permanent acquisition, there could be no such backsliders to worry about. Faith flickers on and off in a believer's life in the same way hope sometimes grows faint and works of charity few.

On the positive side are luminous moments of faith, hope, and charity that guide the inquirer's transformation and encourage him to intensify his search. I shall call them "episodes of virtue." While the inquirer has them, and in the measure he has them, he possesses a Christian mind. Episodes of virtue are expressions of the inquirer's Christianity, though they are only intermittently present. They are among the "huge efforts of the mind to which the soul sometimes rises," but they are not sustained. "[The soul] only leaps up," Pascal notes. "Not as if it mounted the throne forever, but only for an instant."[108]

There appears to be no a priori reason why *episodes of virtue* such as Pascal describes should not be experienced by an inquirer who begins with no more than the meagre resource of concupiscent hope. Nor has the inquirer been expected to take any step in the process of acquiring Christian virtue that a philosopher could not agree to.

## Objections

Nevertheless, my description of inquiry may be suspected of both philosophical and theological distortions. Philosophically, one might object to the idea that Christian virtues can be merely episodic. Philosophers since Aristotle have distinguished between episodic displays of virtuous behaviour and the settled habit in which real virtue consists. The person who is only occasionally temperate or courageous in his actions does not count as possessing the virtue of temperance or courage. Only the habitually virtuous are virtuous at all. Shouldn't Pascal also distinguish between carnal minds, in which only episodic "efforts" at faith, hope, and charity occur, and genuinely Christian minds, in which the virtues are more firmly implanted?

Pascal felt the force of the distinction implicit in this question. He agrees "we must not measure what a man's virtue is capable of by his *efforts*, but by his ordinary way of proceeding (*par son ordinaire*)."[109] A critic can therefore say that I have gotten things backwards, trying to make effort suffice where only the ordinary or habitual will do.

Episodic virtue may also be said to be irreconcilable with Pascal's theology. If Pascal had really said that a Christian mind could come about by natural means, would that not make him a Pelagian of the very sort he denounces everywhere in his writing?[110]

In an effort to ward off philosophical objections to the supernatural, I have been trying to keep grace on the periphery of inquiry. It was assumed that any inquirer we are interested in would be a recipient of it, but grace was not allowed to be an explanatory factor in the Christianizing of the inquirer's mind. Now it looks as if that strategy is catching up with me. The facilitating grace banished to satisfy philosophers must be reinstated to satisfy theologians.

This theological objection might conclude by pointing out that the account of the formation of Christian minds I attributed to Pascal brings him too close to a rationalistic picture like that of Descartes. John McDade reminds us of the many ways in which that would be a mistake:

> [Pascal] does not think that a comprehensive account of [the Cartesian rationalist] kind can work because the conditions are not operative which would make it possible. It would mean ignoring the fragmentation of the human self, the fragility of human knowing, the ambiguous character of God's presence in and to the world and the dialectic of selective divine grace and human freedom which conditions everything. Whatever is said has to accommodate these chasms. For Pascal, whatever truth we can come to about God is not antecedent to the historical dialectic of sin, election and medicinal grace but is disclosed only within this history. The truth about God arises only within this complex, jagged human history: "... without Scripture, without original sin, without a necessary mediator, promised and arrived, one cannot absolutely prove God, nor teach good doctrine nor good morality."[111]

If these objections cannot be answered, then only a miracle will advance the inquirer beyond the point at which Pascal leaves him at the end of the wager. While that would be grist for the mill of those who take Pascal to be anti-philosophical in his outlook, it would be fatal for the interpretation of Pascalian inquiry argued here.

**Reply to the Objections**

Does the virtue text cited above, in which Pascal distinguished between virtues and mere "efforts," mean that my account has confused the two? There would be a couple of dodgy ways to dodge that bullet. I could side with those commentators who see that text as applying only to Aristotelian virtues, not Christian ones, or as merely echoing, without necessarily endorsing, Montaigne.[112] On either interpretation the text in question would not reflect Pascal's understanding of Christian virtue.

Another dodge would be to argue that Pascal simply evinces contradictory opinions about Christian virtues. Given the unfinished and sometimes chaotic character of the *Pensées*, it is a standing temptation to explain away apparent contradictions as mere doctrinal static.

A more interesting response can be given, however, that brings out the deeper integrity of Pascal's thought. He can be shown to have reconciled episodic and Aristotelian conceptions of virtue in an original way.

Two types of person will experience episodes of virtue, Pascal thinks. One type makes up the unfortunate class of what I will call *temporary Christians*. Temporary Christians think like real Christians for a time, but do not persevere. At some point in their lives, such people depart from the Christian way forever, and they die in mortal sin. They are indiscernible from real Christians during the episodes of virtue they experience, but because those episodes stop recurring prior to their death, these people do not count as real Christians. The unfathomable will of God permits their existence, Pascal thinks, for purely instrumental reasons. They exist, as he puts it, "for the good of the elect."[113]

The detachment with which Pascal accepts the instrumentality of temporary Christians is part of what Leszek Kolakowski aptly calls "Pascal's sad religion." But sad or not, the existence of temporary Christians helps clarify Pascal's account of the Christian mind and lends coherence to his larger apologetic project in the *Pensées*.

Here's how it works: as already mentioned, episodes of virtue occur naturally in the minds of temporary Christians and are qualitatively indiscernible from those in the minds of the elect. If the minds of the elect were in any way superior, there would be a reason why they were chosen, a reason by which election and damnation could be justified. But Pascal, like other Jansenists, is a voluntarist on this point, claiming that God decides to save some and damn others simply by an act of will. "The separation of the elect from the damned," he writes, "must be left as God's impenetrable secret."[114] The elect are chosen "by an absolute and irrevocable will ... out of a purely gratuitous goodness. The rest God abandons to their evil desires, as he might justly have abandoned everyone."[115]

God therefore makes no change in nature by supplying grace. As Pascal sees it, the whole conflict between Pelagians and orthodox Catholics arises from the fact that human experience is confined to the natural order of things. Pelagians conclude that the natural order must therefore be sufficient for salvation, while orthodox Catholics conclude that the order of grace must therefore transcend nature. Since all we have to go on is the natural order, experience provides nothing to which either side can appeal to resolve the conflict.[116]

The difference between temporary and persevering Christians can be explained by rightly understanding nature and grace. Episodes of virtue occur naturally to Christians of both kinds. Both may have faith, acquire hope, and perform acts of charity, because they have found reasons for doing so. If the elect are the only ones to persevere, it is because of a critical difference in their relationship to the transcendent causality of grace.

What do the elect have, then, that temporary Christians lack? The elect benefit from "an absolute volition" of God by which they are saved. But this volition makes no immediate change in the elect. It operates indirectly. The salvation of the elect is part of what God was aiming at in the creation of the world. It was one of his front-burner considerations. The will to bring about their salvation led him to create the world in such a way that the elect encounter reasons for acquiring Christian minds, and are receptive to them, on an episodic basis throughout their lives. Although the episodes of virtue experienced by the elect will be qualitatively indistinguishable from those of temporary Christians, only the elect will continue to experience them throughout their lives. That is how the natural order of things has been contrived. The same natural order will ensure that temporary Christians will either stop encountering persuasive reasons to live as Christians, or else encounter them at inopportune moments when they fail to persuade. Temporary Christians' welfare is a back-burner consideration for God. The natural order of things was not established with them in mind.

According to Pascal's sad religion, the episodes of virtue that occur in temporary Christians do not occur for their own sake but because they are instrumental to achieving the good of the elect. Nevertheless, God's absolute and instrumental wills form one single will, and nature is one.[117]

Pascal's doctrine of grace also allows an original way of distinguishing between virtue and habit. If temporary Christians stop exhibiting Christian virtues before the end of their lives, the ordinary explanation would be to say that they never formed the habit, and therefore only appeared at one stage of their lives to possess the virtue. But what about the elect whose individual acts of virtue are indiscernible from those of temporary Christians and yet persevere?

Pascal's interesting and original answer does justice to the Aristotelian insight that virtue must be connected with our nature. For Pascal they are connected. God does not make believers persevere by a miracle. Instead he attunes the natural order to their nature in such a way that the ordinary situations believers encounter in their natural lives naturally persuade them to think and act as Christians. The most important habit of a Pascalian inquirer is inquiry. Those who become inquirers incline to it by their natures. Those among the elect incline to it regularly, though not unfailingly, and it leads them in Christian ways.

The view I am attributing to Pascal is not Cartesian rationalism. Pascal tries to work within Catholic theology, where Descartes often prefers to work around it. Neither is Pascal's account Pelagian. If it were Pelagian, the salvation of the inquirer would depend on his own efforts. But it doesn't. The efforts of inquirers who lack grace are insufficient, as the sad case of temporary Christians makes clear. The inquirer's efforts only suffice if he perseveres in them, but this is just what he will not do, unless nature has been graciously contrived to permit it. In this way Pascal can endorse the position he finds in Augustine, according to which "all who persevere, persevere by a grace which very invincibly causes them to do so, and without which they would not be able to persevere."[118] But at the same time he can also endorse the Aristotelian view that only those who habitually act virtuously are virtuous.

## Balanced Minds

If I am right about how Pascal's inquirer comes to experience episodes of virtue, then there is nothing about the process to which philosophers must object. Supernaturally given grace, though acknowledged to be among the necessary conditions for conversion, determines only the pool from which converts are drawn, not the course their conversion will take. Each episode of virtue arises by natural means. And the "perseverance invincibly caused" by grace is caused through the original setup of the universe in creation, not by ad hoc promptings, once the process of conversion is underway.

Philosophical effort is required of the Pascalian inquirer, in the midst of his search for reasons to believe. He must exhibit in the first place a balanced mind. "You must know when to doubt," Pascal tells us, but also, when to be assured and, where necessary, when to submit. Whoever does not operate this way misunderstands the power of reason. There are people who fall afoul of these three principles either by giving assurance that everything is demonstrated, because they are not proficient in demonstration, or by doubting everything, because they don't know when to submit their judgement, or by submitting to everything, because they don't know when to make a judgement.[119]

In three ways, then, an inquirer can fall short of being reasonable. One is by thinking everything demonstrable.

When Pascal accuses those who make this error of lacking skill in demonstration, he is probably doing so tongue in cheek. On a literal reading such an accusation would be directed against philosophical duffers – ignorant inflators of reason's powers who are not likely to interest Pascal any more than they do anyone else. Therefore, it is more likely to be intellectual high achievers, and their distinctive hubris, that Pascal has in his sights: people who mistake their own remarkable aptitude in supplying demonstrations for a limitless power.

Epictetus and Descartes would be the probable suspects here. Recall, for example, Descartes's triumphal pronouncement in the *Discourse on Method*:

> Those long chains of reasoning, simple and effortless, which geometers habitually use to arrive at their most difficult demonstrations, prompted me to imagine that all things knowable by men are inter-connected in the same way. And so, provided we abstain from receiving anything as true that is not so, and provided we always maintain the order necessary for deducing one thing from another, there can be nothing so distant, that we will not ultimately get to it, nor so hidden that it will not be discovered."[120]

How can even supremely intelligent people like Descartes make this error? It's not because they lack proficiency in demonstration, as Pascal teasingly affirms. They are virtuosos of demonstration. They fall into error because they have the vice of their virtue, and that is exactly where Pascal locates the real problem. So deeply have these talented rationalists entered into geometrical thinking that it makes them shallow about life. Geometry does not give them insight into the fine structure of things, as they believe. It causes them instead to mistake geometric regularities for the lineaments of the world. They confuse theoretical objects with real ones. Beyond the safe and shapely world of geometry there exist "things so delicate and numerous that one needs a delicate and clear sensitivity (*sens*) in order to sense them (*pour les sentir*) and to be able to judge them rightly and astutely through this sensitivity (*sentiment*)."[121] What Pascal here calls "a delicate and clear sensitivity" is what he elsewhere calls *"finesse,"* and elsewhere again attributes to the *heart*. This kind of sensitivity is one of the attributes of reasonable inquiry. Those who possess it avoid the folly of dogmatism and do not overestimate the power of reason, especially their own.

Alas, there are still other ways for reason to go wrong. Some people go too far in the opposite direction: they claim nothing can be demonstrated. Such people end up contesting even the incontestable. In the terminology of L170/S201, they fail to *submit*.

The model here would presumably be the arch-sceptic Pascal sees in Montaigne, though Montaigne may be only playfully titillating his readers with a radical scepticism intended to provoke thought and discussion. If so, then Pascal needs to focus on earnest sceptics, who say nothing can be known with certainty, and reject even the most careful demonstrations.

Diffidence towards *purported* demonstrations is of course perfectly legitimate. Careful inquiry demands it, and Pascal recognizes it as a virtue.[122] Here, however, he is pointing out that diffidence goes too far when it makes us think that reason *never* performs according to specifications. Sometimes reason does its job and demonstrates something. When it does, a reasonable person submits his judgment to the conclusion reached by the demonstration. Refusal to submit to bona fide demonstrations is simply unreasonable. It produces the dysfunctionality discussed in Chapters One and Two under the label of *philosophical failure*.

Radical sceptics are not the only ones to fail in this way. Take some eager beginner in Critical Thinking 101 who is far from being a sceptic. Wishing to make a good impression on the first day of class, he challenges his professor to *demonstrate* that valid argument is more likely to move from true premises to true conclusions than guesswork is. Why should students submit to a class on critical thinking, he asks, before being shown the advantages of doing so?

The beginner is not a sceptic. He thinks he is already embodying the ideal of critical thinking. But in fact he is being unreasonable. The lectures he is putting in question are about to furnish the very proof he is asking for. It cannot be provided in advance of the lectures.

Failures of this kind are failures of *submission*. The Enlightenment motto, *sapere aude* ("dare to know"), is a thrilling exhortation, but it passes over the submission in which learning always has to begin. "I am not seeking understanding in order to believe," say the Augustinians, "but believing in order that I may understand."[123] Pascal considers this Augustinian modesty to be required equipment for a reasonable mind.[124]

Radical scepticism and intemperate enthusiasm for critical thought are two ways of failing to submit when it would be reasonable to do so. Here is a third. Reasonable people also submit to truths that are *revealed*. "How I hate this caviling about not believing in the Eucharist, etc.," Pascal writes. "If the Gospel is true, if Jesus Christ is God, what is the problem?"[125]

This little fragment does not argue that the Gospel is true, or that Jesus Christ is God. It ridicules those who, while accepting revelation in principle, deny it in practice. Theologians who try to demythologize the Bible to make it acceptable to modern sensibilities would be good examples of the kind of unreasonableness Pascal has in view. If Jesus Christ is all-powerful, what prevents him from appearing under the attributes of Eucharistic bread and wine? If God created the universe, what could stop him from causing the Red Sea to part, or raising the dead?

Pascal plays up, as the Enlightenment likes to downplay, the occasions in which the submission of reason is a sign of not intellectual weakness but vitality. Not submitting on these occasions is unreasonable and a sign of mental feebleness.

Pascal admits, of course, that reason can also fail by submitting too readily. It's just that where this kind of unreasonableness figures at the top of the Enlightenment's list, on Pascal's it is found at the bottom. Unwarranted submission is what is called credulity or superstition.

Credulous minds are at the opposite extreme from radical sceptics, but no less vicious. Sometimes credulity is offhandedly attributed to insufficient education, but Pascal sees more deeply. Its real cause, he says, is lack of *judgment*.

He doesn't explain the connection, but it is not difficult to see what he means. A passage from Kant's *Critique of Pure Reason* explains it memorably. "Understanding," Kant tells us, "is capable of being instructed, and of being equipped with rules." Judgment, on the other hand,

is a special talent which can be practised only, and cannot be taught. It is the specific quality of so-called mother wit; and its lack no school can make good. For although an abundance of rules borrowed from the insight of others may be proffered to, and as it were grafted upon, a limited understanding, the power of rightly employing them must belong to the learner himself; and in the absence of such a natural gift no rule that may be prescribed to him for this purpose can ensure against misuse.[126]

Then, in a footnote, Kant adds:

Deficiency in judgement is what is ordinarily called stupidity (*Dummheit*), and for such a failing there is no remedy. An obtuse or narrow-minded person to whom nothing is wanting save a proper degree of understanding and the concepts appropriate to it, may indeed be trained through study, even to the extent of becoming learned. But as such people are commonly still lacking in judgement, it is not unusual to meet learned men who in the application of their scientific knowledge betray that original want, which can never be made good.[127]

*Finesse* is the distinguishing quality of judgment, Pascal thinks.[128] Not only does it teach us things we cannot otherwise learn, it also equips us to acknowledge the unknowable. No matter how much learning they acquire, minds without finesse, or judgment, remain credulous. Reasonable minds must be neither credulous nor sceptical nor dogmatic.

They can, however, be Christian. "If everything were submitted to reason, our religion would have nothing mysterious or supernatural," Pascal says in an exercise of the balanced judgment now under consideration. "If the principles of reason were shocked, our religion would be absurd and ridiculous."[129] Both the foregoing sentences are counterfactuals. They imply, therefore, that a Christian mind recognizes mysterious and supernatural things, which transcend reason, while at the same time perceiving that these things do not offend reason. Judgment balances the Christian mind, teaching it when submission is called for and when not. "No one is as reasonable as a true Christian," Pascal says.[130]

**Reasonable Inquiry**

So far no obstacle has been discovered that would prevent a reasonable inquirer from moving by naturalistic and philosophically transparent means from unbelief to conversion. But the question has been discussed at a very abstract, theoretical level. It is time to consider the *content* of Pascalian inquiry. What precisely is it that brings a reasonable inquirer to believe?

Generally speaking, it is the permeability of God's disguises. They are always permeable somewhere, but not always in the same place. Therefore, different paths have led different inquirers to conversion. Searchers for God must find their way through the gate appropriate to their time or they will never arrive at all. "Our own time has the prophecies," Pascal says:

> Other times have had other indications. All the proofs support each other. If one of them is true they all are ... Those who saw the Flood believed the Creation and the Messiah who was foretold. Those who saw Moses believed in the Flood and in the fulfilment of prophecy. And we who see the fulfilment of prophecy ought to believe in the Flood and in Creation.[131]

Forms of concealment and disclosure change, but the pattern remains the same. Different avenues of approach open up, but they always converge on the same intersection of mutually reinforcing orthodox beliefs, including creation, the flood, prophecy, and, presumably, many more theologically important beliefs, particularly those concerning Jesus Christ, which the Catholic tradition has made matters of dogma. To become a Christian the inquirer must arrive at a point where his beliefs include the teachings of the Church.

The opening in Pascal's time (and presumably in our own) is found in the area of prophecy. By prophecy Pascal means biblical anticipations of the advent and influence of Jesus Christ. Only by grace will anyone find that open door, but no further miracle is required for someone to move through it to the place where Christian dogmas intersect. That step can be taken naturally and transparently, Pascal thinks, through reasonable inquiry. How so?

Pascal did not think that Christianity could be demonstrated, but he thought there were *proofs* that made it *reasonable*.[132] By proofs (*preuves*) he means historical, empirical evidence drawn preeminently from Scripture, particularly from biblical prophecies that were fulfilled. One brief fragment gives a skeletal outline of the big picture for his projected apology. It is entitled "Proofs," and reads, "Prophecy with its fulfilment. What preceded Jesus Christ and what came after."[133]

In a longer fragment Pascal says why he thinks prophecies are so significant: "If one man had made a book predicting the time and manner of the coming of Jesus Christ, and if Christ had then come in the manner prophesied, that book would be infinitely powerful. But," so Pascal argues,

"[in the Christian tradition] we have much more. A whole sequence of men over a span of four thousand years who constantly, and invariably, one after the other, predict the same advent. There is an entire people who proclaim [the Messiah's] coming and who have endured for four thousand years to give corporate witness of the assurances they have received, and who could not be discouraged by whatever threats or persecutions they were subjected to. This is evidence of an entirely different order."[134]

From a lecture Pascal reportedly gave in 1658, and from numerous fragments dealing with prophecies in the *Pensées*, we can infer that he was going to draw on his extensive knowledge of the prophets and the insight born of long reflection on them, which contemporaries assure us he had,[135] to show that the Christian religion has unrivalled historical support, "with many things coming together to establish its certainty."[136] A careful inquirer following Pascal's indications would discover numerous paths of evidence converging on Christian orthodoxy.

We can't be sure exactly how Pascal would have presented the prophecies in the completed apology. "The detached scraps we find of them in the collection known as the *Pensées*," says Filleau de la Chaise, a contemporary of Pascal's who was present at his now lost lecture, "give only an imperfect idea of the body [of evidence] he intended to assemble."[137]

It is of course regrettable that we shall never know how Pascal would have constructed his argument from prophecy. But no matter how adroitly it had been done, it would almost certainly have failed to satisfy the rigorous standards of historical criticism about to be put in place by biblical critics like Richard Simon and Baruch Spinoza, standards that would themselves be refined throughout the Enlightenment and beyond, culminating in the "higher criticism" of the nineteenth and twentieth centuries. Surely no argument alleging exact anticipation of New Testament events by Old Testament prophecies would meet the standards set by modern historical-critical Bible scholarship. Bible scholars today are reluctant to call the prophets "foretellers" of future events at all, but settle instead for understanding them as "forthtellers" of God's message to the prophets' own contemporaries.[138]

Historical and higher criticism would be redoubtable adversaries for certain apologetic uses to which the *Pensées* might have been put. They would certainly block any attempt to use prophecy to demonstrate the truth of Christianity. But nothing these critical approaches can say affects the narrower possibility currently being considered – the possibility, that is, of a rational inquirer's finding in prophecy not demonstrations but *rational grounds* for developing Christian beliefs.

Even if prophecy is the main catalyst in converting the inquirer, there can be no a priori objection. That is because converting does not, for Pascal, begin with a blank slate upon which reason neutrally inscribes its findings. The inquirer is not an indifferent, academic observer. A concupiscent interest in the prospect of life° has put him on a hopeful search for reasons to believe the teachings of the Church, even if the reasons he finds are only provisional ones. He does not expect to find a rigid dogmatic boilerplate that will repel all subsequent assaults of scepticism. Once he finds temporary accommodation within the teachings of the Church, he will look for reasons to prolong his stay. Inquiry will continue for as long as the inquirer finds it profitable. If he is among the elect, it will continue as long as he lives.

There is a trick to reading prophecy, however. Some might even call it a paradox. "In order to examine [prophecies]," Pascal says, "you have to understand them."[139] That assertion is a little like the famous Augustinian idea of believing in order to understand, but Pascal's proposal is even more paradoxical. What can he mean by *understanding in order to examine*? Normally we wouldn't examine something we have already understood, nor could we understand anything we had never examined.

However, Pascal goes on to clarify what he means. It is not individual prophecies that must be understood before we examine them. We have to understand what prophecy itself *is*. If it is speech that simultaneously bears two senses, the literal and the symbolic, then prophets can be both forthtellers and foretellers, and their predictions can furnish reasons for belief. But if prophecy's symbolic sense is disallowed, then it will not give an inquirer reasons to believe.

If the literal sense were the only sense prophecy could bear, then many of the doctrines the Church has drawn from it would lose their warrant. For example, on the day of Pentecost, the Apostle Peter invokes prophecy against certain Jewish sceptics: "Men and brethren, let me speak freely to you about the patriarch David that he is both dead and buried ... He, being a prophet ... foreseeing [the enthronement of Christ], spoke concerning the resurrection of the Christ ... Therefore let all the house of Israel know assuredly, that God has made this same Jesus, whom you crucified, both Lord and Christ."[140]

In the same passage, we are told that out of Peter's large audience three thousand persons were converted.[141] Pascal would not deny that the messianic words King David spoke a thousand years before Christ could be read as mere "forthtellings." They could be read, that is, as if they bore only some literal sense aimed at their original audience. In that case, Pascal realizes, they would not be about Christ at all. "If you think [the prophecies] have only one sense," he says, "then it is certain that the Messiah has not come."[142]

However, if, as a hopeful hearer, you are prepared to give credit to the Church's way of reading prophetic language, which is what Pascal means by *understanding* prophecy, then you will find yourself able at that point to examine it, and see whether what it predicted has come to pass. One has only to entertain the possibility of a figurative reading of the Old Testament, Pascal says, to see that it supplies the proper interpretive key.[143] For, "if [the prophecies] bear two meanings, it is certain that the Messiah has come in Jesus Christ."[144]

Without that key, Scripture will always appear uncertain and contradictory. If the Messiah foretold in the Old Testament had to be a conquering monarch of the line of David, establishing the Jewish people in a secular kingdom that would never end, as a literal reading of many Old Testament passages would make him, then we could be certain that no such Messiah has arrived. But we would also find in the Old Testament puzzling testimony to the coming of another Messiah, one who would be "despised and rejected by men, a man of sorrows and acquainted with grief."[145]

If that lowly Messiah was to be only figuratively a king, if his purpose were to establish a spiritual kingdom "not of this world,"[146] of which only believers would be subjects, then that part of the prophecy could not help but be fulfilled by Jesus Christ.[147] Nor would anything prevent some apparently conflicting parts of the prophecy from being fulfilled at the same time. The figurative reading allows the conqueror and the man of sorrows to be the same man. The prophets' *forthtellings* were spoken in a language suited to the situation of their original audience, while their symbolic *foretellings* spoke of what was to come.

A critic might reply that the secondary meaning is the very thing that historical-critical scholarship puts in question. Pascal could agree. Modern scholarship raises a question, but it does supply any definitive answer. "The whole question," Pascal says, "is whether the prophecies have two meanings."[148]

The inquirer does not need to have answered that question. Inquiry is an open-ended activity, and if anyone purported to demonstrate that the meaning of Scripture was inevitably singular, inquirers would have to be prepared to examine the demonstration. No such demonstrations exist, however, so inquirers are free to continue with their effort to see the world in the light of the Church's teachings.

Reading prophecies for their figurative meaning is not arbitrary, as it would be, for example, to mine them for stock market advice. As Pascal points out, reading prophecy figuratively is sanctioned by Scripture itself, by a long rabbinical tradition, by the Kabbalah, by the Apostles, and explicitly by Jesus Christ.[149]

Critics will be unimpressed with this reasoning perhaps. It takes the truth of Scripture for granted, and therefore reasons in a circle, they will say. And that gives *them* good reason for suspending their judgment about it. However, it gives the inquirer no reason at all.

The inquirer is inside the circle these critics complain about, and they are outside. Where you are makes all the difference. The inquirer is only trying to discover whether, by acting like a serious believer, he will find reasons for becoming one. It's an empirical question. The only way to answer that question is the one Pascal recommends.

But then the inquirer is surrendering his reason too quickly, a critic might reply. However, Pascal thinks otherwise. The inquirer is not surrendering his reason at all; he is exercising it. He will not be content merely to read Scripture as figurative. He will also confront the critics, both within the tradition and outside it, who say he shouldn't. Only when full credit has been given to every dissonant voice is the job of interpretation done, according to the demanding hermeneutic espoused by Pascal. Interpretation involves the most rigorous possible dialectical engagement. First within the Scripture itself:

> In order to understand Scripture we need to find a meaning in which all the contrary passages are harmonized. Without that there is no sense to it at all. It is not enough to find an interpretation in which several passages concur. You need one that can harmonize even contrary ones ...
>
> If you take the law, the sacrifices and the kingdom to be [temporal] realities, you will not be able to harmonize all the passages. Therefore they must necessarily be figurative.
>
> The true sense is therefore not that of the Jews, but in Jesus Christ all the contradictions are harmonized.[150]

But there are also critics outside the Catholic tradition. They, too, have to be addressed. In Pascal's time, the Church was preoccupied with Protestant objections to many of its interpretations of Scripture. Protestants held, for example, that the bread and wine of the Eucharistic celebration, on which the Catholic Mass is centred, are merely symbolic of the body and blood of Christ. The Pascalian inquirer replies,

> On the subject of the Blessed Sacrament we believe that, when the substance of the bread is changed and trans-substantiated into the body of Our Lord, then Jesus Christ is really present there. There is one of our truths. The other is that this sacrament is also a figure for the cross, and for Christ's glory, and a commemoration of the two. That is the Catholic faith, and it unites the two truths that seem opposed.
>
> The heresy of our day does not suppose the sacrament involves both the presence of Jesus Christ and its figuration, and that it is both a sacrifice and the commemoration of a sacrifice. It does not believe that we can admit one of these truths without for that reason excluding the other.
>
> The heretics cling to the one point – that the sacrament is figurative – and to that extent they are not heretics. But they believe that we are denying that truth. That is why they make so many objections against us based on passages from the Church Fathers who [stress the figurative nature of the sacrament]. [Protestants] end up denying the real presence and in that point they are heretics.[151]

It is so easy to fall into heresy, Pascal thinks. All it takes is to over-emphasize a single word, or to underemphasize it. He illustrates what he means by citing the way Protestants overestimate the meaning of *omnes* (Latin for "all") in one of their teachings, and underestimate it in another. The lesson to be learned from these dangers is that "one must follow the Fathers and the tradition."[152] In other words, a reasonable person submits his judgment to that of the Church. It is true that no one would feel inclined to submit his judgment to the Church if he had not made a prior commitment to understanding through belief. But there is nothing unreasonable about making such a commitment, because it proclaims itself to be a path to life∞, the goods of which everyone instinctively and even concupiscently desires. And once that commitment is made, there is nothing unreasonable about submitting one's judgment to the Church.

A Pascalian inquirer begins inside the circle, and thinks from the inside out. 'Out,' in this context, means all the way out: out of the Church into secular history. "How beautiful it is," Pascal writes, "to see with the eyes of faith how Darius and Cyrus, Alexander, the Romans, Pompey and Herod, act without knowing it for the glory of the Gospel."[153] These historical figures are all mentioned in the Bible as having unwittingly helped advance the coming of Christ's kingdom.

Any attempt to understand secular history in Christian terms will, of course, be opposed by secular critics, and their criticisms have to be addressed if inquiry is to be a serious undertaking. In Chapter Three I sketched how a critical Pascalian inquirer might respond to the secularism of his own time, as well as responses he could be imagined giving to the secular anthropology of later ages, as it is expressed by Voltaire or Nietzsche or Thomas Nagel. The general principles governing reasonable inquiry were outlined earlier in the present chapter in the section called "Balanced Minds."

From Pascal's point of view, the difficulty presented by secular adversaries does not lie in the power of their arguments but in the depth of their misconceptions about Christianity. "Let [Christianity's critics] at least learn what religion they are fighting against before they start fighting," he says, and then launches into a study of some of their common misapprehensions:

- The critics reproach the Faith for the obscurity of its notion of God. But the Faith teaches that God's nature is a mystery.
- Critics reproach the Church because of the difficulty they experience in coming to a ready understanding of Scripture or the Creeds. But why is that a reproach, when the Church itself teaches the necessity of meditating on these matters day and night, and ascribes to them a depth that passes human understanding?[154]

Since it is an empirical question, whether or not Pascalian inquiry leads to conversion, critics cannot deny the possibility that it does. Moreover, the conversion to which it leads is cognitive as well as transformative, and transformative *because* it is cognitive. Thinking from the inside out brings the inquirer into contact with arguments against Christianity as well as with evidence for its truth. The encounter with criticism transforms the inquirer by giving him a new understanding of God and himself:

The God of Christians is not merely a God who is author of the geometric truths and the order of the elements. That is what the pagans and

Epicureans think. He is not only a God who exerts his providence on the lives and possessions of men, in order to assure those who worship him a happy span of years. That's how the Jews think of God. But the God of Abraham and Isaac, the God of Jacob and of Christians is a God of love and consolation. He fills the soul and heart of those whom he possesses. He is a God who makes them inwardly sense their misery and his infinite mercy, who joins himself to the depth of their soul, filling it with humility, joy, confidence, love, making them incapable of striving for anything but him.[155]

An inquirer who begins with a concupiscent examination of the possibility of life∞ may progress to a state where he is filled, at least episodically, with humility, joy, confidence, and love. As long as grace is a providential arrangement of natural events rather than a supernatural suspension of them, an inquirer can arrive at belief by means that are both natural and philosophically transparent on the one hand, and God's gracious provision on the other. Inspiration and reason are reconciled in inquiry.

> The Christian religion, the only one with reason on its side, does not admit as its children those who believe without inspiration. Not that it excludes reason and custom. On the contrary! One must open one's mind to proofs, and steep oneself in them (s'y confirmer) by custom, but one must also prepare oneself for inspiration through acts of humility. They alone can accomplish the true and salutary effect, lest the cross of Christ be rendered inessential.[156]

## The Primacy of Dialectic

A critic may say that in order to make the inquirer's path a cognitive one Pascal divorces cognitivity from validity and soundness. The inquirer finishes up with whatever set of beliefs he finds persuasive, regardless of whether they are sound. Such a procedure cannot count as philosophical because no objective standards of evaluation are applied to the arguments he encounters.

The easiest way to refute this criticism is to consider the worst case it warns against. Suppose, then, that some or all of the arguments the now believing inquirer accepts are unsound. That would only be a decisive criticism, if his inquiry were assumed to be at an end. But reasonable inquiry never comes to an end. There will always be new criticisms and new episodes of doubt. Recurring dialectical engagement with our current beliefs is the inseparable counterpart of the episodic nature of our virtues.

Luckily, dialectic is also one of life's chief delights, at least according to Pascal. Battle pleases us more than victory, he observes (though in my experience that cast of mind is less universal than Pascal thinks). However, he connects it with the almost universal fondness for games:

> [as with games] so also in the search for truth. In disputes we love to witness the battle of opinions, but are not at all keen on contemplating the truth we discover. Truth is known in a pleasurable way only when it is born of argument."

It would be fortunate if believers liked arguing as well as Pascal thinks they do, because they are certain always to be engaged in it. There are several reasons for this. One is the hiddenness of God:

> That is what Scripture is pointing out in the many places where it says that those who search for God find him. Scripture is not speaking of a light like the noonday sun. We don't say that those who look for daylight at noon, or water in the sea, will find some. Thus the evidence for God in nature cannot be so clear. Scripture also tells us elsewhere, "truly you are the hidden God.[157]

Inquiry is also made necessary by the episodic character of Christian virtue. It is true that these episodes become habitual, and hence real virtues, in inquirers who belong to the elect. But habits only guide our thoughts and actions most of the time. Living faith, which is the most important of the theological virtues in this context, can be challenged, and, when it is challenged, inquirers may be plunged back into doubt. The search on which they are embarked cannot end before death. According to Pascal, this should not amaze us. The Christian religion teaches,

> that men are in the dark and estranged from God, that he has hidden himself from their knowledge ... that God has established certain sensible marks in the Church that will cause him to be recognized by those who are sincerely searching for him, but that he has disguised them nevertheless in

such a way that he will only be perceived by those are searching for him with all their hearts.[158]

The inquirer's search will be interminable, even if he is searching with all his heart. "The heart *feels* God," Pascal says (my emphasis), "but reason doesn't. That's what faith is: God felt by the heart, not by reason."[159] An inquirer is a man of reason who will therefore never be entirely satisfied and will have no choice but to continue to inquire. He is a finite inquirer seeking to understand an infinite God. So inquiry is an endless task.

Pascal tells his inquirer never to despair, even though his search "never amounts to anything."[160] There are several reasons why even consistent failure to produce lasting conviction ought not to make him despair. First, he knew the object of his search would be hidden. Second, he knew it was infinite. Third, search is itself fulfilling. Most important of all, inquirers do, at times, discover God, though only intermittently, and in a glass darkly.

At the end of IR, in summoning the inquirer to his task, Pascal foretold not merely its rigours, but also what would be its rewards: "I tell you," Pascal wrote,

> you will profit in this life and with every step you take on this path you will see such certainty of gain, and so much nothingness in what you put at risk, that you will know at last that you wagered for something certain and infinite, which cost you nothing.[161]

When Pascal says the inquirer knows something "at last," he doesn't mean at the end, for the inquiry he is engaged in has no end. By "at last" Pascal means after many dialectical battles. What the inquirer learns at last by experience is that the faith he has set out to find is indeed supported by many reasons worthy of belief, even though it is not nailed down by irrefragable demonstrations. His sense of assurance grows slowly, empirically, as might his confidence in any empirical theory. His firm belief in the defensibility of his faith is forged in the act of defending it. That is encouragement enough to keep him on the only road he thinks will lead to life$^\infty$. It remains a road of inquiry – cautious, humble inquiry – because there is no prospect of decisive rational proof, "lest the cross of Christ should be made of none effect" – that is, lest grace should be thought unnecessary.[162]

## The Garber Questions Revisited

It is now time to revisit the questions of Daniel Garber with which this chapter began. He asked in the first place whether inquiry might not be a form of self-deception. Next he raised the question whether inquiry's noncognitive (ritual-based) point of departure does not in some way cast doubt upon any conclusions that might be reached within the inquiry itself. Lastly, he asked about the contingency of the process that makes our inquirer a Christian, when another inquirer, meeting a different wager argument, might have ended up as a Jew or a Muslim. If inquiry can be understood as an ongoing dialogue with unbelief, in which the inquirer lays no claim to certainty, but only faith, these questions should look less formidable than they did at first.

First the question of self-deception. It is true that there is no guarantee that the inquirer is not deluding himself, but that is not peculiar to Christian beliefs. To recognize the danger of self-deception is merely to embrace fallibilism, which Pascal thinks a highly reasonable thing for any inquirer to do. A Pascalian inquirer is, of all people, the least likely to be self-deceived precisely because he is so aware of human proneness to deception. He has every reason to avoid complacency. Engaged in a search of infinite promise, but one that can never be concluded, it is in an inquirer's interest to view every challenge with the utmost seriousness, whether it arises from considerations intrinsic to his search or from an external criticism posed by an unbeliever.

What must be said, then, about the noncognitive religious rituals with which inquiry begins and which the inquirer continues to practise? Could they give rise to some form of brainwashing? The worst outcome they could produce would be to convince the inquirer of some untenable position, while making him psychologically incapable of seeing his error. The second worst would be for his noncognitive beginnings to lead him to believe a tenable position but not equip him to defend it.

True, Pascal can answer, either thing could happen. But neither need happen. Our question has been whether an inquirer who decides to treat the Catholic faith as true can end up with views that are dialectically defensible. And we have found no reason to think that he could not, though other outcomes are also possible.

It also seems undeniable that there may be Jewish or Muslim inquirers in the world, and nothing rules out the possibility that our own inquirer could at some point go through a Muslim or Jewish phase.

If Pascal is right, however, there is preponderant evidence in favour of Christianity. Both Judaism and Islam, for example, hold empirically false views about Jesus Christ. And therefore any inquirer who received grace would meet persuasive Christian arguments at an opportune time.

Pascal's position is that the strength of these arguments is only apparent to those who have made a decision to believe. While Garber is right to point out that philosophers strain at such things, still, if what I have argued in this chapter is correct, the circularity in Pascal's argument is not a vicious one. It does not mean that no inquirer can be a philosopher. A Pascalian convert is not someone who gives up philosophy for religion. It is someone who finds the natural place for philosophical inquiry within the Catholic Church's continuing dialogue with the world.

In so responding to Garber I am not moving far off the position he himself finally adopts in answer to his own questions. After the wager, he says,

> I have a feeling of conviction based on evidence, and that is a kind of certainty to which I am entitled, in a sense ... I should continue to examine my reasons for belief, and continue to hunt for good reasons.[163]

This much is exactly what I take Pascal to be saying. However, when the parts I omitted from the passage just quoted are restored to it, Garber's position no longer, in my opinion, corresponds exactly to what Pascal means. What I have left out Garber summarizes a little later on the same page. He takes Pascal's view to be that the wagerer:

> should hesitate to give full trust to [his belief in God] in practical situations, and hedge [his] bets. [His] belief may be grounded on a cognitive illusion, and [he] should be cautious.

Garber's interpretation differs from mine in treating the episodes of doubt through which almost all believers pass as constitutive of the believing mind. As I understand Pascal, doubt is the privation of religious belief, not a part of it. To act as we would in a state of belief is always the right thing to do, because it is what Christian action consists in. Sometimes, however, episodic doubts may reinvigorate our pre-religious fears, including the fear that we are victims of a cognitive illusion, and so limit our ability to act as we should.

Another way to look at the difference between our interpretations is to consider the label "mitigated scepticism," which Garber attaches, if not to Pascal's own philosophy, at least to the attitude he sees Pascal recommending to the wagerer.[164] The tournament of champions shows us that Pascal could never accept such a label. He recognizes no form of scepticism except the Pyrrhonian, which itself is destroyed in its fight to the death with dogmatism. The wager argument is part of post-tournament inquiry, which only begins when scepticism and dogmatism have been left behind. In my view, Pascalian inquiry is better understood as a thoughtful, cautious, and interminable ascent out of the valley of the shadow of doubt.[165]

* * *

I have tried to show how Pascal can answer the most daunting technical objections that can be raised to the idea of his being a philosopher. But if these objections have now been laid to rest, it may only pave the way to another disquieting question: is Pascal perhaps *just barely a philosopher*? Maybe the powerful writing that enchants us derives from his literary gifts alone or from style mixed with depth of religious insight. Perhaps what I am calling his philosophy is only the exiguous fruit of an almost barren methodology. In the final chapter I shall address the question of Pascal's philosophical greatness.

# 6 Measuring Pascal

## Fragments

The route to this point has been strewn with textual, historical, theological and philosophical obstacles, which had to be sidestepped or surmounted. Therefore, it has been circuitous and slow. A more direct approach to Pascal's philosophy would have been to itemize his noteworthy contributions to important philosophical subdisciplines, such as epistemology, metaphysics, or ethics and base an assessment of his philosophy on them. More direct certainly, but it has been taken by others, and I am not satisfied it does justice to Pascal.

Pascal's philosophical contributions, though often memorable, are fragmentary. A recent doctoral thesis on Pascal's theory of knowledge is appropriately subtitled *Fragments of an Epistemology*. The Pascal scholar Vincent Carraud asserts that Pascal's philosophy, though a powerful one, is made up of "heterogeneous and incoherent" metaphysical and theological fragments. A.W.S. Baird's *Studies in Pascal's Ethics* acknowledges, both at its outset and in its conclusion, that Pascal adopts "different moral stances" and makes "seemingly inconsistent judgements," which Baird undertook to explain but never promised to reconcile.[1] These studies have their merits, but they cannot show that any coherent philosophy underlies the fragmentary contributions to which they point.

When viewed against a background of systematic philosophy, Pascal illuminates dark places with isolated flashes of light. Admirers give him credit for the light, but detractors accuse him of magnifying the darkness. The first attitude makes Pascal a minor philosopher; the second makes him no philosopher at all. However, we don't need to be drawn into that debate in the first place. Instead we can stop judging him by the standard of systematic philosophy and assess him on his own terms. Then, of course, we have to decide what the terms are on which an appropriate judgment can be founded. This is the question I will attempt to answer in the present chapter. The materials have already been gathered in earlier chapters. Now is the time to assemble them.

Pascal rejected philosophy as he found it. Neither scholasticism nor the modern insurgents who challenged it in the name of the new science seemed to him to be on the right track. Instead their quarrels belonged to the interminable annals of philosophical warfare, whose mutually destructive instability Pascal depicted so memorably in his "Conversation with M. de Saci." There he described philosophy as a tournament of champions in which scepticism and dogmatism destroy one another. That tournament is the showpiece of his reflections on *philosophical failure*, but in the *Pensées* and other writings he reflects further on failure, anchoring it ultimately in that *ur*-crisis of human history theologians call the Fall.

The connection Pascal establishes between failure and Fall constitutes the most comprehensive account of philosophical failure ever given. The whole package – tournament, failure, and Fall – provides a sober Pascalian counterpoint to the optimism of the early modern era.

Many of Pascal's contemporaries believed, as many still believe today, that lasting happiness can be achieved by applying the empirical and mathematical methods of the new science to life, or to politics, or both. Pascal didn't think so. How could science give us happiness or justice, he asked, when it cannot even produce knowledge?

We are finite creatures of a middle realm, unable to grasp the extremes. The middle-sized objects that surround us, and the middle-sized subjects who we are, emerge mysteriously out of the infinitesimal, and are mysteriously swallowed again in the infinite. All things, therefore, are mysterious to us, and we are riddles to ourselves.

Politics is even more likely to disappoint us. Offices cannot be distributed on merit, first, because merit cannot be objectively evaluated as justice demands, and, second, because even the most conscientious of our rulers are imperceptibly warped by their own concupiscence.

Pascal's attack on philosophy was as freewheeling as it was fragmentary. The angles of attack were as clever as they were unconventional. Philosophers, however, have been more willing to call them dazzling than illuminating. Which would have come as no surprise to Pascal. His own analysis of philosophical failure predicts that even the best arguments for unpopular conclusions will be ill received.

Certainly his attack on philosophy has been ill received. It leads many philosophers to treat Pascal as a religiously motivated moralist, who, having rejected their discipline in its entirety, can be safely ignored. Here are a few illustrations.

William Kelly Wright's *History of Modern Philosophy*, in its single mention of Pascal, describes him as one who "seeks refuge in mysticism" from the scepticism to which Descartes's philosophy seems to lead. The 10 erudite pages on Pascal in Émile Bréhier's 500-page history of modern philosophy begin with the assertion, "Pascal was no philosopher." G.N. Clarke's history of the seventeenth century refers to Pascal as a mathematician, a religious thinker and a stylist but is silent about him in the chapter devoted to philosophy.

Among more recent histories of modern philosophy, Peter Sedgwick's makes no mention of Pascal, while Roger Scruton's, in its only reference to him, has him advocating "mesmerizing ourselves into a state of unfounded belief." Jean-Michel Besnier's recent history is exceptional in the thorough and insightful treatment it accords Pascal.[2]

The simplest way for philosophers to undervalue Pascal is to ignore his work. Their habit of ignoring him leads to the strange result that such philosophical studies of his work as exist are often authored by members of other disciplines. For example, Richard Scholar, author of one of the most insightful studies of the Conversation with Saci (2003), is a professor of French literature. So are the editor and eight of the fourteen contributors to Cambridge University Press's excellent *Companion to Pascal*.[3] It is fortunate that Nicholas Hammond, the collection's editor, was able to overcome the initial reluctance of the Press to include a volume on Pascal in a series reserved for "major philosophers."[4] Yet even this volume to some extent reflects the common conception of him as a contributor of fragments. It emphasizes the "astonishingly wide range of disciplines" to which he contributed, while promising "to offer a balanced view of his work."[5] These are, of course, laudable goals, and they are achieved in Hammond's collection, but one wonders whether Cambridge (or any other major press) would commission a volume devoted to Pascal's philosophy alone. Let us see why they should.

The tournament of champions leaves the edifice of traditional philosophy in ruins. As the dust of battle settles, however, a narrow pathway is disclosed along which it is still possible to advance by reasoned investigation. I have been calling this kind of investigation *inquiry*. But how far and in what direction does inquiry lead?

Part of Pascalian inquiry consists in dialectic, and part of dialectic involves playing the role of critic to one's critics. Pascalian inquiry is a versatile dialectical weapon, well equipped for critical dialogue in different registers. It has sufficient resources to take the measure of predecessors like Epictetus or Montaigne, or of successors like Voltaire or Nietzsche, or even to assess the ersatz religion of therapy, which attempts to console modern man for his unachievable aspirations. Pascalian rejoinders can be found to an impressive variety of philosophical positions, and critical versatility is thus the first of Pascal's philosophical perfections.

## Scepticism

Pascal's success as a dialectician tempts some of his readers to classify him as a kind of sceptic. Daniel Garber attributes a "mitigated scepticism" to Pascal, or at least believes that an attitude of mitigated scepticism is what Pascal wants the wagerer to adopt.[6] Richard Popkin seemed to classify Pascal as a Christian Pyrrhonist.[7] However, notwithstanding the strong influence of scepticism in Pascal's thought, he would not have applied either label to himself. Mitigated sceptics are reducible to Pyrrhonian ones in Pascal's view, and Pyrrhonian scepticism proves incoherent in the tournament of champions. We must think of Pascal as a versatile critic, but not a sceptic. He cannot be a sceptic, because he embraces dogma.

## Dogma

It may seem paradoxical to attribute dogma to the author of the tournament of champions, but there is in fact a large dogmatic component to Pascal's thought, though it is often overlooked, because Pascal never offers any philosophical justification for it. If he did, he would be a dogmatist. But Pascal sees no need to defend the dogmas he accepts.

First, he would not defend the ones he called "reasons of the heart." They are matters of which we are intuitively or instinctively assured without argument, and which are so fundamental to our understanding that any argument in their favour would be likely to presuppose them.

Pascal's dogmas also include the teachings of the Roman Catholic Church, which any Catholic, and therefore any Catholic philosopher, take for granted. These teachings Pascal treats like a fortress, which only needs defending where it is under attack. Foundational dogmas are assumed to be revealed, and what tradition has built upon them may also be taken for granted, except where it is the subject of ongoing internal debate within the Church. The debate about grace was such an exception in the time of Pascal. Yet both parties to the debate, Jansenist and Jesuit, participated as Catholics. Pascal reflected the attitude of both sides in saying that tradition is the source of truth, and the Pope its guardian.[8]

Treating the Catholic tradition as a fortress also allowed Pascal convenient access to Catholic philosophy without making him into a systematic or dogmatic philosopher in his own right. Although Saint Augustine is his philosopher of choice, he draws on others, including, to a surprising degree, Descartes. Catholic orthodoxy, as Pascal understands it, forms the horizon of his dazzling, fragmentary thoughts and, as one student of his theology observes, "supplies their coherence." It is because of his underlying Catholicism, the same author continues,

> that Pascal never feared to stretch his ideas to their limits, for in so doing he felt neither contradiction nor anguish but only the omnipresence of a central and substantial truth.[9]

Pascal used his talents as Pope Leo X had summoned philosophers to do a century before. In his struggle with the doctrine of "double truth," Leo X charged philosophers to "attempt with all their strength to make evident to their students the truth of the Christian Religion and to refute the quite refutable arguments to the contrary put forward by philosophers." Recent Catholic thought has renewed the appeal to philosophers to engage with the whole range of positions that are antagonistic to Catholic belief while drawing on the tradition for their ammunition.[10]

There is an advantage to Pascal's quiet way of embracing Catholic doctrine. If you put forward no argument in defence of your core beliefs, you offer your adversary nothing to refute. But such a tactic could also be expected to exact a heavy price. Can beliefs Pascal acquires without philosophical expenditure give him buying power in an open market? In other words, can Pascal hope for anything better than a stalemate between himself and an articulate unbeliever?

## Obstacles Briefly Revisited

Some think Pascal has no use for arguments against unbelievers, because he has an ace up his sleeve in the form of "efficacious grace."

As Jansenists understood it, grace of this kind transcends reason, and receiving it logically entails conversion. Once efficacious grace enters the picture, conversion is assured, and reasons anyone might have for converting are superfluous. To the extent that conversion is under-determined by arguments and overdetermined by grace, these critics think, Pascal is no philosopher.

To be short on argument and long on grace is certainly not what we expect of a philosopher. But in addition to that, the kind of evidence Pascal offers in favour of belief is itself controversial. Pascal says the pathway to faith passes through Old Testament prophecies which, when interpreted in the symbolic way sanctioned by a long Christian tradition, can be regarded as fulfilled in the life of Christ. Yet he admits that fulfilled prophecies fall short of being demonstrative and will only seem persuasive *after* the faith has already been embraced. Not surprisingly, philosophers wonder whether offering them as evidence is not viciously circular.

Furthermore, it is doubted, even by many Christians, that prophecies can stand as evidence in the way Pascal assumes, let alone stand as proof. Utterances traditionally classified as prophecies may not have been intended to *foretell* anything, one line of biblical criticism contends, and certainly they did not refer to specific details of the life of Christ. Therefore, these texts cannot function in the way Pascal wants them to.

Lack of conclusive arguments in favour of Christianity, the over-whelming character of grace, and the possible misunderstanding of prophecy can look like significant obstacles to reading Pascal as a phi-losopher. They make it easier to see him as a religious moralist who may mock and criticize philosophy when it suits him, but who, when it comes to conversion, simply invokes grace as a miraculous deus ex machina yielding belief.

## Obstacles Overcome

That is the wrong way to look at Pascal, however, as I attempted to show in Chapter Five. Grace is a gift to the elect, but it is given with infinite tact, folded into the events of their lives in such a way that they regularly encounter reasons for belief at moments when they are able to receive them. It is the reasons, not the grace, which account for belief. And these reasons become the material for the ongoing inquiry in which Catholic philosophy, and reflective Christian life, consist.

Though miracles or prophecy can be occasions of belief, they can just as well be occasions for examination, doubt, and even loss of belief.

Faith can be lost as well as won. Pascal treats it as episodic. The only necessary difference between the elect and what I called "temporary Christians" is that the elect finish their lives as believers. A member of the elect, for Pascal, is like an exceptionally lucky person who keeps finding enough money to meet his needs. The difference is that in the religious cases of interest to Pascal, they find reasons, rather than money, and they arise from provident grace rather than luck.

Faith, then, is a recurrent commitment to inquiry, and grace is the arrangement of events such that the commitment to inquiry will define a person's life. So understood, faith and grace are not obstacles to reason, but vehicles for reason's expression in the form of philosophical inquiry. It is also reason's supreme expression, because grace enables philosophical inquiry to involve recurrent encounters with the truth.

In the end, Pascalian inquiry is very simple. An inquirer finds prophecy believable and commits himself to a life of faith. If there is any circle here, it is at least not a vicious one.

### Pascalian Apodeixis

Pascal thinks he can dispose his reader towards becoming a committed inquirer, which is to say, towards conversion. He can do more than merely reach a stalemate with unbelievers; he can change their minds. The wager argument is Pascal's main instrument for that task.

In fact, Pascal's chief goal in the *Pensées* is to take the battle to those outside the Christian fortress and bring them back not as captives but as converts. There needs to be, therefore, what I shall call an *apodictic* element to Pascalian inquiry. Just as inquiry puts dialectic in place of scepticism, so it puts what I am calling *apodeixis* in place of philosophical dogmatism.

What, then, does Pascalian apodeixis amount to? To understand its place in inquiry we must acknowledge, as Pascal did, the emotional dimension of both belief and unbelief.

Whatever we believe about substantive questions, we *hope*, or sometimes *fear*, that we are right; we are *afraid* we could be mistaken; and there is some way we *wish* the world to be.

Pascal acknowledges that the rational arguments by which unbelievers defend their unbelief may be just as good as the ones believers have for faith. Believers and unbelievers may also be equally passionate about their differing beliefs. Nevertheless, Pascal thinks believers have a more stable emotional foundation for their beliefs than unbelievers have. Unbelievers are emotionally vulnerable, because they have immutable longings that can only be satisfied by belief.

The intellectual standoff between believer and unbeliever therefore need not result in stalemate. When emotions are also taken into consideration, the position of believers can be shown to be objectively more advantageous than that of unbelievers. Showing the advantages of belief to an unbeliever can make an effective move against his unbelief, and Pascal thinks it is also a philosophical move. That is the direction in which the narrow path of post-tournament apodeixis leads.

For Pascal, the unbeliever is in conflict with his own hopes and desires. He is like someone betting everything on a result that is not only uncertain but also the one least in his interest, if it comes to pass. Betting on a different outcome, Pascal will argue, will have better consequences in the here and now, even if the anticipated result does not come to pass, and infinitely better consequences if it does.

Betting, in this context, is a metaphor for what, in religious language, is called conversion. In a brief fragment concerning order, Pascal announced his intention to make emotion the focus of an argument for conversion. He then wove together the ideas of betting, emotion, and conversion in the complex fragment known as the wager.

Post-tournament inquiry, for Pascal, thus consists in dialectical defence of the Christian fortress on the one hand, and, on the other hand, in apodictic struggle with unbelief. Except for his work in mathematics, and in what we now call the natural sciences, his fragmentary contributions to philosophy's subfields arise in the course of inquiry, not as supplements to it. As I read Pascal's philosophy, then, it is pure inquiry.

## Embedding Pascal

If this is Pascal's philosophy, it is certainly a subtle one. In some quarters that is a strike against it. Compared to the systematic thought of a Descartes or a Leibniz, this philosophy also looks thin. Another strike against it. Nothing can be done about its subtlety. But those who have experienced the power of Pascal's philosophical writing and fallen under its spell, sometimes think they can fatten it up a little, and so justify their fascination, by embedding him in a plump, healthy-looking philosophical school.

The urge to do so is easy to understand. It is almost commendable. In Pascal they encounter a writer whose philosophical authority mysteriously exceeds the few chaotic pages in which it is expressed. It is natural, then, to look for its source in some adequate and commensurable cause. Also, as with other admired philosophers, one envies their power of expression and hopes through study to learn to command it in one's own practice of philosophy. Embedding Pascalian inquiry in some respectable philosophical school looks like an answer to both demands. If Pascal is expressing the views of such a school, *that* may be the source of his philosophical authority. And, if it is the source, then, by thinking with the school in question, we too might tap into its power.

In the postwar period, when existentialism was in vogue, so was an existentialist Pascal.[11] His stylish thoughts on such themes as human wretchedness, ennui, anxiety, and diversion seemed to fit well with a brand of philosophy whose nature was difficult to nail down, and so could easily take on board another outsider like Pascal.

On the other hand, Pascal is certainly not among the philosophers who, in Sartre's famous definition, believe that existence precedes essence. For Pascal, essence is the central concern of our existence. We live our lives in tension between the concupiscent essence we were born with and the innocent prelapsarian essence that beckons from an infinite distance, to which we feel an impotent, yet inextinguishable, desire to return.

Existentialism's impatience with systematic thought also sits precariously with Pascal's acceptance of Christian thinking in general and Augustinian thought in particular. And, finally, Pascal's apodictic philosophy appeals to nothing like the subjective leap of faith that is encouraged by some Christian existentialists. Instead it is rooted in the objective and almost plebeian self-interest that attracts us to a good bet. To classify Pascal as an existentialist is, then, to distort or overlook some of the most important aspects of his thought.

## The Will to Believe

Others find a home for Pascal in the big tent of pragmatism.[12] Jeff Jordan not only thinks there is clear affinity between Pascal's apodictic thought and Jamesian pragmatism, but he argues that Pascal needs James's help to accomplish what he sets out to do in the wager fragment.

According to Jordan, Pascal's wager only works if it is formulated the way William James has it in his famous essay, "The Will to Believe."[13]

It is ironic that that essay, which has fascinated so many readers since it first appeared in print, was a paradigm case of philosophical failure when given as a talk. James complained of the "remote and listless audience" who came out to hear him at the Yale Philosophy Club in 1896, and criticized his host for uttering "no syllable of comment on the words to which his ears had been exposed."[14] Despite James's popular style, the idea of *willing to believe* required more effort to understand than he had anticipated.

And yet the idea is not so much difficult as shocking. The thesis, briefly stated, is that "our passional nature not only lawfully may, but must, decide an option between propositions, whenever it is a genuine option that cannot by its nature be decided on intellectual grounds."[15] Roughly paraphrased, James is saying that, under certain conditions, you not only *may* believe what you want, you *must* do so.

That is radical stuff! No wonder his live audience was not instantly persuaded. Any critical listener would want to think carefully about the conditions that bestow such unparalleled licence.

What James meant in that context by an "option" was any proposition we are asked to believe but for which there is no available proof. Not all such propositions, of course, would be of interest to philosophers. James is only concerned with options he calls "genuine," which must meet three further conditions in addition to their want of demonstration.

First, genuine options are "momentous" ones. A momentous option is a proposition that, if believed, is existentially significant. The proposition that you must get a haircut, for example, doesn't count as momentous, unless you are Samson.

In the second place, a genuine option must be "forced." It is the kind of option that permits only one alternative course, not the kind you can weasel out of by thinking up ingenious ways of avoiding the issue. Choosing life rather than death is a forced option. Choosing one career rather than another is not. You could always drift.

Finally, genuine options are also "living options," by which James means propositions we can picture ourselves embracing. For example, many people today cannot even imagine how a celibate life could be a good choice. Celibacy, for them, is not a living option. On the other hand, many of those same people do think of moderate asceticism as a living option, provided it will help to reduce what they like to call their "ecological footprint." This option is also forced. There are but two ways to go. You must either participate in the prescribed asceticism or not. Those who don't participate include not only those who reject the relevant claims of ecology but also those who merely have sufficient doubts about it not to make it their guide.

James writes as if the momentousness of an option were never controversial, but the example of eco-asceticism shows otherwise. Some people think it self-evidently momentous, while for many it fails to be a living option not because it looks difficult but because it looks insignificant.

Fortunately, in the matter with which James is chiefly concerned – namely religious belief – liveliness and momentousness can safely be taken for granted. Religion has almost always and everywhere been considered to be of the first importance. It is true that professional secularists like to pretend that religion, for them, is an inconsiderable thing, but there is usually a telltale swagger in their profession that gives the game away.

In addition to being living and momentous, religion is also a *forced* option. You must either choose it or not. Any benefit available to religious people is conditional upon belief. Therefore agnostics miss out on it just as surely as militant atheists do.

In "The Will to Believe" James stipulates that he is talking about religion in general, not Christianity, making it sound as if this stipulation were just a way of not getting sidetracked with details. "Religions differ so much in their accidents," he says, "that in discussing the religious question we must make it very generic and broad."

This, however, is a little disingenuous. Believers do not see any difference between their religion and "the religious question." And if conciseness were all we wanted, it could be achieved by discussing some particular religion as one token of the religious type, just as a particular apple may stand for apples in general.

James's unstated reason for preferring a general discussion is that his own religion is general. It is a religion without accidents, so to speak. His religion is religion as such. Certainly it is not Christian. To one of his Christian correspondents James wrote, "I believe myself to be (probably) permanently incapable of believing the Christian system of vicarious salvation." And in the essay, "Is Life Worth Living," he writes "A man's religious faith ... means for me essentially his faith in the existence of an unseen order of some kind in which the riddle of the natural order may be found explained."[16] I point out this tendency to generic religion not to be critical of James but to clarify his position.

Religion, then, whether of James's abstract kind or attached to a particular creed, confronts us with a choice in which the stakes are high and where both the religious and the nonreligious life are living options for most people. Like Pascal, however, James thinks we will never have decisive "intellectual grounds" for choosing one way or the other. His famous and influential claim (quoted earlier in full) can now be simplified as follows in the light of the preceding discussion:

> Not only "may" we decide in favour of religious belief when it is proposed to us. We "must" do so. And "our passional nature" not only urges us to choose in favour of belief, it provides an intellectually valid warrant for doing so.

When religion is at issue, in other words, we may (indeed, we *must*) believe what we *want* to believe. We must believe what we *hope* is true, or disbelieve what we *fear* may be true. Our "passional nature," by which James means our emotional nature, justifies us in forming our beliefs this way.

Passions don't normally justify us in believing what we want. And it is difficult to see how they can ever do so, even when we restrict the claim to genuine religious options for which conclusive evidence is unavailable. James knows that anyone of a scientific or philosophical disposition is going to be sceptical, and even indignant, regarding this supposed entitlement. What he calls "scientific absolutists" will say we must only believe things for which there is conclusive evidence. He quotes W.K. Clifford, a nineteenth-century standard-bearer for scientific absolutism, to the effect that it is "wrong always, everywhere and for everyone, to believe anything upon insufficient evidence." All religious believers, as far as Clifford is concerned, are morally corrupt.

Clifford is not altogether wrong, according to James; he is simply too absolute. His maxim applies to most, but not all, of life's intellectual quandaries. His critique of religious belief may apply to some believers, but not to all. Clifford issues a blanket condemnation, but his blanket is too short and narrow to cover everything and everyone.

Most decisions about what to believe fall short of being momentous. It does not much matter whether you think the coming winter will be a cold one or not. So why decide? Follow Clifford instead and suspend belief.

Also, few decisions are forced, in James's sense of requiring us to choose between two options. You are not to blame if you have not yet made up your mind as to string theory's chances of unifying physics. In matters unforced, as in matters trivial, Clifford's maxim is an excellent one. The wise thing is to be informed, not opinionated. Wisdom desires to preserve itself from error, and therefore does not draw conclusions about controversial things, when no penalty is attached to remaining neutral.

But things look different when religion lays before us living options that are both momentous and forced. In these cases we discover that the desire to preserve ourselves from error, though very good in itself, takes second place to another legitimate desire, of which religious options make us vividly aware. Religions put before us a game-changing choice. They declare the existence of a reality that is perfect and eternal, transcending our ordinary experience, in which a kind of mystical participation is possible *to those who believe*. There is, in other words, according to religion, something intrinsically and intensely desirable to which faith alone gives access.

If this putative reality is as religion describes it, then those who categorically reject it miss out. But because religion is a forced option, you also miss out if you merely follow Clifford's maxim and withhold belief. To follow Clifford in religious questions is, therefore, James concludes, a grave error. Diffidence towards religion's claims is not just questionable; it is absurd. "[W]here faith in a fact can help create the fact," James says, "that would be an insane logic which should say that faith running ahead of scientific evidence is the 'lowest kind of immorality' into which a thinking being can fall. Yet such is the logic by which our scientific absolutists pretend to regulate our lives."

In religious cases, then, according to James, it is not merely our privilege but our intellectual duty to embrace a faith that so intensely engages our passions. In his own words, he is making "a defence of our right to adopt a believing attitude in religious matters, in spite of the fact that our merely logical intellect may not have been coerced."

## James vs. Pascal

The resemblance between James's argument and Pascal's is obvious. James openly acknowledges it. He considers Pascal's version an important, though crude, anticipation of his own. It is crude because, as James puts it, Pascal "tries to force us into Christianity by reasoning as if our concern with truth resembled our concern with the stakes in a game of chance." Both the wager argument's Christian content and the wager metaphor itself blur the argument's logic as far as James is concerned.

Pascal's recommendation of "masses and holy water" must have been only "a last desperate snatch at a weapon," James declares – one that, in any case, would be useless today to "Turks" and "Protestants" and, indeed, to anyone in whom there was not already a "pre-existing tendency to believe" in such things. And James is confident his reader will "feel that when religious faith expresses itself thus, in the language of the gaming-table, it is put to its last trumps."

James's version of the argument is exactly what you get once Pascal's version is liberated from both its alleged defects. James congratulates himself for having successfully detached the religious and logical kernel of Pascal's argument from its Christian and aleatory husk.

### Embedding Pascal in Jamesian Pragmatism

No one has written more about the wager argument than Jeff Jordan, and he finds in James a guide to understanding its logic. He streamlines James's critique, however. Jordan thinks the wagering metaphor can remain as the organizing principle, provided Pascal's argument is stripped of its Roman Catholic focus and made, like James's version, a defence of generic theism. Jordan even claims that generic theism was what Pascal intended, though, as I pointed out in Chapter Four, such a construal of the argument cannot withstand comparison with the text. I also pointed out in Chapter Four that purging the argument of its Catholicism serves no purpose, since, *pace* Jordan, it is not needed to answer the perennial, but overrated, "many gods" objection.

However, Jordan's last and most philosophical reason for embedding Pascal in Jamesian pragmatism is of greater interest. He advocates this move out of the charitable wish to extend Pascal's philosophical reach. It is the same generous intention that prompts other readers of Pascal to embed his thought in existentialism and that causes many more simply to marvel at the strange disparity between the power they sense in Pascalian inquiry and the narrow limits within which what I have called Pascalian apodeixis seems to be confined. How can a philosopher so rich in insight be so poor in applications?

Embedding Pascal in Jamesian pragmatism is Jordan's way of addressing that disparity. "Unlike the wager," Jordan writes,

the focus of James's argument extends far beyond the issue of the rationality of theistic belief to include various philosophical issues (for instance,
whether to embrace determinism or indeterminism), and even matters of
practical life.[17]

The wager argument is the key to Pascalian apodeixis, and Jordan
thinks he can strengthen and extend it by integrating it into Jamesian
pragmatism. Can he?

Jordan's intention is generous and charitable, but like his other modi-
fications to the wager argument, it is also gratuitous. It is surprising
that Jordan, who knows Pascal's writings so well, can think Pascal
requires James's assistance to discuss the problem of determinism, or
that he can believe Pascal silent about matters of practical life. It never
occurs to Jordan that the thin and ineffectual Pascal, whom pragmatism
is brought in to fortify, is partly his own creation. He cuts Pascal off
from his Catholicism and marvels that the geldling is unfruitful. But,
like most of us, Pascal performs better when he is left intact.

Just consider Jordan's examples of what pragmatism will enable
Pascal to discuss. The first problem, that of determinism and indeterminism, is a great theme in Pascal's writings on grace, and though he
defends a controversial view of grace, he does so as a Catholic and in
the conviction that it is orthodox. The radical determinism and limited
freedom he defends is, he claims, "the view of the disciples of Saint
Augustine, or rather of the Fathers and of the entire tradition and,
therefore, of the Church."[18] It's hard to see what Jamesian pragmatism
could add to this view except, perhaps, contradiction.

As to matters of practical life, Jordan's second example of a theme
pragmatism would open to Pascal, he is the author of reflections on
human grandeur and wretchedness, charity and cupidity, finesse and
folly, imagination and inconstancy, dignity and diversion, and on and
on. How could Pascal require pragmatism's help in these matters,
where he has been, for centuries, an acknowledged guide?

## Minor Philosopher?

To recognize the philosophical importance of Pascal's Catholicism is to
recognize a fact, but it does not do a great deal for his stature as a philosopher. The Enlightenment taught us to value philosophical originality and therefore not to give a philosopher much *philosophical* credit
for ideas he borrows from the tradition. It also taught us to expect

conflict between religion and philosophy, and therefore to view as non-philosophical whatever religious doctrines a philosopher accepts on faith. If we apply these standards to Pascal, he may get some credit for the dialectical part of his philosophy, a little for the narrowly focused apodictic part that expresses itself through the wager argument, and a little more for the fragmentary contributions to philosophy's subfields that arise in the course of inquiry. He might be as much as a minor Catholic philosopher.

On my account, Pascalian inquiry is nothing more than dialectic, apodeixis, and the fragmentary contributions that arise from them. They are all Pascal *has*. But is a minor Catholic philosopher all he *is*?

To read Pascal is to sense that he is more than that. Authority indwells his captivating prose. But I doubt that any convincing account of it can be given by embedding him in some respectable philosophical school. I shall therefore try a different approach. My account will take the form of a story within a story within a story.

## Gorgias

The frame story, the one enclosing the other two, is quickly told. In one of the longest and most challenging of Plato's dialogues, Socrates contends with three orators: Gorgias, after whom the dialogue is named, who was famous throughout the Greek-speaking world for his feats of oratory; Polus, who is a teacher of rhetoric and an admirer of Gorgias; and Callicles, of whom nothing is independently known but who is portrayed by Plato as a Nietzsche-like orator with an unmastered urge for self-assertion.

Socrates's three interlocutors remind me of three evils, which candidates for baptism are asked to foreswear: the world, the flesh, and the devil. Gorgias is a worldly man, though basically a decent one; Polus, like the flesh, is weak; and Callicles is diabolical, one of the nastiest people Socrates meets in all the dialogues.

The *Gorgias* opens with an investigation into what oratory is and what it is good for, but soon the question becomes whether studying oratory makes a person just. Gorgias says it does, but he can't prove it. Polus admits it doesn't but claims that it makes the orator powerful. Callicles, like Cole Porter, says it doesn't matter, because anything goes. Up is down today. Socrates's bad is Callicles's good.

Each interlocutor reveals his character under Socratic questioning. Gorgias's superficiality is exposed in a gentle manner that never puts his fundamental decency in doubt. Puny Polus is quickly shaken up and dumped. Callicles, who is neither decent like Gorgias nor weak like Polus, is a more formidable interlocutor. Socrates's big question for Callicles, as it eventually is for every interlocutor, is how to lead a life worth living. There are other questions, of course, but they are not pertinent to my tale.

On the main question Callicles and Socrates are far apart. For Callicles, the greatest good is limitless self-indulgence. He is disappointed to find he cannot prove his point as easily as he thought he could. But as Socratic questioning edges closer to putting even the coherency of his position in doubt, Callicles begins to answer morosely and uncooperatively, eventually lapsing into resentful silence. Which leads Socrates to tell him what will be the second of my stories.

## Myth or Logos?

Sulking Callicles is to listen to what Socrates promises will be a very fine "discourse" (*logos*), though Socrates suspects that Callicles will dismiss it as mere "myth" (*mythos*). Socrates, however, tells it "as the truth" (523a).

In the age of Cronos, there was a law which is still in effect that after death those who had lived pious and just lives should be sent to the Isles of the Blessed, while unjust and godless people should be sent to Tartarus, "the prison for punishment and justice" (523b).

When the rulers of both regions began complaining to Zeus that undeserving people were arriving at both destinations, Zeus said it was because of the custom, then in effect, of judging people on their last day of life, when their souls were still imprisoned like breath in their bodies. Living bodies did not always reflect the state of the soul. People of wealth and leisure sometimes presented attractive bodies to their judges, and so disguised their wizened and corrupted souls. And people with beautiful souls might limp to the Meadow of Judgment full of wounds and scars inflicted on their bodies in a lifetime of struggle against evil. So Zeus decreed that judgment from that time forth would be administered after death. Souls would be presented naked before their judges, whose own naked souls would be visible to those they judged (523a–524a).

## A Sacred Logos

Socrates says this is what he has heard, and he assures Callicles that he believes it to be a true *logos*. But what is a *logos* in this context? I have translated it neutrally as discourse, but now we need to know what type of discourse Socrates has in mind. It must have some philosophical traits in order to permit Socrates to *reason* about it, as he says he does, using the word *logizomai*, a close and obvious cognate of *logos* (524b).

On the other hand, discourses of this kind cannot be merely philosophical arguments. Socrates says he believed this one first, and only reasoned about it afterward.[19] And that is no way to treat a philosophical argument.

What kind of *logos* would it be prudent to believe first and reason about later? A religious one, you might think, and the Seventh Letter shows that to be Plato's view as well.[20] There we learn of a religious obligation to believe *sacred logoi* of precisely the kind Socrates discusses in the *Gorgias*, namely, those dealing with the immortality of the soul, the judgment it will receive, and the chastisements it will have to endure.

"Sacred discourses" (*hieroi logoi*) was a term applied by the ancient Greeks to the holiest of texts, some of which, for reasons of piety, were never even written down, but passed on orally only to the initiated.[21] The discourse Socrates recounts in the *Gorgias*, then, is best understood as a *hieros logos*, and Socrates's manner of introducing it to Callicles, as something to be believed first and reasoned about afterward, reflects its religious character.

One thing Socrates has learned by reasoning about this *logos* is that our own naked souls will be seen for what they are on Judgment Day and dealt with accordingly. Those who have been pious and just in their lives will be sent to the Isles of the Blessed. But two destinations are possible for the misshapen souls of the wicked. If they are redeemable, they will be sent to a sort of Purgatory, where they can, through punishment and penance, be restored to psychic health. But those who are incurably evil will be sent to Tartarus forever, where their excruciating torments will serve as an example to others of how not to live their lives.

E.R. Dodds, in his classic commentary on the *Gorgias*, detects what he calls "an obvious difficulty" at this point in Socrates's story. Who could benefit from the torments of the incurably wicked in Tartarus, he asks? Not the living, because they will not see what goes on in Tartarus until they arrive there. And for the dead, Dodds supposes, the lesson must come too late. He concludes that "the passage makes sense only on the assumption that these dead will one day return to earth: it presupposes the doctrine of rebirth, which Plato evidently already held when he wrote the *Gorgias* but did not choose to expound in this context."[22]

I am not persuaded. The dead are obviously not the only ones aware of what happens to the incurably wicked. Socrates is aware of it, and he is still alive. So will anyone else become aware of it who reasons as Socrates does about the sacred discourse. It is true that many people will not believe the discourse to be a sacred one, and therefore will not reason about it as Socrates does, and so will arrive at the underworld unprepared. However, as Socrates will soon say, he has made it his vocation to see that as many people as possible join him in reasoning about this *logos* as they should. It should first be believed, then interpreted.

But there is another important step to take with such a *logos*. As with any religious text, believing and interpreting are necessary but not sufficient. It must also be *applied* to the believer's life. And Socrates lists the five ways in which he applies this discourse in his own life (526d).

First, he takes steps to make his soul as healthy as possible, so that he will be able to present it in that state to his judge. Second, he lives modestly, rejecting the honours coveted by the many. Third, he practises the truth, and, fourth, he tries as much as possible to live as the best kind of man. His fifth and last measure is the most significant for the story I am telling. Socrates appeals to other people, and especially Callicles, to embrace the same kind of life. "Callicles," he says,

> I am fully persuaded by these *logoi* ... and I also exhort all other men, as much as I can, and especially I exhort you (in response to your earlier call to me) to take up this life and struggle, which I hold to be worth all the struggles of our present existence.[23]

The reasons Socrates offers Callicles at this point are subjective ones. The first is that *Socrates* is "persuaded by these *logoi*," and the second is that *he* upholds the struggle to live the moral life as "worth all the struggles of our present existence." Since Callicles is vociferously committed to a different view, it is legitimate to ask what *objective* reasons Socrates has given him for changing course? Why should Callicles not treat the *logos* as "an old wives tale and regard it with contempt" (527a), as Socrates suspects he will? The answer Socrates gives is my third story, the pearl at the centre of the other two, and their point.

Socrates does not claim to *know* how things are. Here as elsewhere he professes to be ignorant (509a). He offers Callicles no knock-down argument for changing his present beliefs or altering his present course of life. What he offers instead are *inducements,* but they are powerful ones.

His first inducement begins with a concession: "It would in no way be shocking to disdain these *logoi,*" Socrates tells Callicles, "if, by searching, we could somehow find better and truer ones" (527a).

Searching, of course, for Socrates, consists in the kind of elenctic examinations to which, in the course of the dialogue, Gorgias, Polus, and Callicles have all submitted ... and succumbed. Not only philosophical questions are investigated in elenctic examinations, the interlocutors themselves are put on trial and their lives held up for scrutiny.

Now, at this late moment of the dialogue, Socrates reminds Callicles that elenctic inquiry, the most powerful method Socrates has been able to devise, has revealed nothing truer or better than the sacred *logos* he has recounted here. And in spite of themselves Gorgias, Polus, and Callicles have been made witnesses to its power. "As you see," Socrates says, "here are three of you, the wisest among the Greeks today ... and you have not been able to demonstrate that any life ought to be lived other than this one" (527a/b).

Defeated views of life sprawl left and right on Socrates's elenctic path. One vision of the good life, however, survives "unshaken" (527b). It is the life that conducts us to the Islands of the Blessed, according to the sacred *logos* Socrates spent a lifetime defending. Many interlocutors have tried to put it in question. None has succeeded. Callicles himself has tried and failed that very day, as have Gorgias and Polus.

This brings Socrates to offer Callicles a second inducement for making the triumphant *logos* his own. Not only will embracing it cause him to join the side he cannot defeat, it will also make him happy "both in life and at life's end" (527c). The Socratic *logos* is of value, whereas the discourse Callicles has been defending, and which he tried to persuade Socrates to believe, "is worth nothing" (527e).

What Socrates has offered Callicles are inducements, not proofs. Commentators therefore do well to raise the question of what, if anything, Socrates has *proved.*[24] It is the same question that is raised about the apodictic argumentation of Pascal. But no commentator on the *Gorgias,* to my knowledge, has been prompted to doubt that the Socrates portrayed there is really a philosopher. He is no systematizer like Aristotle or Leibniz or Descartes, yet we recognize him as more than a minor practitioner of philosophy. He is the iconic founder of the discipline.

## Pascal and Socrates

The philosophical practice of Socrates sheds a revealing light on Pascal. In the first place, each holds unbendingly to a sacred discourse for which he offers no dogmatic justification. Pascal's sumptuous Catholicism differs in obvious ways from the lean *logos* of Socrates.[25] But the differences do not change the fact that both Socrates and Pascal recognize sacred teachings, and whatever moral commitments they entail, as preconditions of their own thinking.

The two philosophers are also alike in their professions of ignorance. Both are conscious of a paradoxical self-knowledge – the knowledge that they do not know – elevating them above people who imagine themselves knowledgeable. Neither sees any conflict between his profession of ignorance and the philosophical assurance he derives from sacred teachings in which he believes.

To each of them the sacred *logos* comes as a divine gift, one that enables him to see that all human beings are ignorant, though few are aware of their ignorance. Socrates's statements to this effect in the *Apology* are well known. Pascal's less temperate ones deserve to be. "Learn, proud one," he exclaims,

> what a paradox you are to yourself! Humble yourself, impotent reason! Be silent imbecile nature! Recognize that man infinitely surpasses man, and learn from your master your actual condition, of which you are ignorant. Hear God![26]

Each philosopher is not only strongly committed to certain sacred teachings but feels chosen by them to be their apostle. Hence the mixture of dialectic and apodeixis in their thinking. Dialectic is brought in to defeat the claims of those who take up views that cannot be reconciled with what has been revealed. The apodictic task, which they view as a calling, consists in persuading unbelievers how much wiser they would be if they accepted the claim the sacred teachings make on their lives.

In neither Socratic nor Pascalian philosophy, finally, do the arguments in favour of the sacred teachings take the form of metaphysical proofs. All that is offered are inducements. The first inducement is the invitation to the interlocutor to join the side that he and others have found it impossible to defeat. The second inducement is the evidence offered to the interlocutor that conversion will bring him happiness both in life and in the afterlife.

* * *

Let that suffice for comparisons. Here is what we now need to consider: the Socrates of the *Gorgias* reasons from within a religious fortress and remains a philosopher. Pascal does it, and by many accounts forfeits the title of philosopher for that reason.[27] Can that asymmetry be justified?

I don't think it can. Examples of such a mixture of dialectic and apodeixis may be rare in the history of philosophy, but they are far from eccentric. They belong where Socrates is: at the centre of the discipline.

My story is meant to show that, although the volume of Pascal's philosophy is slight and the way of apodeixis narrow, the grandeur of his thinking lies elsewhere. It lies in his manner of inquiry. Pascal holds the secular modern (or postmodern) reader to account in a personal way that recalls the manner and power of Socratic investigations. He mocks our pieties, challenges our certainties, and provokes us with the thought that we have settled for an impoverished life when infinite riches are within our grasp.

Pascal's philosophy is not on trial. We, his readers, are.

# Appendix A: Infini rien

(a>) Notre âme est jetée dans le corps où elle trouve nombre, temps, dimensions, elle raisonne là-dessus et appelle cela nature, nécessité, et ne peut croire autre chose. (<a

(b>) L'unité jointe à l'infini ne l'augmente de rien, non plus que un pied à une mesure infinie; le fini s'anéantit en présence de l'infini et devient un pur néant. Ainsi notre esprit devant Dieu, (<b) ainsi notre justice devant la justice divine. Il n'y a pas si grande disproportion entre notre justice et celle de Dieu qu'entre l'unité et l'infini.

Il faut que la justice de Dieu soit énorme comme sa miséricorde. Or la justice envers les réprouvés est moins énorme et doit moins choquer que la miséricorde envers les élus.

Nous connaissons qu'il y a un infini, et ignorons sa nature comme nous savons qu'il est faux que les nombres soient finis. Donc il est vrai qu'il y a un infini en nombre, mais nous ne savons ce qu'il est. Il est faux qu'il soit pair, il est faux qu'il soit impair, car en ajoutant l'unité il ne change point de nature. Cependant c'est un nombre, et tout nombre est pair ou impair. Il est vrai que cela s'entend de tout nombre fini.

Ainsi on peut bien connaître qu'il y a un Dieu sans savoir ce qu'il est.

N'y a-t-il point une vérité substantielle, voyant tant de choses vraies qui ne sont point la vérité même?

Nous connaissons donc l'existence et la nature du fini parce que nous sommes finis et étendus comme lui.

Nous connaissons l'existence de l'infini et ignorons sa nature, parce qu'il a étendue comme nous, mais non pas des bornes comme nous.

Mais **(c>)** nous ne connaissons ni l'existence ni la nature de Dieu, parce qu'il n'a ni étendue, ni bornes. **(<c)**

Mais **(d>)** par la foi nous connaissons son existence, **(<d)** par la gloire, nous connaîtrons sa nature.

Or j'ai déjà montré qu'on peut bien connaître l'existence d'une chose sans connaître sa nature.

O. Tournez

O. **(aP1>)** Parlons maintenant selon les lumières naturelles. **(<aP1)**

**(aP2>)** S'il y a un Dieu il est infiniment incompréhensible, puisque n'ayant ni parties ni bornes il n'a nul rapport à nous. Nous sommes donc incapables de connaître ni ce qu'il est, ni s'il est. **(<aP2)** Cela étant qui osera entreprendre de résoudre cette question? Ce n'est pas nous qui n'avons aucun rapport à lui.

**(aP3>)** Qui blâmera les chrétiens de ne pouvoir rendre raison de leur créance, eux qui professent une religion dont ils ne peuvent rendre raison; ils déclarent en l'exposant au monde que c'est une sottise, *stultitiam*, et puis vous vous plaignez de ce qu'ils ne le prouvent pas. S'ils la prouvaient, ils ne tiendraient pas parole. C'est en manquant de preuve qu'ils ne manquent pas de sens. **(<aP3)** Oui mais encore que cela excuse ceux qui l'offrent telle, et que cela les ôte du blâme de la produire sans raison **(bI>)** cela n'excuse pas ceux qui la reçoivent. **(<bI)** **(cP1>)** Examinons donc ce point. Et disons: Dieu est ou il n'est pas; mais de quel côté pencherons-nous? la raison n'y peut rien déterminer. Il y a un chaos infini qui nous sépare. Il se joue un jeu à l'extrémité de cette distance infinie, où il arrive croix ou pile. Que gagerez vous. **(<cP1)** **(cP2>)** Par raison vous ne pouvez faire ni l'un ni l'autre; par raison vous ne pouvez défaire nul des deux. **(<cP2)**

**(cP3>)** Ne blamez donc pas de fausseté ceux qui ont pris un choix, car vous n'en savez rien. **(<cP3)** Non, mais je les blâmerai d'avoir fait **(dI>)** non ce choix, mais un choix, car encore que celui qui prend croix et l'autre soient en pareille faute ils sont tous deux en faute; le juste est de ne point parier. **(<dI)**

Oui, mais il faut parier. Cela n'est pas volontaire, **(eP1>)** vous êtes embarqué.[1] **(<eP1)** **(eP2>)** Lequel prendrez-vous donc? Voyons; puisqu'il faut choisir voyons ce qui vous intéresse le moins. **(<eP2)** **(eP3>)** Vous avez deux choses à perdre : le vrai et le bien, et deux choses a engager: votre raison et votre volonté, votre connaissance et votre béatitude,

---

1  Following Sellier. Plural in Lafuma.

et votre nature a² deux choses à fuir: l'erreur et la misère. (**<eP3**) (**eP4>**) Votre raison n'est pas plus blessée puisqu'il faut nécessairement choisir, en choisissant l'un que l'autre. Voilà un point vidé. (**<eP4**) (**fP/I>**) Mais votre béatitude? (**<fP/I**) (**gP1>**) Pesons le gain et la perte en prenant croix que Dieu est. Estimons ces deux cas: si vous gagnez vous gagnez tout, et si vous perdez vous ne perdez rien : gagez donc qu'il est sans hésiter. (**<gP1**) (**gP2>**) Cela est admirable. (**<gP2**) (**hI>**) Oui il faut gager, mais je gage peut-être trop. (**<hI**) (**iP1>**) Voyons puisqu'il y a pareil hasard de gain et de perte, si vous n'aviez qu'à gagner deux vies pour une vous pourriez encore gager, mais s'il y en avait 3 à gagner? (**<iP1**)

(**iP2>**) Il faudrait jouer (puisque vous êtes dans la nécessité de jouer) et vous seriez imprudent lorsque vous êtes forcé à jouer de ne pas hasarder votre vie pour en gagner 3 à un jeu où il y a pareil hasard de perte et de gain. (**<iP2**) (**iP3>**) Mais il y a une éternité de vie de bonheur. Et cela étant quand il y aurait une infinité de hasards dont un seul serait pour vous, vous auriez encore raison de gager un pour avoir deux, et vous agirez de mauvais sens, en étant obligé à jouer, de refuser de jouer une vie contre trois à un jeu où d'une infinité de hasards il y en a un pour vous, s'il y avait une infinité de vie infiniment heureuse à gagner : (**<iP3**) (**iP4>**) mais il y a ici une infinité de vie infiniment heureuse à gagner, un hasard de gain contre un nombre fini de hasards de perte et ce que vous jouez est fini. (**<iP4**) (**iP5>**) Cela ôte tout parti partout où est l'infini et où il n'y a pas infinité de hasards de perte contre celui de gain. Il n'y a point à balancer, il faut tout donner. Et ainsi, quand on est forcé a jouer, il faut renoncer à la raison pour garder la vie plutôt que de la hasarder pour le gain infini aussi prêt à arriver que la perte du néant. (**<iP5**)

Car il ne sert de rien de dire qu'il est incertain si on gagnera, et qu'il est certain qu'on hasarde, et que l'infinie distance qui est entre la certitude de ce qu'on expose et l'incertitude de ce qu'on gagnera égale le bien fini qu'on expose certainement à l'infini qui est incertain. Cela n'est pas ainsi. Tout joueur hasarde avec certitude pour gagner avec incertitude, et néanmoins il hasarde certainement le fini pour gagner incertainement le fini, sans pécher contre la raison. Il n'y a pas infinité de distance entre cette certitude de ce qu'on expose et l'incertitude du gain: cela est faux. Il y a, à la vérité, infinité entre la certitude de gagner et la certitude de perdre, mais l'incertitude de gagner est proportionnée à la

---

2 Following Sellier. Verb missing in Lafuma

certitude de ce qu'on hasarde selon la proportion des hasards de gain et de perte. Et de là vient que s'il y a autant de hasards d'un côté que de l'autre le parti est à jouer égal contre égal. Et alors la certitude de ce qu'on s'expose est égale à l'incertitude du gain, tant s'en faut qu'elle soit infiniment distante. Et ainsi **(jP1>)** notre proposition est dans une force infinie, quand il y a le fini à hasarder, à un jeu où il y a pareils hasards de gain que de perte, et l'infini à gagner. **(<jP1)**

**(jP2>)** Cela est démonstratif et si les hommes sont capables de quelque vérité celle-là l'est. **(<jP2)**

Je le confesse, je l'avoue, **(KI>)** mais encore n'y a(-t-) il point moyen de voir le dessous du jeu? **(<kI)** Oui **(mP>)** l'Écriture et le reste, **(<mP)** etc. Oui mais j'ai les mains liées et la bouche muette, **(nI>)** on me force à parier, et je ne suis pas en liberté, on ne me relâche pas et je suis fait d'une telle sorte que je ne puis croire. Que voulez-vous donc que je fasse? **(<nI)** – Il est vrai, mais **(oP1>)** apprenez au moins que votre impuissance à croire vient de vos passions **(<oP1)**. **(oP2>)** Puisque la raison vous y porte et que néanmoins vous ne le pouvez, **(<oP2)** **(op3>)** travaillez donc non pas à vous convaincre par l'augmentation des preuves de Dieu, mais par la diminution de vos passions. **(<oP3)** Vous voulez aller à la foi et vous n'en savez pas le chemin. Vous voulez vous guérir de l'infidélité **(oP4>)** et vous en demandez des remèdes, **(<oP4)** **(oP5>)** apprenez de ceux, etc. qui ont été liés comme vous et qui parient maintenant tout leur bien. Ce sont des gens qui savent ce chemin que vous voudriez suivre et guéris d'un mal dont vous voulez guérir; **(<oP5)** **(oP6>)** suivez la manière par où ils ont commencé. C'est en faisant tout comme s'ils croyaient, en prenant de l'eau bénite, en faisant dire des messes, etc. Naturellement même cela vous fera croire **(<oP6)** **(oP7>)** et vous abêtira. **(<oP7)** **(pI>)** Mais c'est ce que je crains. **(<pI)** – Et pourquoi? **(qP1>)** qu'avez-vous à perdre? mais pour vous montrer que cela y mène, c'est que cela diminue les passions qui sont vos grands obstacles, etc. **(<qP1)**

### Fin de ce discours

**(qP2>)** Or quel mal vous arrivera (-t-il) en prenant ce parti? **(<qP2)** **(qP3>)** Vous serez fidèle, honnête, humble, reconnaissant, bienfaisant, ami sincère, véritable ...À la vérité vous ne serez point dans les plaisirs empestés, dans la gloire, dans les délices, mais n'en aurez-vous point d'autres?

Je vous dis que vous y gagnerez en cette vie, et que à chaque pas que vous ferez dans ce chemin, vous verrez tant de certitude de gain, et tant de néant de ce que vous hasardez, que vous connaîtrez à la fin que vous avez parié pour une chose certaine, infinie, pour laquelle vous n'avez rien donné.(<qP3)

(rI>)O ce discours me transporte, me ravit,(<rI) etc. Si ce discours vous plaît et vous semble fort, sachez qu'il est fait par un homme qui s'est mis à genoux auparavant et après, pour prier cet être infini et sans parties, auquel il soumet tout le sien, de se soumettre aussi le vôtre pour votre propre bien et pour sa gloire; et qu'ainsi la force s'accorde avec cette bassesse.

# Appendix B: Infinity-Nothing

(a>) Our soul is flung into the body where it finds number, time, dimensions. Our soul reasons about this and calls it nature, necessity, and can believe in nothing else. (<a)

   (b>) Unity joined to infinity adds nothing to it, any more than one foot would increase an infinite distance. The finite disappears before the infinite and becomes pure nothing. That is how our spirit is before God (<b); such is our justice before divine justice. The disproportion between our justice and God's is not so great as that between unity and infinity.

   God's justice must be immense, like his mercy. Now his justice toward the damned is not so immense and should be less shocking to us than his mercy toward the elect.

   We know there is an infinite without knowing its nature, since we know it is false that numbers are finite. Therefore it is true that there is a numerical infinite, but we do not know what it is. It is false to call it even; it is false to call it odd, for adding a unit to it does not change its nature. Nevertheless it is a number, and every number is either even or odd. It is true that this is obvious for all finite numbers.
   In the same way we can know that there is a God without knowing what he is.
   Is there not a substantial truth, seeing there are so many true things that are not truth itself?

   We therefore know both the existence and the nature of the finite because we are finite and extended in the same way.

We know the existence of the infinite and are ignorant of its nature, because it has extension as we do, but lacks our limits.

But **(c>)** we know neither the existence nor the nature of God, because he has neither extension, nor limits. **(<c)**

But **(d>)** we know his existence by faith **(<d)**, by his glory we will know his nature.

Now I have already shown that we can definitely know the existence of a thing without knowing its nature.

[...]

**(aP1>)** Let us now speak according to natural lights. **(<aP1)**

**(aP2>)** If there is a God he is infinitely incomprehensible, because having neither parts nor limits he has no connection (*rapport*) with us. We are therefore incapable of knowing either what he is or whether he is. **(<aP2)** That being so, who will dare to try to resolve this question? It's not a task for us, who have no connection with him.

**(aP3>)** Who will blame Christians then for not being able to give a reason for their belief, when they profess a religion for which no reason can be given? In offering their faith to the world they declare it to be folly, *stultitiam*, and then you complain when they don't prove it. If they did prove it they would not be keeping their word. Their want of proof is just what absolves them of a want of sense **(<aP3)**. Yes but although that may excuse those who offer their faith as unprovable, and exempt them from blame when they bring it forward without proof, **(bI>)** it does not excuse anyone who accepts it **(<bI)**. **(cP1>)** Let us examine that point. Put it this way: God either exists or he doesn't. But which way do we lean? Reason is no help. An infinite chaos separates us from God. A game is being played at the limit of that distance in which either heads or tails is the outcome. What will you wager **(<cP1)**?

**(cP2>)** Reason will not lead you one way or the other; reason undermines neither **(<cP2)**.

**(cP3>)** Therefore don't condemn those who have made a choice, since you know nothing about it **(<cP3)**. No, but I will blame [Christians] **(dI>)** for having made not this choice but any choice. For although the one who takes heads and the one who takes tails are equally blameworthy, both are to blame. The right thing is not to wager **(<dI)**.

Yes but you must wager. It is not voluntary. **(eP1>)** You are embarked **(<eP1)**. **(eP2>)** Which will you take then? Look, since you have to choose, let's look for what is least in your interest **(<eP2)**.

**(eP3>)** You have two things to lose: the true and the good; and two things to draw on: your reason and your will, your knowledge and your beatitude. Your nature seeks to avoid two things: error and misery **(<eP3)**. **(eP4>)** Because you must choose, your reason is not wounded any more in choosing one side than the other. One point is thus disposed of **(<eP4)**. **(fP/I>)** But what of your beatitude **(<fP/I)**? **(gP1>)** Let us weigh the gain and the loss if you choose "heads," that God exists. Let us appraise the two cases: if you win, you win everything, and if you lose, you lose nothing. Wager then on his existence without hesitation **(<gP1)**. **(gP2>)** That is wonderful **(<gP2)**! **(hI>)** Yes, I have to bet, but perhaps I am betting too much **(<hI)**. **(iP1>)** Let's see. Since there is equal chance of winning or losing, if you had only two lives (to win) against one (to lose) you could wager, but what if there were three to win **(<iP1)**?

**(iP2>)** You would have to bet (because you have no choice) and you would be imprudent when you are forced to play not to bet your life to win three in a game where the odds of losing and winning are equal **(<iP2)**. **(iP3>)** But there is an eternity of happy life. And that being so, even if there were an infinite number of possible outcomes of which only one was in your favour, you would still be right to bet one to get two, and you would be making a mistake if, when obliged to play, you refused to stake one life against three in a game where only one of an infinite number of outcomes is in your favour, provided there was an infinity of infinitely happy life to win **(<iP3)**. **(iP4>)** But in this case there is an infinity of infinitely happy life to win, one chance of winning against finite chances of losing and what you risk is finite **(<iP4)**. **(iP5>)** Wherever the infinite is present and the risks of loss are not infinite as against the likelihood of winning, there is no place for opinion. There is nothing to deliberate about; you have to risk everything you've got. And thus, when you're forced to play, you'd be crazy to keep your life instead of risking it for an infinite gain, an outcome no less likely to occur than a loss which amounts to nothing. **(<iP5)**

For nothing is accomplished if you say that winning is uncertain while it is certain that we take a risk, and that the infinite distance between the certainty of what we put at risk and the uncertainty of what we stand to win makes the finite good one certainly puts at risk equal to the infinity we are not certain to win. That is not how things stand. Every player takes risks that are certain for wins that are not. And even if he takes a certain finite risk for an uncertain finite gain, he still does not sin against reason. There is no infinite distance between that certainty of what we put at risk and the uncertainty of winning: that is false. There really is infinity between the certainty of winning and the certainty of losing, but the uncertainty of winning is in the same proportion to the certainty of what we put at risk as the chances of winning and losing. And that is why, when there are as many chances on one side as on the other the game is to be played at equal odds. Then the certainty of what you put at risk, far from being infinitely distant, is equal to the uncertainty of what you stand to gain. Thus **(jP1>)** our proposition has infinite force when a finite amount is risked in a game where the odds of losing or winning are the same, and there is infinity to be won. **(<jP1)**

**(jP2>)** That is demonstrative, and if there is any truth men are capable of grasping, that is it. **(<jP2)**

**(kI>)** I confess, I admit it. But still, is there no way of knowing the outcome of the game? **(<kI) (mP>)** Yes, Scripture and the rest, **(<mP)** etc. Yes but my hands are tied and my tongue is mute. **(nI>)** I am forced to wager and yet not free to do so. I am not released from betting, and yet am so made that I cannot believe. What do you expect me to do **(<nI)**? It is true, but **(oP1>)** recognize at least that your inability to believe arises from your passions **(<oP1). (oP2>)** Since reason draws you toward wagering and yet you cannot do it **(<oP2), (oP3>)** try to convince yourself not by working through proofs for the existence of God, but by weakening your passions **(<oP3)**. You wish to move toward the Faith, but you don't know the way. You want to cure yourself of unbelief **(oP4>)** and you ask about remedies **(<op4). (oP5>)** Learn from those who were bound like you and who now wager all they have. They are people who are familiar with the way you wish to travel and are cured of the illness from which you seek to recover **(<oP5); (oP6>)** follow the method by which they began. They got there by doing everything as if they believed, taking holy water, having masses said, and so on. This will make you believe by natural means **(<oP6) (oP7>)** and will make you stupid. **(<oP7) (pI>)** But that is what I fear **(<pI)**. But why? **(qP1>)** What have you got to lose? But to show you that it will work, it's what weakens the passions that are your great obstacles, etc. **(<qP1)**.

### End of This Conversation

**(qP2>)** Well, what harm will it do you to take this bet? **(<qP2) (qP3>)** You will be faithful, honest, humble, grateful, beneficent, a sincere friend, authentic ... It is true you will not be involved in poisoned pleasures, in glory, in voluptuousness, but will you not have other joys?

I tell you, you will profit in this life and with every step you take on this path you will see such certainty of gain, and so much nothingness in what you put at risk, that you will know at last that you wagered for something certain and infinite, which cost you nothing. **(<qP3)**

**(rI>)** O these words carry me away. They delight me, **(<rI)** etc. If this proposal pleases you and seems powerful to you, know that it was put forward by a man who fell to his knees beforehand and afterwards, to pray to that infinite, undivided being, to whom he submits all that is his own, that he might also submit to himself all that is yours, both for your good and for his glory, so that power would be reconciled with lowliness.

# Notes

## Introduction

1 Chateaubriand (1802), *Le génie du christianisme*, III.ii.6.
2 Voltaire (1777): "Dernières remarques sur *les pensées* de M. Pascal et sur quelques autres objets," CXXIII: "Pascal a été géomètre et éloquent; la réunion de ces deux grands mérites était alors bien rare; mais il n'y joignait pas la vraie philosophie."
3 Kolakowski (1998), p. 82.
4 Russell (1946), p. 795.
5 See Wetsel (1981), p. xv.
6 Harrington (1982).
7 Though see Fallon (1991).
8 Carraud (1992), p. 22[3], "ouvrage qui, malgré son titre, ne voit en rien la difficulté."
9 I give some examples in endnote 2 of Chapter Six.
10 French biographies range from the massive one of Fortunat Strowski (1922) to the slim but authoritative one by Jean Mesnard (1967). In English, the best place to begin is with Marvin O'Connell (1997).
11 See Ronald Knox's fine discussion of Jansenism in Knox (1950), pp. 204-20. I follow it in this and the next paragraph.
12 Arnauld, Malebranche, and the context of their dispute are brought colourfully back to life in Steven Nadler (2008), who hints (p. 53) that Arnauld may have been called "great" ironically, because of his diminutive size.
13 See, for example, L532/S457; L694/S573. Also Pascal (1963), p. 350: "les hommes sont dans une impuissance naturelle et immuable de traiter quelque science que ce soit, dans un ordre absolument accompli."

14 "Je vous demande pardon, Monsieur, dit M. Pascal à M. de Saci, de m'emporter ainsi devant vous dans la théologie, au lieu de demeurer dans la philosophie, qui seule était mon sujet." Pascal (1963), p. 296b.

15 See O'Connell (1997), p. 129.

## 1. Against Philosophy

1 Sextus Empiricus, *Outlines of Pyrrhonism* 1.i.3: "Those who believe they have discovered [truth] are the dogmatists."

2 See A.A. Long (1986), pp. 75–76

3 Pascal refers to academic scepticism only four times in the *Pensées*. There are thirty-eight explicit references to Pyrrhonism.

4 L131/S164: "Voilà la guerre ouverte entre les hommes, où il faut que chacun prenne parti, et se range nécesssairement ou au dogmatisme ou au pyrrhonisme. Car qui pensera demeurer neutre sera pyrrhonien par excellence."

5 As it did for Montaigne. He thought of Academic scepticism as a kind of "negative dogmatism" because of its certainty that we can know nothing. See Montaigne (1962), vol. 2, p. 193 (= Montaigne (2003), p. 64). See also Neto (1997), esp. p. 201.

6 See Kant, "Preisschrift über die Fortschritte der Metaphysik," Akademieausgabe vol. 20, p. 263: "Die Ausdehnung der Zweifellehre, sogar auf die Prinzipien der Erkenntniß des Sinnlichen, und auf die Erfahrung selbst kann man nicht füglich für eine ernstliche Meynung halten, die in irgend einem Zeitalter der Philosophie statt gefunden habe, sondern ist vielleicht eine Aufforderung an die Dogmatiker gewesen, diejenigen Prinzipien *a priori*, auf welchen selbst die Möglichkeit der Erfahrung ruht, zu beweisen, und da sie dieses nicht vermochten, die letztere ihnen auch als zweifelhaft vorzustellen."

7 Kant, *Prolegomena*, preface, *Werke*, Akademieausgabe vol. 4, p. 260.

8 L773/S637.

9 L745/S618.

10 See, e.g., Ross (1986) and Hunter (1993).

11 See Pascal (1960), where Courcelle comments on Pascal's detailed knowledge of Epictetus pp. 91f, and of Montaigne pp. 98ff.

12 Copleston (1953), pp. 228f.

13 Friedrich (1949), pp. 163f: "So ist in der Tat das Äußerste erreicht in der Selbstpotenzierung des skeptischen Verfahrens, – und in der Auslieferung der schon von allen Seiten problematisch gewordene menschlichen Lage an die völlige Unsicherheit."

14  Conche (1996), p. 42.

15  Popkin (1979), p. 54.

16  Cave (2009), p. 109.

17  Cave (2009), p. 125. See also Scholar (2010), pp. 9f, 101f; and Force (2009), esp. p. 526 and the extensive critical bibliography given in footnote 17.

18  Cave (2009), p. 125.

19  Scholar (2010), p. 102.

20  See Scholar (2010), pp. 187ff.

21  Cicero, *Academica* 2.x.32: "Volunt enim ... probabile aliquid esse et quasi veri simile, eaque se uti regula et in agenda vita et in querendo ac disserendo."

22  See Sextus Empiricus, *Outlines of Pyrrhonism* 1.xix.190.

23  Richard Scholar tells us that no medal bearing the device was ever struck, despite rumours to the contrary. Scholar (200), p. 98.

24  "Entretien avec M. de Saci, » Pascal (1994), p. 101, (1960), p. 293b. This "enigmatic" text presents numerous problems for Pascal scholars and cannot be used as evidence for Pascal's views in every context. However, it has been shown to be accurate in its depiction of Epictetus and Montaigne and also in the views it attributes to Pascal. And it is only for such points that I appeal to it here. See Pascal (1960), esp. pp. 91f, 98, 165. I cite it according to the edition of the recently recovered original edition (Pascal (1994)), but include references as well to the more easily available Pascal (1963).

25  Pascal (1994), p. 101; (1963), p. 293b.

26  Sextus Empiricus, *Outlines of Pyrrhonism* 1.i.4.

27  Pascal (1994), p. 122; (1963), p. 296a.

28  Friedrich (1949), p. 138: "Von Pascals Ansprüchen aus erscheint Montaigne als Sprecher verzweifelten Menschentums. Das ist eine Verdüsterung, die ihn ganz enstellt."

29  Cf. Boyle (2005), chapter 10.

30  Pascal (1994), pp. 99f; (1963), p. 293b: "Il met toutes choses dans un doute universel et si général que ce doute s'emporte soi-même ... dans un cercle perpétuel et sans repos."

31  Pascal only refers twice to the Epicureans in the *Pensées*. At L208/S240, he speaks of "les diverses sectes des stoïques et des épicuriens, des dogmatistes et des académiciens, etc." L449/S690 attributes to "pagans and Epicureans" the false idea of God as merely "auteur des vérités géometriques et de l'ordre des éléments." Cf. Carraud (1992), pp. 187ff.

32  The transcriptions are called *Discourses* (*Diatribai*), and the summary is called the *Handbook* or *Manual* (*Encheiridion*).

33  Long (2002), p. 2.

34 Long (2002), pp. 2f. For a brief account of Epictetus's influence, see Robert Dobbin's introduction to *Epictetus: Discourses and Selected Writings*, London/ New York, Penguin, 2008, pp. xvff.

35 Stockdale (1993).

36 See, e.g., Le Guern (1971), pp. 26f. Later (pp. 130f) Le Guern thinks Pascal was not ready to be critical of Descartes at the time of the "Conversation with M. de Saci" (generally dated 1655) because he was still under Descartes's influence then. Perhaps so. But Pascal would have to have been under the influence of something stronger than Descartes not to have recognized him as the arch-dogmatist even then.

37 Pascal (1994), p. 122; (1963); p. 296a.

38 L110/S142: "et c'est sur ces connaissances du coeur et de l'instinct qu'il faut qu la raison s'appuie."

39 See L110/S142; L424/S680.

40 See Diogenes Laertius (1988), p. 297.

41 L380/S412.

42 Pascal (1994), pp. 97f; (1963), p. 293a/b.

43 L430/S683: "Levez vos yeux vers Dieu, disent les [dogmatistes] ... voyez celui auquel vous ressemblez, et qui vous a fait pour l'adorer ... la sagesse vous y égalera, si vous voulez le suivre. 'Haussez la tête, hommes libres', dit Épictète."

44 As can be verified in Pascal (1960), p. 16. The editor documents Pascal's attributions to Epictetus on facing pages of the text of the Conversation with Saci.

45 L553/S462.

46 Descartes, *Discours de la méthode*, Pt 2, AT 6, p. 19.

47 *Discours de la méthode*, Pt 6, AT 6, p. 62.

48 Pascal (1994), p. 104; (1963), p. 294a.

49 Scholar (2003), pp. 82f.

50 de la Bruyère (1965), p. 388.

51 See http://the-brights.net/; also "An Idea That Is Not Very Bright," *Montreal Gazette*, 10 Nov. 2003.

52 See L150/S183: "Les impies qui font profession de suivre la raison doivent être étrangement forts en raison."

53 Pascal (1994), p. 104; (1963), p. 294a: "Il leur demande sur quels principes ils s'appuient; il les presse de les montrer. Il examine tous ceux qu'ils peuvent produire."

54 The French term is *l'âme*, but in this context it means "mind."

55 Pascal (1994), pp. 108–10); (1963), p. 294b. The Lafuma text (1963) is gappy and defective.

56  L423/S680.

57  L406/S25.

58  Cicero, *Tusc. quaest.* 5.2.5.

59  Pascal (1994), p. 126; (1963), p. 296b: "ces sages du monde plaçaient ces contraires dans un même sujet."

60  For an excellent introduction to the modern logic of terms, see Englebretsen (1990). For the point I am about to make, see pp. 3ff.

61  Pascal (1994), p. 126; (1963), p. 296b: "ils se brisent et s'anéantissent."

62  See, e.g., L140–6/S172–9.

63  Pascal (1994), p. 126; (1963), p. 296b: "ils se brisent et s'anéantissent pour faire place à la vérité de l'Evangile."

64  See, e.g., Carraud (1992), pp. 119ff; Gouhier, cited in Carraud (1992), p. 119.

65  L12/S44: "[Rendre la religion aimable] ... et puis montrer qu'elle est vraie."

66  L149, p. 521a/S182, p. 140.

67  L160/S192.

68  Pascal (1963), p. 290b.

69  L149, p. 520b/S182, p. 139: "Les philosophes vous l'ont promis et ils n'ont pu le faire. Ils ne savent ni quel est votre véritable bien, ni quel est votre véritable état."

70  L190/S222: "quand [une preuve de Dieu] servira a quelques-uns, cela ne servirait que pendant l'instant qu'ils voient cette démonstration, mais une heure après ils craignent de s'être trompés."

71  Nozick (1981), p. 4.

72  Ibid., p. 4.

73  van Inwagen (2006), pp. 37–55.

74  Ibid., p. 37.

75  Ibid., p. 38.

76  Ibid., p. 39.

77  Ibid., p. 54. Italics in original.

78  Plantinga (1965), p. vii.

79  I take for granted that Anselm's argument was ontological, though this, like almost everything else one can say about the argument, has been questioned by someone. See, e.g., Jean-Luc Marion (1992) and Losoncy (1992).

80  *Proslogion*, §3: "si id quo maius nequit cogitari, potest cogitari non esse: id ipsum quo maius cogitari nequit, non est id quo maius cogitari nequit; quod conuenire non potest."

81  It is arguable that in Anselm's cloistered setting neither the metaphysical nor the psychological questions were irrelevant and that prolonged contemplation of them would lead the contemplative into a deeper grasp of

the divine reality whose existence Anselm was trying to establish. To dismiss such factors may be to take too narrow a view of the argument.

82 As Leibniz points out critically in a passage cited below ("Meditationes de Cognitione, Veritate et Ideis" (1684), GP 4, 425.

83 *Meditation* 5, AT 7, p. 65, lines 16–19: "Jam vero si ex eo solo, quod alicujus rei ideam possim ex cogitatione mea depromere, sequitur ea omnia, quæ ad illam rem pertinere clare et distincte percipio, revera ad illam pertinere."

   For rhetorical purposes, Descartes puts his principle as the antecedent of a conditional, implying, however, that it is true, much as we might say, "If we may take for granted that two plus two equals four, then ..." My translation simplifies by stating the principle categorically.

84 AT 7, p. 65, lines 19f: "nunquid inde haberi etiam potest argumentum, quo Dei existentia probetur?"

85 Descartes says "a valley" instead of "a slope." Unfortunately, solitary mountains are possible and they have no valley. And since Descartes's analogy has to be analytically true in order to illustrate his point, I have amended it to make it so.

86 Reading *minus* for *majus* as in the canonical French translation (AT 9, p. 52).

87 *Meditation* 5, AT 7, p. 66, lines 8–15: "non magis posse existentiam ab essentia Dei separari, quam ab essentia trianguli magnitudinem trium ejus angulorum aequalium duobus rectis, sive ab idea montis ideam vallis: adeo ut non *minus* repugnet cogitare Deum (hoc est ens summe perfectum) cui desit existentia (hoc est cui desit aliqua perfectio), quam cogitare montem cui desit vallis."

88 See Oppy (1995), pp. 24f.

89 Nouveaux essais, 4, 10, §7: "n'est pas un paralogisme, mais c'est une démonstration imparfaite qui suppose quelque chose qu'il falloit encore prouver pour le rendre d'une evidence Mathematique. C'est qu'on suppose tacitement que cette idée de l'Etre tout grand, ou tout parfait, est possible, et n'implique point de contradiction."

90 E.g., at GP 4, 403: "la voye des idées qui est en vogue aujourd'huy et qui souvent est un asyle d'ignorance aussi bien que les qualités occultes d'autres fois."

91 "Meditationes de Cognitione, Veritate et Ideis," GP 4, 425: "[n]ec minus abuti ... nostri temporis homines jactato illo principio: *quicquid clare et distincte de re aliqua percipio, id est vermum seu de ea enuntiabile.* Saepe enim clara et distincta videntur hominibus temere judicantibus, quae obscura et confusa sunt. Inutile ergo axioma est, nisi clari et distincti *criteria* adhibeantur."

92 Paraphrasing Anselm's version, Leibniz says (*Nouveaux essais* 4, 10, 7): "Dieu est le plus grand ou (comme parle Descartes) le plus parfait des êtres."

93 *Journal de Trévoux* in 1701, GP 4, 405: "on pourroit former une demonstration encore plus simple, en ne parlant point des perfections, pour n'être point arresté par ceux qui s'aviseroient de nier que toutes les perfections soient compatibles, et par consequent que l'idée en question soit possible."

94 GP 4, 406: "une proposition modale qui [est] un des meilleur fruits de toute la Logique, scavoir que *si l'Estre necessaire est possible, il existe.*"

95 GP 4, 402: "proposition la plus belle sans doute et la plus importante de la doctrine des modales, parce qu'elle fournit un passage de la puissance à l'acte, et c'est uniquement icy qu'*a posse ad esse valet consequentia.*"

96 As can easily be proved. Let '$\Diamond p$' mean 'p is possible' and '$\Box p$' mean 'p is necessary'. Now suppose $\Diamond p \to p$. Then, since $p \to \Diamond p$, $p \leftrightarrow \Diamond p$. Thus, $\sim p \leftrightarrow \Diamond \sim p$, and $\sim\sim p \leftrightarrow \sim\Diamond\sim p$. Hence, $p \leftrightarrow \Box p$. Therefore, $\Diamond p \leftrightarrow p \leftrightarrow \Box p$.

97 I.e., $\Diamond\Box p \to \Box p$.

98 For details, see, e.g., Hughes and Cresswell (1968), p. 49.

99 I am referring here to what logicians call "accessibility relations." These points are developed in more detail in Hunter (1989), pp. 3–10.

100 Dumoncel (1983), esp. p. 419.

101 Kalinowski (1985).

102 Ibid., pp. 96f.

103 Dumoncel (1985).

## 2. Failure and Fall

1 Hirstein (2005), p. 4.

2 Hirstein (2005), p. 10.

3 Reported in Hirstein (2005), p. 154.

4 Hirstein (2005), p. 8.

5 Hirstein (2005), p. 187. I have slightly altered the order and punctuation of the criteria.

6 A good survey of the issue including an argument for the separability of epistemic and moral obligation can be found in Haack (2001).

7 Hirstein (2005), pp. 171f. See also Pinker (2002), p. 43.

8 Hirstein (2005), p. 179. The term originally comes from Quine (1969).

9 van Inwagen (2006), p. 37.

10 The entire passage from which I shall be quoting is found at AT 7, pp. 4f. For a fuller account of the context of this remarkable letter, see Hunter (1998).

11 "certitudine & evidentia Geometricas aequare, vel etiam superare."

12 "non spero me illarum ope magnum operae pretium esse facturum, nisi me patrociniis vestro adjuvetis."

13 "[I]n eo differentia est, quod in Geometria, cum omnibus sit persuasum nihil scribi solere, de quo certa demonstratio non habeatur, saepius in eo peccant imperiti, quod falsa approbent, dum ea videri volunt intelligere, quam quod ver refutent: contra vero in Philosophia, cum credatur nihil esse de quo non possit in utramque partem disputari, pauci veritatem investigant, & multo plures, ex eo quod ausint optima quaeque impugnare, famam ingenii aucupantur."

14 It is ironic that Descartes attempted to exploit precisely this cast of mind a few years earlier when he was seeking collaborators for his work in the sciences. As noted in Chapter One, he tried to attract researchers to assist him with his project by pointing to the power and wealth science promised in addition to knowledge.

15 Aristotle, *Metaphysics* 5.22, 1022b, trans. Richard Hope, Ann Arbor, University of Michigan Press, 1968.

16 See, e.g., Thomas Aquinas, *Summa Theologica* I q. 48.

17 The Manicheans held that the world was created by the struggle between the two equally matched powers of good and evil. See Augustine, *Confessions*, Book 7.

18 For an excellent account of both the meaning and the possible limitations of this doctrine, see Kane (1980). Susan Neiman's important discussion of the idea's recent history, *Evil in Modern Thought* (2002), recounts the attempts that have been made since the Enlightenment both to banish the idea of evil and to confront it. A contemporary analytic discussion of both tendencies can be found in Kekes (1990).

19 L149/S182.

20 L934/S762.

21 Pope, "Essay on Man," Epistle 2, lines 13–18. Pascal's original words, L131/S164: "Quelle chimère est-ce donc que l'homme? quelle nouveauté, quel monstre, quel chaos, quel sujet de contradictions, quel prodige? Juge de toutes choses, imbécile ver de terre, dépositaire du vrai, cloaque d'incertitude et d'erreur, gloire et rebut de l'univers."

22 L821/S661.

23 Though it is usually published along with "L'esprit de la géométrie" and often treated as if it were the completion of that work, in fact the two are independent, the "Art de persuader" having been written five years after the other. See the edition with commentary Pascal (1979) for details, esp. p. 10. I shall be following that edition of the "Art de Persuader" here.

24 Pascal (1979), p. 32 = Pascal (1963), p. 355a.

25 Pascal (1979), p. 20, §38 = Pascal (1963) 351b: "tout ce que la géométrie propose est parfaitement démontré, ou par la lumière naturelle, ou par les preuves."

26 Pascal (1979), p. 35 = Pascal (1963), p. 356a.

27 Pascal (1979), p. 32 = Pascal (1963), p. 355a.

28 Ibid..

29 L821/S540. See also L410/S29.

30 See, e.g., L97/S131.

31 Pascal (1979), p. 33 = Pascal (1963), p. 355a: "Dieu a établi cet ordre surnaturel, et tout contraire à l'ordre qui devait être naturel aux hommes dans les choses naturelles."

32 Genesis 3:14–24 (Revised Standard Version).

33 Pascal (1979), p. 33 = Pascal (1963), p. 355a.

34 For a fine introduction to this vast subject, see Jonsen and Toulmin (1988).

35 *Lettres provinciales,* 5, Pascal (1963), p. 390. See also Bras (2009), esp. chapter 2.

36 I am grateful to Hugh Hunter for this observation.

37 Ovid, *Metamorphoses*, 7, pp. 20f: "video meliora proboque, deteriora sequor." St Paul, *Romans*, 7:9.

38 Aristotle, *Nicomachean Ethics*, 7.ii.1f (1145b 22–28) trans. H. Rackham, Loeb Classical Library, Cambridge, MA, Harvard University Press, pp. 1926ff. (Translation slightly modified.)

39 Pascal (1979), p. 33 = Pascal (1963), p. 355a.

40 For a brief explanation of it, see Moriarty (2003), p. 147.

41 Pascal (1979), p. 33 = Pascal (1963), p. 355b.

42 Pascal (1979), pp. 34f = Pascal (1963), pp. 355b–356a: "[I]l y a [des rencontres] où les choses qu'on veut faire croire sont bien établies sur des vérités connues, mais qui sont en même temps contraires aux plaisirs qui nous touchent le plus. Et celles-là sont en grand péril de faire voir, par une expérience qui n'est que trop ordinaire ... que cette âme impérieuse, qui se vantait de n'agir que par raison, suit par un choix honteux et téméraire ce qu'une volonté corrompue désire, quelque résistance que l'esprit trop éclairé puisse y opposer."

43 Chesterton (1908), pp. 22f.

44 The theme of van Fraassen (1980).

45 L401/S20.

46 L136/S168.

47 L434/S686. The crucial last sentence, "C'est l'image de la condition des hommes," does not occur in the Sellier text.

48 L421/S680: "la pente vers soi est le commencement de tout désordre, en guerre, en police, en économie, dans le corps particulier de l'homme. La volonté est donc dépravée."

49 Lorenzen (1987), p. 176.

50 L199/S230.

51 Pascal (1963), p. 231b.

52 L199/S230.

53 L65/S99.

54 L199/S230.

55 L199/S230.

56 W.V.O. Quine's disturbing essay, "On Simple Theories of a Complex World," can be read as a Pascalian meditation on this point. See Quine (1976), pp. 255–8.

57 See Descartes's preface to the original French translation of his *Principia Philosophiae*, esp. AT 9, *Principes*, p. 20.

58 L199, p. 526b/S230, p. 165.

59 L199/S230.

60 In the first draft of the fragment from which I have been extensively quoting, Pascal wrote, "It is as absurd as it is impious to deny that man is composed of two parts of different natures, that is, of mind (*âme*) and body." Cited in Le Guern (1971), p. 151.

61 L199/S230.

62 L27/S61.

63 L199/S230. Contemporary philosophers of science would see in Pascal's critique a variant of what is called "pessimistic induction."

64 For a survey of the problematic role of science in policy making, see Dryzek (1993).

65 L44/S78.

66 Fleischacker (2004), p. 205.

67 See Ferreyrolles (1984), esp. chapter 6.

68 Lafuma (1963), pp. 366–8.

69 The essentials of Pascal's thoughts on justice can be found in Laurent Thirouin's collection (2011). Ferreyrolles (1984) draws also on the *Provinciales* and other writings.

70 L533/S457.

71 Thirouin (2011), p. 10.

72 See Fleischacker (2004), p. 3 passim.

73 Cicero, *De officiis*, 1.7.20: "iustitia, in qua virtutis est splendor maximus, ex qua viri boni nominantur, et huic conjuncta beneficentia."

74 Cicero, *De officiis*, 1.14.45: "in beneficentia dilectus esset dignitatis; in quo et mores eius erunt spectandi, in quem beneficium congeretur."

75 See Fleischacker (2004), p. 20 passim. See also Nussbaum (2000), esp. p. 179.

76 Fleischacker, (2004), pp. 38ff.

77 Lafuma (1963), p. 366a: "une infinité de hasards."

78 Ibid., p. 366a/b: "Cet ordre n'est fondé que sur la seule volonté des législateurs qui ont pu avoir de bonnes raisons, mais dont aucune n'est prise d'un droit naturel."

79 *Summa Theologica* I², q. 94, resp: "Quantum ergo ad illa principia communia, lex naturalis nullo modo potest a cordibus hominum deleri in universali. Deletur tamen in particulari operabili."

80 My understanding of Pascal's political thought has been advanced by André Clair's (2003) thorough review of the texts. But the Pascalian text I am in the midst of citing shows that Pascal did not "abandon every form of the doctrine of natural right," as Clair claims at one point (p. 419), though he seems to have second thoughts later (p. 424). On this point, see also Hammond (1994), p. 174.

81 L60/S94.

82 Sellier as quoted in Hammond (1994), p. 171 q. v.

83 Lafuma (1963), p. 368a.

84 L149/S182: "la concupiscence qui vous attache à la terre"; L460/S699: "l'amour-propre et la concupiscence qui arrêtent [l'amour de Dieu]." Jean Mesnard (1988), p. 33, says concupiscence "implies self-love and has love of God for its contrary."

85 L97/S131: "La concupiscence et la force sont les sources de toutes nos actions. La concupiscence fait les volontaires, la force les involontaires."

86 L74/S108.

87 L210/S243.

88 L106/S138; L118/S150.

89 Roland Desné (1972), p. 54, quotes R. Pomeau as having "very aptly said [that] Pascalian anguish was attuned to the state of mankind at the time of and just after the Thirty Years War."

90 Gross (1948), p. 39.

91 See in particular *Essais* 2, 12.

92 L60/S94.

93 See, e.g., Steil and Hinds (2009), pp. 39–43.

94 L81/S116.

95 Not everyone has noticed this. André Clair goes through contortions to show peace to be absolutely the highest good. See Clair (2003), p. 417.

96 See esp. L118/S150: "Grandeur de l'homme dans sa concupiscence même, d'en avoir su tirer un règlement admirable et en avoir fait un tableau de charité."

97 Hammond (1994), p. 181.
98 L60/S94.
99 L60/S94.

## 3. His Critics' Critic

1 Friedrich (1949), p. 182.
2 L16/S50.
3 Pintard (1962), pp. 113–16. Cited in Wetsel (1994), pp. 113f.
4 For a summary of their candidates, see Wetsel (1994), pp. 119–29.
5 Kolakowski (1998), p. 132.
6 Voltaire (1958), pp. 93f: "Il me paraît qu'en général l'esprit dans lequel M. Pascal écrivit ces *Pensées* était de montrer l'homme dans un jour odieux. Il s'acharne à nous peindre tous méchants et malheureux. Il écrit contre la nature humaine à peu près comme il écrivait contre les jésuites. Il impute à l'essence de notre nature ce qui n'appartient qu'à certains hommes. Il dit éloquemment des injures au genre humain.
7 See, e.g., Whelan (1992).
8 Voltaire (1958), §6, p. 99: "Pourquoi nous faire horreur de notre être? Notre existence n'est point si malheureuse qu'on veut nous le faire accroire. Regarder l'univers comme un chachot, et tous les hommes comme des criminels qu'on va exécuter, est l'idée d'un fanatique."
9 Ibid., p. 94: "J'ose prendre le parti de l'humanité contre ce misanthrope sublime ; j'ose assurer que nous ne sommes ni si méchants ni si malheureux qu'il le dit."
10 Desné (1972), p. 45.
11 Ibid., p. 47.
12 Ibid., p. 44.
13 Voltaire (1958), §11.
14 That, at least, is the classic understanding of Mandeville, though there is, of course, more to him. See, e.g., Lynch and Walsh (2003).
15 Mandeville (1988), p. cxxvi.
16 Ibid., p. cxvi.
17 Smith (1790), pp. 341f.
18 E.g., 1 John 2:15ff; Romans 12:2.
19 For an introduction to the vast literature of *contemptus mundi*, see Hühn (1971) and Gnädiger et al. (1977–99), vol. 3, cols 186–94.
20 The Holocaust, however, revived the idea in the mid-twentieth century, for example in the theology of Dietrich Bonhoeffer, and the postwar philosophy of T.W. Adorno. See Kenneth Surin's (1985) insightful piece.

21 Douglass, (1857), pp. 159f. This book can also be read online through several providers.

22 Augustine, *Confessions* 1.13.

23 L427/S681: "qu'il se trouve des hommes indifférents à la perte de leur être et au péril d'une éternité de misères ... C'est un enchantement incompréhensible et un asoupissement surnaturel."

24 Letter to Franz Mehring, 14 July 1893.

25 L418/S680: "La raison n'y peut rien déterminer."

26 L149, p. 520b/S182, p. 47. "Voilà l'état où les hommes sont aujourd'hui. Il leur reste quelque instinct impuissant du bonheur de leur première nature, et ils sont plongés dans les misères de leur aveuglement et de leur concupiscence qui est devenue leur seconde nature."

27 *Ecce Homo* 2.3, "Dass ich Pascal nicht lese, sondern liebe."

28 *Gesammelte Werke (Musarionausgabe)*, vol. 21, p. 98: "daß [sein] Blut in dem meinen rollt." Cited in Natoli (1985), p. 17.

29 Zwierlein (2001), p. 234.

30 Cf. Natoli (1985), p. 101.

31 Ibid., p. 174[4].

32 See, e.g., *Morgenröthe* 1, §69: "Wenn unser Ich, nach Pascal und dem Christenthume, immer hassenswerth ist."

33 See, e.g., *Zarathustra* 4, "Vom höheren Menschen," §1: "auf dem Markt glaubt niemand an höhere Menschen."

34 *Die fröhliche Wissenschaft* 4, §283, "Vorbereitende Männer."

35 Robinson (1964), p. 157.

36 Ibid.

37 Lyotard (1979), p. 30.

38 L6/S40: "(1.) Partie. Misère de l'homme sans Dieu."

39 L199/S230: The extremes touch one another.

40 L434. The phrase is missing from the copy used in the Sellier edition.

41 Moskowitz (2001), p. 2.

42 Ibid.

43 Rieff (1966), p. 12.

44 For a partial list, see Moskowitz, (2001), p. 6.

45 Moskowitz (2001), pp. 2f.

46 Ibid., p. 283.

47 Ibid., p. 7

48 Martin (2006), p. 10.

49 Sorensen (1997), p. 743.

50 Bovens (1999), p. 232.

51 Ibid., p. 235.

52  Martin (2006), p. vii.
53  Ibid., p. 4.
54  Ibid., p. 194.
55  L136/S168: "Sans divertissement il n'y a point de joie. Avec le divertisse-
    ment il n'y a point de tristesse. Et c'est aussi ce qui forme le bonheur des
    personnes de grande condition qu'ils ont un nombre de personnes qui les
    divertissent, et qu'ils ont le pouvoir de se maintenir en cet état."
56  L136, p. 517a/b/S168, p. 123.
57  L148/S181.
58  L44/S78.
59  L43/S127.

## 4. Reluctant Inquirer

 1  L12/S46.
 2  See Pascal's "Prière pour demander à Dieu le bon usage des maladies,"
    Pascal (1963), pp. 362ff.
 3  The role of spiritual blindness will be discussed in detail with textual doc-
    umentation in Chapter Five.
 4  Girard (1999), p. 130.
 5  Reporting on all three articles as they were at time of consultation.
 6  Taylor (2007), p. 25.
 7  Nagel (1997), p. 130.
 8  Ibid., p. 131.
 9  To think otherwise is to commit what is called "the genetic fallacy."
10  L157/S189; L449/S690: "Athéisme marque de force d'esprit, mais jusqu'à un
    certain degré seulement"; "je ne me sentirais assez fort pour trouver dans
    la nature de quoi convaincre des athées endurcis."
11  L237/S269.
12  L427, p. 553a/S681, p. 470.
13  The references in order are L273/S304, L273/S304, and L310/S341.
14  L427, p. 533/S681, p. 473.
15  See, for example, *Catechism of the Catholic Church* (1994), articles 157ff.
16  Pascal (1963), "Préface sur le traité du vide," p. 230b.
17  All passages quoted from Thomas are from *Summa Theologica* Ia.q1.a8,
    resp. The last one quoted runs: "Si vero adversarius nihil credat eorum
    quae divinitus revelantur, non remanet amplius via ad probandum articu-
    los fidei per rationes, sed ad solvendum rationes, si quas inducit, contra
    fidem."
18  Pascal (1963), "Préface sur le traité du vide," p. 231a.

19  Newman (1910), pp. 466f.
20  To see the remarkable and underappreciated degree to which Pascal was a follower of Descartes, consult Ariew (2007) and Carraud (2007).
21  *Meditations*, Dedicatory Letter, AT 7, p. 2. For a discussion of the apologetic significance of this passage, see Hunter (1998).
22  Leo X (1860), p. 602.
23  Lohr (1976), p. 213. For more on the context, see Hunter (1998).
24  L808/S655.
25  Gilberte Périer, "Vie de Monsieur Pascal," in Pascal (1963), p. 24b.
26  L83/S117. Sceptics in the tradition of Montaigne would be doubters without being know-it-alls, as an anonymous reader of this book has pointed out. But they might still be *knowing*, in the pejorative sense of that term, which also falls within the semantic field of 'know-it-all.'
27  L241/S273.
28  L404/S23.
29  Parish (2010), pp. 32f.
30  Pascal (1963), p. 496b.
31  L131/164.
32  L215/S248.
33  The jury is still out on the question of whether this must be so. See Garber (2009), p. $9^1$.
34  Some book-length treatments of IR are Lønning (1980), Rescher (1985), Armour (1993), and Jordan (2006).
35  Brunet (1956), p. 7.
36  Hacking (1972), p. 188.
37  See, e.g., Edwards (2003) and Elster (2003).
38  Hájek (2003), p. 49.
39  Brunet (1956), p. 129.
40  Pascal's conception of original sin and its effects were discussed in Chapter Two.
41  L131/S164.
42  L149, p. 520b/S182, p. 139.
43  See, e.g., *Summa Theologiae* 1a, q. 88 a.3 reply: "cum intellectus humanus, secundum statum praesentis vitae, non posit intelligere substantias immateriales creates ... multo minus potest intelligere essentiam substantiae increatae."
44  See, e.g., Thomas Aquinas, *De ente et essentia*, 4, §26: "possum enim intelligere quid est homo vel phoenix, et tamen ignorare an esse habeat in rerum natura."
45  Descartes, *Meditation* 2, AT 7, p. 25: "Nondum vero satis intelligo, quisnam sim ego ille, qui jam necessario sum."

46 Jordan (2006), p. 9. Though it would be easier to agree with Jordan's notion of "extended theism" (p. 10), which is close to what I would mean by Christianity.

47 L577/S480.

48 For a helpful introduction to this rule, see Laurent Thirouin (1991), pp. 135–9. A.W.F. Edwards (2003) covers the same material in English, but it is more technical.

49 See Jordan (2006), 164ff.

50 L577/S480.

51 Cf. Edwards (2003), p. 44.

52 See, e.g., Edwards (2003), pp. 49f.

53 Port Royal Logic 4.16 = Arnauld and Nicole (1970), p. 428.

54 Ibid., p. 429.

55 See Lønning (1980), pp. 75f.

56 See Hájek (2003), p. 29 for some references.

57 'Now' signifies the religious idea of *kairos*, the opportune moment. In chronological time, it may correspond to an extended period or even to the whole of life. Or it may be a recurrent but not permanent possibility. But there are also possible changes and chances in life* that can render life* unchoosable.

58 Taleb (2007), p. 210. One thesis of Taleb's book is that the failure to learn this lesson puts in jeopardy the economic stability of the West.

59 Hume, *Enquiry* 4: "[A]ll inferences from experience suppose, as their foundation, that the future will resemble the past," but it is impossible to prove it, since all arguments in its favour "are founded on the supposition of that resemblance." *Treatise* 2.iii.3: "Reason is, and ought only to be the slave of the passions and can never pretend to any other office than to serve and obey them."

60 L835/S423.

61 Port Royal Logic 4.16 = Arnauld and Nicole (1970), p. 429.

62 See *Summa Theologica* 1–2, q. 5, art. 8, resp.

63 Boethius distinguishes '*mendax felicitas*' from '*vera beatitudo*'; Aristotle distinguishes between '*eudaimonia*' and '*makaria*.' For an introduction to these distinctions, see Celano (1987).

64 "I am the Lord, and there is none else. There is no God beside me" (Isaiah 45:5).

65 For a partial bibliography, see Jordan (2002), p. 220, fn. 19.

66 Jordan (2002), p. 220.

67 See esp. Jordan (2005).

68 James (1956), p. 103.

69 Michael Martin does this in *Atheism: A Philosophical Justification* (1990), pp. 232ff. Cited in Jordan (2002).

70 L242/S275.

71 Acts 17:23.

72 L180/S211.

73 Ibid.

74 L198/S229.

75 Pascal's theory of grace would enter into a full discussion of this question, since he thinks that only recipients of grace are able to appreciate evidence relating to God. However, since it is not necessary to deal with it here in order to resolve this problem, I shall defer discussing it until it cannot be avoided.

76 L929/756.

77 Normally this exclamation is attributed to the interlocutor, but I follow Lønning (1980), pp. 84f, in attributing it to Pascal. See Lønning for his reasoning.

78 Pascal (1963), p. 267b.

79 Spinoza to Ludovico Meyer, 20 April 1663, in *Opera* (1925), p. 53.

80 See Hájek (2003), p. 29.

81 See Rescher (1985), pp. 13f, for a careful exposition of the mathematical side of Pascal's reasoning.

82 For a masterful overview of them and of the pertinent secondary literature, see Hájek (2003).

83 L427, p. 553a/S681, p. 471.

84 Lønning (1980), pp. 91f. I am also indebted to Lønning for some points in my statement of what the wager argument accomplishes.

85 The translation I offer contains only one of the meanings the original could support. Those who read French should consult Appendix A.

86 L410/S29.

87 Brian Foster's (1963) masterful survey of the strengths and weaknesses of a number of readings is still a useful introduction.

88 Pascal (2005), p. 214.

89 L5/S39.

90 L11/S45: "de preparer la machine, de chercher par raison."

91 L741/S617.

92 Claims very like it are made in the psychological literature. See, e.g., Bem (1966). The article opens with this bold claim: "An individual's beliefs and attitudes can be manipulated by inducing him to role play, deliver a persuasive communication, or engage in any behavior that would characteristically imply his endorsement of a particular set of beliefs."

93  L419/S680, p. 215.
94  L936/S751, p. 582.
95  L816/S659.
96  For more on Pascal's notion of grace, see Moriarty (2003), also Kolakowski (1998), pp. 113f.
97  L45/S78 (p. 73). See also L380/S412, L382/S414.
98  Technically, since reason teaches him nothing about it (cP1), he must also believe it is less than one, but that is not at issue here.
99  Compare Appendix A.
100  L44/S78.
101  See, e.g., Brunet (1956), pp. 91f, and Lønning (1980), pp. 105f.

## 5. Burdens of Proof

1  L110/S142: "Ceux à qui Dieu a donné la religion par sentiment de coeur sont bienheureux et bien légitimement persuadés."
2  Garber (2009), 17
3  Supposing that the line of thought begun in the wager argument continues in the *Pensées*. Apparently not everyone thinks that it does. See Garber (2009), p. 9.
4  Garber (2009), pp. 32f.
5  Hélène Bouchilloux (2002), p. 4, acknowledges both versions of the question on her way to offering quite a different answer from the one found here: "La nature est corrompue, la raison est corrompue. La nature et la raison ne sont guéries que par la grâce. Il est impossible de croire le christianisme par la seule raison ou par une foi purement humaine (c'est-à-dire par une foi donnée par l'homme): on ne peut le croire que par une foi divine (c'est-à-dire par une foi donnée par Dieu) ... Il reste visiblement à s'interroger sur le rôle exact dévolu à la raison et au discours de la preuve, en tenant compte à la fois de la théologie de Pascal ... et des éléments contenus dans les *Pensées*."
6  "Second Writing on Grace," Pascal (1963), p. 318b.
7  L149, p. 520b/S182, p.138.
8  L119/S151.
9  L618/S511.
10  L449, p. 558a/S690, pp. 488f.
11  L45/S78, p.73.
12  See for example, St Thomas Aquinas, ST 1–2, q. 110, art. 3, ad 3.
13  "First Writing on Grace," Pascal (1963), p. 313a.
14  "Third Writing on Grace," Pascal (1963), p. 330b.
15  The nature of the Pelagian heresy will be discussed later in this chapter.

16  L232/S264.
17  L347/S379.
18  L432, p. 605a/S662, p. 439. The same point has also been made about vociferous critics of religion writing today. Scorners of Christianity like Richard Dawkins and Christopher Hitchens seem strangely blind to the Christian character of their own moral imaginations. See Feser (2008); also McDade (2010), pp. 176f.
19  Matthew 13:13–16.
20  L233/S265.
21  L487, p. 569b/S734, p. 537.
22  L596/S493.
23  L236/S268.
24  McDade (2004), p. 127.
25  I discuss this doctrine and the use made of it by modern philosophers in Hunter (1996) and (2004).
26  Descartes, *Discours de la méthode*, Pt 5, AT 6, p. 45.
27  See L84/S118.
28  On the ideological aspect of the new atheism, see Feser (2008).
29  Pascal (1963), p. 267a/b.
30  For a brief account of this miracle, see Hunter (1996), pp. 114ff.
31  The brief account of Pascal's view that follows borrows from the neat summary of it Gouhier (1971) p. 188; See also McDade (2004), pp. 124f.
32  The interesting ways in which this is and is not the case are discussed by Frede (1999), pp. 41–68.
33  L416/S35.
34  L449, p. 557b/S690, p. 487.
35  L622/S515.
36  L908/S451.
37  Brémond (1967), p. 373.
38  Ibid.
39  St Thomas, ST 2–2, q. 4, art. 5, resp: "Distinctio fidei formatae et informis est secundum id quod pertinent ad voluntatem, id est secundum caritatem."
40  Davidson (1979), p. 63.
41  L308/S339.
42  In his account of it, to which I am in several places indebted, Mesnard (1988) calls it P.
43  Mesnard (1988), pp. 30, 48.
44  More comprehensive treatments can be found in Mesnard (1988) and Grasset (2008).

45 Contra Mesnard (1988), p. 31, who writes that Pascal uses the term 'order' "non pas en son sens usuel ... de disposition réfléchie, calculée, méthodique."

46 Sellier (1990), p. 76.

47 L933/S761. For an excellent discussion of the content and relationship of both fragments, see Mesnard (1988). On the question of priority, see p. 35.

48 L298/S329.

49 See Davidson (1979), p. 63: "Each plane has its people."

50 See, e.g., L222/S255; L270/S301.

51 Mesnard (1988), p. 46, provides the evidence for putting Epicurus here.

52 Pascal (1963), pp. 367f.

53 The letter accompanied Pascal's gift to Christina of one of his reckoning machines. See Cailliet (1945), pp. 95ff.

54 Letter to Her Highness the Queen of Sweden, June 1652, Pascal (1963) p. 280a. Perhaps Christina took Pascal's letter to heart. Two years later she abdicated her throne.

55 François Mauriac notes that Pascal's silence regarding the level of charity reflects the degree to which his later religious preoccupations had slipped from his mind. See Mauriac (1931), p. 105.

56 See Davidson (1979), p. 54.

57 L598/S495.

58 L287/S319.

59 L502/S738.

60 L615/S508.

61 Thirouin (2011), p. 17.

62 L502/S738.

63 Philippe Sellier's example. See Sellier (1979), p. 77.

64 L933/S761. The choice of abbreviation is that of Mesnard (1988).

65 The biblical reference is 1 John 2:16, "the lust of the flesh, and the lust of the eyes, and the pride of life."

66 Mesnard (1988), esp. pp. 36–9. I am exploiting his results but not adopting his interpretation of them.

67 L502/S738.

68 Compare L421/S560, pp. 466f.

69 "Third Letter on the Condition of Great Ones," Pascal (1963), p. 368b.

70 Ibid.

71 Davidson (1979), pp. 68f. (Quotation slightly amended for grammar.)

72 See, e.g., Garcia (2002); Grasset (2005).

73 Garcia (2002), p. 89.

74 Ibid., p. 90.

75 See Appendix B, oP6.

76  See, e.g., Hatfield (2003), pp. xiv, 42.
77  See Descartes's letter to Elizabeth, 28 June 1643, AT 3, p. 695.
78  L44/S78.
79  L200, pp. 620f/S231f, pp. 513f.
80  Garcia (2002), p. 90.
81  Ibid., p. 91.
82  von Balthasar (1991), p. 102.
83  L512/S670.
84  Vincent Carraud (1992), pp. 455f, goes so far as to call it "antimystical."
85  "First Writing on Grace," Pascal (1963), p. 313b
86  Ibid., p. 313a.
87  Pascal (1963), p. 640b, fragment xv among the "pensées inédites."
88  *Traité de la confiance chrétienne*, cited in *Dictionnaire des livres jansénistes*, 4, pp. 124, 125. Cited in turn by Brémond (1967), p. 373.
89  L712/S590.
90  Pascal (1963), p. 313b.
91  Though any hope we do achieve, he also says, mitigates our fear. L208/S240.
92  "Nous voguons sur un milieu vaste, toujours incertains." L199, p. 527a/S230, p. 167.
    Compare Russier (1956), p. 238.
93  L913/S742.
94  Which had been brewing for the previous year. See Gouhier (1956), p. 298. "Dénouement" is Gouhier's term.
95  See Gouhier (1956), pp. 298–307.
96  Bernard Grasset's fine phrase. See Grasset (2008), p. 22.
97  Gouhier (1956), p. 318.
98  Pascal quotes from the Vulgate, "Non obliviscar sermones tuos" and follows the Septuagint/Vulgate numbering. In Jewish and Protestant Bibles, the reference would be Psalm 119, v. 16.
99  Pascal's sister Gilberte recalls that he had many parts of this the longest of the Psalms by heart, always found fresh insight in it, and delighted to recite it. See Pascal (1963), p. 31a/b.
100  L921/S752.
101  L774/S638.
102  "Third Writing on Grace," Pascal (1963), p. 322.
103  Romans 8:24f.
104  L774/638.
105  The connection between "living faith" and acts of charity goes back ultimately to James 2:17: "Faith without works is dead."
106  L781/S644.

107  L781/S644.

108  L829/S668.

109  L724/S605. My italics on the word 'efforts.'

110  Pelagius, a British monk (ca 360–420 A.D.), defended the view that, even after Adam and Eve's original sin, mankind retained the ability not to sin. We are born, Pelagius said, "without virtue as without vice, and before the activity of our personal will there is nothing in man but what God has stored in him" (Bettensen (1954), p. 75). This view was attacked by St Augustine and condemned as heretical in the Synod of Carthage (418 A.D.). A related view, which came to be known as "Semi-Pelagian," held that the beginning of saving faith lies in an unconditioned act of free will (see *The Catholic Encyclopedia*, "Semi-Pelagianism").

111  McDade (2010), p. 187.

112  See Pascal (2000), p. 390[4], where both possibilities are mentioned.

113  "First Writing on Grace," Pascal (1963), p. 313a.

114  Ibid., p. 313b.

115  "Second Writing on Grace," Pascal (963), p. 318a.

116  See L662/S544.

117  "First Writing on Grace," Pascal (1963), p. 313a.

118  "Third Writing on Grace," Pascal (1963), p. 328a.

119  L170/S201.

120  Descartes, *Discours de la méthode*, Pt 2, AT 6, 19.

121  L512/S670.

122  When he criticizes those who "[submit] to everything, because they don't know when to make a judgement." L170/S201, p. 52.

123  Anselm, *Proslogion*, §1.

124  Pascal actually believes he can prove Augustine's principle (L577/S480). What he means by this claim was discussed in Chapter Three.

125  L168/S199.

126  *Critique of Pure Reason*, A133/B172. Translation of Norman Kemp Smith, slightly revised.

127  *Critique of Pure Reason*, A134/B172f.

128  L513/S671.

129  L173/S204.

130  L357/S389.

131  #15 of the *Pensées* "inédites," Pascal (1963), p. 640b.

132  L835/S423.

133  L240/S272.

134  L332/S364.

135  E.g., Étienne Périer, Preface to the Port Royal Edition of the *Pensées*, Pascal (1963), p. 496, Filleau de la Chaise (1922), pp. 62ff.

136  Filleau de la Chaise (1922), p. 63.

137  Ibid., p. 73.

138  See *Oxford Dictionary of the Christian Church* (1997), article "Prophecy."

139  L274/S305.

140  Acts 2:29–36.

141  Acts 2:41.

142  L274/S305.

143  L267/S298.

144  L274/S305.

145  Isaiah 53:3.

146  John 18:36.

147  See L256/S288.

148  L274/S305.

149  L274/S305.

150  L257/S289. I have reversed the order of the last two paragraphs.

151  L733/S614.

152  L571/S474.

153  L317/S348.

154  L427/S681. Cf. also L449/S690, "they blaspheme what they do not know."

155  L449/S690.

156  L808/S655.

157  L781/S644.

158  L427, p. 552a-b/S681, p. 468.

159  L424/S680, p. 467.

160  L5/S39.

161  See Appendix B, qP3.

162  1 Cor 1:17, quoted in L842/S427.

163  Garber (2009), p. 53.

164  Ibid., pp. 45f.

165  I am grateful to Daniel Garber for comments that helped me clarify the point of our disagreement.

## 6.  Measuring Pascal

1  Moran (2006); Carraud (1992), p. 450; Baird (1975), pp. vii, 93.

2  Wright (1941), p. 87; Bréhier (1983 reprint of 1933), p. 114; Clarke (1960); Sedgwick (2001); Scruton (1995), p. 46; Besnier (1993), pp. 93–106.

3  Hammond (2003).

4  Nicholas Hammond, personal communication. For the series' focus on "major philosophers," see the cover blurb on any volume in the series.

5  Hammond (2003), p. 1.

6 Garber (2009), pp. 45f.
7 See Popkin (1979), p. xviii.
8 L865/439.
9 Miel (1969), p. 193.
10 Leo X's call to philosophers is from "Apostolici Regiminis (1513)" in Gaude (1860), p. 602. John Paul II's encyclical *Fides et ratio* makes an even broader and more urgent appeal, as does Alasdair Macintyre in his discussion of that encyclical in *God, Philosophy, Universities* (2009), esp. pp. 165–80.
11 See, e.g., Mounier (1949), p. 9; Roberts (1959), pp. 15–59.
12 See, e.g., Jordan (2005; 2006); McCullagh (2007), pp. 21–34.
13 The argument is briefly presented in Jordan (2005).
14 Richardson (2006), p. 351.
15 James (1956), p. 108. Subsequent citations from this short and famous article will not be footnoted. It is collected in many places with differing paginations.
16 Quoted in Richardson (2006), pp. 406, 355.
17 Jordan (2005), p. 180.
18 Pascal (1963), p. 313b.
19 Ταῦτ᾽ ἔστιν, ὦ Καλλίκλεις, ἃ ἐγὼ ἀκηκοὼς πιστεύω ἀληθῆ εἶναι. καὶ ἐκ τούτων τῶν λόγων τοιόνδε τι λογίζομαι συμβαίνειν (524a/b).
20 Seventh Letter, 335a/b. Tradition holds this letter to be authentic. Even those who deny it think it the work of someone with a good grasp of Plato's thought.
21 See Heinrichs (2003).
22 Plato (1985), p. 381.
23 Ἐγὼ μὲν οὖν, ὦ Καλλίκλεις, ὑπὸ τούτων τῶν λόγων πέπεισμαι ... παρακαλῶ δὲ καὶ τοὺς ἄλλους πάντας ἀνθρώπους, καθ᾽ ὅσον δύναμαι, καὶ δὴ καὶ σὲ ἀντιπαρακαλῶ ἐπὶ τοῦτον τὸν βίον καὶ τὸν ἀγῶνα τοῦτον, ὃν ἐγώ φημι ἀντὶ πάντων τῶν ἐνθάδε ἀγώνων εἶναι (526d/e).
24 See, for example, Plato 1989), pp. 249f.
25 Josef Pieper (2011) is a recent commentator in a long line stretching back as far as Eusebius who sees the gap between the Socratic *logos* and the Catholic tradition as narrower than what the secular commentary tradition assumes.
26 L131, p. 515b/S164, p. 117.
27 That is the only justification given by Émile Bréhier for the dramatic words, "Pascal is no philosopher," with which the entry on Pascal begins in his history of philosophy. Bréhier (1983), p. 114.

# Bibliography

Ariew, Roger. 2007. "Descartes and Pascal." *Perspectives on Science* 15, no. 4: 397–409. http://dx.doi.org/10.1162/posc.2007.15.4.397.

Armour, Leslie. 1993. *Infini Rien*. Journal of the History of Philosophy Monograph Series. Carbondale, IL: Southern Illinois University Press.

Arnauld, Antoine, and Pierre Nicole. 1970. *La logique ou l'art de penser*. Paris: Flammarion.

Baird, A.W.S. 1975. *Studies in Pascal's Ethics*. The Hague: Martinus Nijhoff.

Bem, Daryl J. 1966. "Inducing Belief in False Confessions." *Journal of Personality and Social Psychology* 3, no. 6: 707–10.

Besnier, Jean-Michel. 1993. *Histoire de la philosophie moderne et contemporaine*. Paris: Grasset, 1993.

Bettensen, Henry. 1954. *Documents of the Christian Church*. Oxford: Oxford University Press.

Bouchilloux, Hélène. 2002. "Apologie et théologie dans *Les Pensées* de Pascal." *Revue Philosophique de la France et de L'etranger* 127, no. 1: 3–19. http://dx.doi.org/10.3917/rphi.021.0003.

Bovens, Luc. 1999. "Two Faces of Akratics Anonymous." *Analysis* 59, no. 4: 230–6.

Boyle, Nicholas. 2005. *Sacred and Secular Scriptures: A Catholic Approach to Literature*. Notre Dame, IN: University of Notre Dame Press.

Bras, Mathieu. 2009. *Blaise Pascal: Apologie et Probabilités*. Thesis, University of Ottawa.

Bréhier, Émile. 1983. *Histoire de la philosophie*. Vol. 2, *XVIIe–XVIIIe siècles*. Paris: Presses Universitaires de France.

Brémond, Henri. 1967. *Histoire littéraire du sentiment religieux en France*. Vol. 4. Paris: Librairie Armand Colin.

Brunet, Georges. 1956. *Le pari de Pascal*. Paris: Desclée de Brouwer.

Cailliet, Émile. 1945. *Pascal*. Philadelphia: Westminster Press.

Carraud, Vincent. 1992. *Pascal et la philosophie*. Paris: Presses Universitaires de France.

–––. 2007. "Pascal's Anti-Augustinianism." *Perspectives on Science* 15, no. 4: 450–92. http://dx.doi.org/10.1162/posc.2007.15.4.450.

Catholic Church. 1994. *Catechism of the Catholic Church*. 2nd. ed. Vatican: Libraria Editrice Vaticana.

Cave, Terence. 2009. "Imagining Scepticism in the Sixteenth Century." In *Retrospectives: Essays in Literature, Poetics, and Cultural History*, eds Neil Kenny and Wes Williams, 109–29. Leeds, Legenda: Modern Humanities Research Association and Maney Publishing.

Celano, Anthony J. 1987. "The Concept of Worldly Beatitude in the Writings of Thomas Aquinas" *Journal of the History of Philosophy* 25, no. 2: 215–26.

Chesterton, G.K. 1908. *Orthodoxy*. London: Bodley Head.

Clair, André. 2003. "Justice, imagination et symbole." *Revue Philosophique de Louvain* 101, no. 3: 413–33. http://dx.doi.org/10.2143/RPL.101.3.750.

Clarke, G.N. 1960. *The Seventeenth Century*. Oxford: Clarendon Press.

Conche, Marcel. 1996. *Montaigne et la philosophie*. Paris: Presses Universitaires de France.

Copleston, Frederick S.J. 1953. *A History of Philosophy*. Vol. 3, *Ockham to Suárez*. London: Burns Oates & Washbourne.

Davidson, Hugh M. 1979. *Means and Meanings in Pascal's Pensées*. Chicago: University of Chicago Press.

de la Bruyère, Jean. 1965. *Les caractères*. "Des esprits forts" §1. Paris: Garnier-Flammarion.

Descartes, René. 1996. *Oeuvres de Descartes*. Eds Charles Adam and Paul Tannery. Paris: Vrin. Abbreviated AT.

Desné, Roland. 1972. "The Role of England in Voltaire's Polemic Against Pascal: Apropos the Twenty-Fifth *Philosophical Letter*." In *Eighteeenth Century Studies*, ed. Peter Gay, 42–57. Hanover, NH: University Press of New England.

Diogenes Laertius. 1988. *Life of Pyrrho*, 9.196. In *Hellenistic Philosophy*, trans. and eds. Brad Inwood and L.P. Gerson. Indianapolis: Hackett.

Douglass, Frederick. 1857. *My Bondage and My Freedom*. New York: Miller, Orton.

Dryzek, John S. 1993. "Policy Analysis and Planning: From Science to Argument." In *The Argumentative Turn in Policy Analysis and Planning*, eds. Frank Fischer and John Forester, 213–32. Durham, NC: Duke University Press.

Dumoncel, Jean-Claude. 1983. "Le système de Leibniz: Sa structure et son centre." *Revue Philosophique de la France et de L'etranger* 173, no. 4: 401–25.

———. 1985. "La théologie modale de Leibniz." *Studia Leibnitiana* 17, no. 1: 98–104.

Edwards, A.W.F. 2003. "Pascal's Work on Probability." In *The Cambridge Companion to Pascal*, ed. Nicholas Hammond, 40–52. Cambridge, UK: Cambridge University Press.

Elster, Jon. 2003. "Pascal and Decision Theory." In *The Cambridge Companion to Pascal*. ed. Nicholas Hammond, 53–74. Cambridge, UK: Cambridge University Press.

Englebretsen, George. 1990. *Essays on the Philosophy of Fred Sommers*. Lewiston, NY: Mellen.

Fallon, Stephen M. 1991. *Milton among the Philosophers*. Ithaca, NY: Cornell University Press.

Ferreyrolles, Gérard. 1984. *Pascal et la raison du politique*. Paris: Presses Universitaires de France.

Feser, Edward. 2008. *The Last Superstition: A Refutation of the New Atheism*. South Bend, IN: St Augustine's Press.

Filleau de la Chaise. 1922. *Discours sur les Pensées de M. Pascal*. Ed. Victor Giraud. Paris: Bossard.

Fleischacker, Samuel. 2004. *A Short History of Distributive Justice*. Cambridge, MA: Harvard University Press.

Force, Pierre. 2009. "Montaigne and the Coherence of Eclecticism." *Journal of the History of Ideas* 70, no. 4: 523–44. http://dx.doi.org/10.1353/jhi.0.0052.

Foster, Brian. 1963. "Pascal's Use of *Abêtir.*" *French Studies* 17, no. 1: 1–13.

Frede, Michael. 1999. "Monotheism and Pagan Philosophy in Later Antiquity." In *Pagan Monotheism in Late Antiquity*, eds Polymnia Athanassiadi and Michael Frede, 41–68. Oxford: Clarendon Press.

Friedrich, Hugo. 1949. *Montaigne*. Bern: Franke Verlag.

Garber, Daniel. 2009. *What Happens After Pascal's Wager?* Milwaukee: Marquette University Press.

Garcia, Laura L. 2002. "St. John of the Cross and the Necessity of Divine Hiddenness." In *Divine Hiddenness*, eds Daniel Howard-Snyder and Paul K. Moser, 83–97. Cambridge, UK: Cambridge University Press.

Gaude, Francisco, ed. 1860. *Bullarum diplomatum et* privilegiorum. Turin: Seb. Franco et Henrico Dalmazzo.

Gheeraert, Tony. 2008. "Pages arrachées à *l'Apologie pour la religion*: Les premières liasses des *Pensées* de Blaise Pascal." Lecture given at the Académie de Rouen, 18 November. Text at lettres.ac-rouen.fr/sequences/tl/gheeraert_pascal_TL2009.doc

Girard, René. 1999. *Je vois Satan tomber comme l'éclair.* Paris: Grasset.

Gnädiger, L. et al. 1977–99. "Contemptus mundi." In *Lexikon des Mittelalters.* 10 vols. Stuttgart: Metzler.

Gouhier, Henri. 1971. *Blaise Pascal: Commentaires.* 2nd ed. Paris: Vrin.

———. 1956. "Le mémorial est-il un texte mystique?" In *Blaise Pascal: L'homme et l'œuvre,* 296–341. Paris: Éditions de Minuit.

Grasset, Bernard. 2005. "Poésie, philosophie et mystique." *Laval théologique et philosophique* 61, no. 3: 553–81.

———. 2008. "Le sens pascalien du mot *esprit* et les trois ordres." *Revue Philosophique de la France et de L'etranger,* no. 1: 3–30.

Gross, Leo. 1948. "The Peace of Westphalia, 1648–1948." *American Journal of International Law* 42, no. 1: 20–41.

Haack, Susan. 2001. "'The Ethics of Belief' Reconsidered." In *Knowledge, Truth and Duty,* ed. Mathias Steup, 21–33. New York: Oxford University Press.

Hacking, Ian. 1972. "The Logic of Pascal's Wager." *American Philosophical Quarterly* 9, no. 2: 186–92.

Hájek, Alan. 2003. "Waging War on Pascal's Wager." *Philosophical Review* 112, no. 1: 27–56. http://dx.doi.org/10.1215/00318108-112-1-27.

Hammond, Nicholas, ed. 2003. *The Cambridge Companion to Pascal.* Cambridge, UK: Cambridge University Press.

———. 1994. *Playing with Truth.* Oxford: Clarendon Press. http://dx.doi. org/10.1093/acprof:oso/9780198158936.001.0001

Harrington, Thomas More. 1982. *Pascal philosophe.* Paris: Société d'édition d'enseignement supérieur.

Hatfield, Gary. 2003. *Descartes and the Meditations.* London: Routledge.

Heinrichs, Albert. 2003. "*Hieroi Logoi* and *Hierai Bibloi*: The (Un)written Margins of the Sacred in Ancient Greece." *Harvard Studies in Classical Philology* 101: 207–66.

Hirstein, William. 2005. *Brain Fiction: Self-Deception and the Riddle of Confabulation,* Cambridge, MA: MIT Press.

Hughes, G.E., and M.J. Cresswell. 1968. *An Introduction to Modal Logic.* London: Methuen.

Hühn, H. 1971. "Weltverachtung." In *Historisches Wörterbuch der Philosophie,* Vol. 12, ed. Joachim Ritter, 521–7. Basel/Stuttgart: Schwabe.

Hunter, Graeme. 1996. "Arnauld's Defence of Miracles and Its Context." In *Interpreting Arnauld,* ed. Elmar J. Kremer, 111–26. Toronto: University of Toronto Press.

———. 1998. "Descartes' Apology." *Studies in Religion* 27, no. 2: 179–91.

———. 1989. "Kant and the Ontological Argument." In *Proceedings of the Sixth International Kant Congress* 2, no. 2: 3–10. Washington, DC: Center for Advanced Research in Phenomenology and University Press of America.

— — —. 1993. "Russell Making History: The Leibniz Book." In *Russell and Analytic Philosophy*, eds A.D. Irvine and G.A. Wedeking, 397–414. Toronto: University of Toronto Press.

— — —. 2004. "Spinoza on Miracles." *International Journal for Philosophy of Religion* 56, no. 1: 41–51. http://dx.doi.org/10.1007/s11153-004-8034-5.

James, William. 1956. "The Will to Believe." In *Selected Papers on Philosophy*, 99–124. London: Dent.

Jonsen, Albert R., and Stephen Toulmin. 1988. *The Abuse of Casuistry*. Berkeley: University of California Press.

Jordan, Jeff. 2002. "Pascal's Wagers." *Midwest Studies in Philosophy* 26, no. 1: 213–23. http://dx.doi.org/10.1111/1475-4975.261063.

— — —. 2005. "Pascal's Wagers and James's Will to Believe." In *The Oxford Handbook of Philosophy of Religion*, ed. William J. Wainwright, 168–87. Oxford: Oxford University Press.

— — —. 2006. *Pascal's Wager: Pragmatic Arguments and Belief in God*. Oxford: Oxford University Press.

Kalinowski, George. 1985. "Sur l'argument ontologique de Leibniz." *Studia Leibnitiana* 17, no. 1: 93–7.

Kane, G. Stanley. 1980. "Evil and Privation." *International Journal of the Philosophy of Religion* 11: 43–58.

Kekes, John. 1990. *Facing Evil*. Princeton, NJ: Princeton University Press.

Knox, Ronald. 1950. *Enthusiasm*. Oxford: Oxford University Press.

Kolakowski, Leszek. 1998. *God Owes Us Nothing*. Chicago: University of Chicago Press.

Lafuma, Louis. 1963. *Pascal: Oeuvres complétes*. Paris: Seuil.

Le Guern, Michel. 1971. *Pascal et Descartes*. Paris: Nizet.

Leibniz, G.W. 1978. *Die philosophischen Schriften*. 7 vols. Ed. C.I. Gebhardt. Hildesheim: Olms. References abbreviated as GP + volume number + page number.

Leo X (pope). 1860. "Apostolici regiminis." In *Bullarum diplomatum et privilegiorum*, ed. Francisco Gaude. Turin: Seb. Franco et Henrico Dalmazzo.

Lohr, C.H. 1976. "Jesuit Aristotelianism and Sixteenth-Century Metaphysics." In *Paradosis*, ed. Edwin A. Quain. New York: Fordham University Press.

Lønning, Per. 1980. *Cet effrayant pari*. Paris: Vrin.

Long, A.A. 2002. *Epictetus: A Stoic and Socratic Guide to Life*. Oxford: Clarendon Press.

— — —. 1986. *Hellenistic Philosophy*. 2nd ed. Berkeley: University of California Press.

Lorenzen, Paul. 1987. *Constructive Philosophy*. Trans. Karl Richard Pavlovic. Amherst: University of Massachusetts Press.

Losoncy, Thomas A. 1992. "More on an Elusive Argument." *American Catholic Philosophical Quarterly* 66, no. 4: 501–5.

Lynch, Tony, and Adrian Walsh. 2003. "The Mandevillean Conceit and the Profit-Motive." *Philosophy* 78, no. 303: 43–62.

Lyotard, Jean-François. 1979. *La condition postmoderne*. Paris: Les éditions de minuit.

Macintyre, Alasdair. 2009. *God, Philosophy, Universities*. New York: Rowman & Littlefield.

Mandeville, Bernard. 1988. Introduction to *The Fable of the Bees*. Ed. F.B. Kaye. Indianapolis: Liberty Classics.

Marion, Jean-Luc. 1992. "Is the Ontological Argument Ontological? The Argument According to Anselm and Its Metaphysical Interpretation According to Kant." *Journal of the History of Philosophy* 30, no. 2: 201–18.

Martin, Michael. 1990. *Atheism: A Philosophical Justification*. Philadelphia: Temple University Press.

Martin, Mike W. 2006. *From Morality to Mental Health: Virtue and Vice in a Therapeutic Culture*. Oxford: Oxford University Press.

Mauriac, François. 1931. *Blaise Pascal et sa soeur Jacqueline*. Paris: Hachette.

McCullagh, C. Behan. 2007. "Can Religious Belief Be Justified Pragmatically?" *Sophia* 46, no. 1: 21–34.

McDade, John. 2010. "The Contemporary Relevance of Pascal." *New Blackfriars* 91, no. 1032: 185–96. http://dx.doi.org/10.1111/j.1741-2005.2009.01349.x.

———. 2004. "Divine Disclosure and Concealment in Bach, Pascal and Levinas." *New Blackfriars* 85, no. 996: 121–32. http://dx.doi.org/10.1111/j.0028-4289.2004.00001.x.

Mesnard, Jean. 1967. *Pascal*. Paris: Hatier.

———. 1988. "Le thème des trois ordres dans l'organisation des *Pensées*." In *Pascal: Thématique des Pensées*, eds Lane M. Heller and Ian M. Richmond, 29–55. Paris: Vrin.

Miel, Jan. 1969. *Pascal and Theology*. Baltimore: Johns Hopkins University Press.

Montaigne, Michel de. 2003. *Apology for Raymond Sebond*. Trans Roger Ariew and Marjorie Greene. Indianapolis: Hackett.

———. 1962. *Essais*. 3 vols. Ed. Maurice Rat. Paris: Garnier. http://dx.doi.org/10.1051/apido:19620305

Moran, Patrick Quinn. 2006. "Pascal's Pensées: Fragments of an Epistemology." PhD Dissertation, University of Ottawa.

Moriarty, Michael. 2003. "Grace and Religious Belief in Pascal." In *The Cambridge Companion to Pascal*, ed. Nicholas Hammond, 144–61. Cambridge, UK: Cambridge University Press.

Moskowitz, Eva S. 2001. *In Therapy We Trust: America's Obsession with Self-Fulfillment*. Baltimore: Johns Hopkins University Press.

Mounier, Emmanuel. 1949. *Introduction aux existentialismes*. Paris: Garnier/Denoël.

Nadler, Steven. 2008. *The Best of All Possible Worlds: A Story of Philosophers, Good and Evil*. New York: Farrar, Straus and Giroux.

Nagel, Thomas. 1997. *The Last Word*. Oxford: Oxford University Press.

Natoli, Charles M. 1985. *Nietzsche and Pascal on Christianity*. New York: Peter Lang.

Neiman, Susan. 2002. *Evil in Modern Thought*. Princeton, NJ: Princeton University Press.

Neto, José R. Maia. 1997. "Academic Skepticism in Early Modern Philosophy." *Journal of the History of Ideas* 58, no. 2: 199–220.

Newman, John Henry. 1910. "Christianity and Scientific Investigation." In *The Idea of a University*, 456–79. London: Longmans, Green.

Nozick, Robert. 1981. *Philosophical Explanations*. Cambridge, MA: Belknap Press.

Nussbaum, Martha. 2000. "Duties of Justice, Duties of Material Aid: Cicero's Problematic Legacy." *Journal of Political Philosophy* 8, no. 2: 176–206.

O'Connell, Marvin R. 1997. *Blaise Pascal: Reasons of the Heart*. Grand Rapids, MI: Eerdmans.

Oppy, Graham. 1995. *Ontological Arguments and Belief in God*. Cambridge, UK: Cambridge University Press.

*Oxford Dictionary of the Christian Church*. 1997. Ed. F.L. Cross. 3rd ed., ed. E.A. Livingstone. Oxford, Oxford University Press.

Parish, Richard. 2010. *Catholic Particularity in Seventeenth-Century French Writing*. Oxford: Oxford University Press.

Pascal, Blaise. 1960. *L'entretien de Pascal et Sacy: ses sources et ses énigmes*. Ed. Pierre Courcelle. Paris: Vrin.

– – –. 1994. *Entretien avec M. de Sacy*. Eds Pascale Mengotti and Jean Mesnard. Paris: Desclée de Brower.

– – –. 1979. *L'Esprit de la géométrie et De l'art de persuader: Textes et commentaires*. Eds B. Clerté and M. Lhoste-Navarre. Paris: Éditions Pédagogie Moderne.

– – –. 1963. *Oeuvres complètes*. Ed. Louis Lafuma. Paris: Seuil.

– – –. 2000. *Pensées*. Ed. Philippe Sellier. Paris: Livre de poche.

– – –. 1966. *Pensées*. Translation following Pascal (1963) by A.J. Krailsheimer. London: Penguin.

– – –. 2005. *Pensées*. Translation following Pascal (2000) by Roger Ariew. Indianapolis: Hackett.

Pieper, Joseph. 2011. *Über die platonischen Mythen*. Munich, 1965. Translated as *The Platonic Myths*, South Bend, IN: St Augustine's Press.

Pinker, Stephen. 2002. *The Blank Slate: The Modern Denial of Human Nature*. New York: Penguin.

Pintard, René. 1962. "Pascal et les libertins." In *Pascal présent*, 113–16. Clermont-Ferrand, France: G. de Bussac.

Plantinga, Alvin, ed. 1965. *The Ontological Argument*. New York: Doubleday.

Plato, 1989. *Gorgias*. Translated with notes by Terence Irwin. Oxford: Clarendon Press.

–––. 1985. *Gorgias: A Revised Text with Introduction and Commentary*. Ed. E.R. Dodds. Oxford: Clarendon Press.

Popkin, Richard. 1979. *The History of Scepticism from Erasmus to Spinoza*. Berkeley: University of California Press.

Quine, W.V.O. 1969. "Epistemology Naturalized." In *Ontological Relativity and Other Essays*, 69-90. New York: Columbia University Press.

–––. 1976. "On Simple Theories of a Complex World." In *The Ways of Paradox*, 255–8. Cambridge, MA: Harvard University Press.

Rescher, Nicholas. 1985. *Pascal's Wager*. Notre Dame, IN: University of Notre Dame Press.

Richardson, Robert D. 2006. *William James: In the Maelstrom of American Modernism*. New York: Houghton Mifflin.

–––. 1966. *The Triumph of the Therapeutic*. New York: Penguin.

Robinson, Richard. 1964. *An Atheist's Values*. Oxford: Clarendon Press.

Roberts, David. 1959. *Existentialism and Religious Belief*. New York: Oxford University Press.

Ross, G.M. 1986. "Leibniz's Role as a Type in English Language Philosophy." In *Beiträge zur Wirkungs-und Rezeptionsgeschichte von Gottfried Wilhelm Leibniz*, ed. Albert Heinekamp. *Studia Leibnitiana Supplementa* 26: 376–84.

Russell, Bertrand. 1946. *A History of Western Philosophy*. London: George Allen and Unwin.

Russier, J. (1956), "L'expérience du Mémorial et conception pascalienne de la connaissance." In *Pascal: L'homme et l'œuvre*, 225–40. Paris: Éditions de minuit.

Scholar, Richard. 2003. *Entretien avec Sacy sur la philosophie*. Arles, France: Actes sud.

–––. 2010. *Montaigne and the Art of Free-Thinking*. Witney, UK: Peter Lang.

Scruton, Roger. 1995 *A Short Introduction to Modern Philosophy*. 2nd ed. London: Routledge.

Sedgwick, Peter. 2001. *Descartes to Derrida: An Introduction to European Philosophy*. Oxford: Blackwell.

Sellier, Philippe. 1990. "Seminar: Pascal's 'Trois Ordres.'" In *Meaning, Structure and History in the Pensées of Pascal*, ed. David Wetsel, 71–83. Paris: Biblio 17–56: Papers on French Seventeenth Century Literature.

Smith, Adam. 1790. *Theory of Moral Sentiments*. 6th ed. London: Strahan. http://galenet.galegroup.com/servlet/MOME?af=RN&ae=U102312049&srchtp=a&ste=14.

Sorensen, Roy. 1997. "Advertisement: A Cure for Incontinence." *Mind, New Series* 106: 424.

Spinoza to Ludovico Meyer, 20 April 1663. In *Opera*. Vol. 4, ed. Carl Gebhardt. Heidelberg: Winters, 1925.

Steil, Benn, and Manuel Hinds. 2009. *Money Markets and Sovereignty*. New Haven, CT: Yale University Press.

Stockdale, James. 1993. *Courage under Fire: Testing Epictetus' Doctrines in a Laboratory of Human Behaviour*. Hoover Essays. Stanford, CA: Stanford University.

Strowski, Fortunat. 1922. *Pascal et son temps*. 3 vols. Paris: Plon-Nourrit.

Surin, Kenneth. 1985. "*Contemptus mundi* and the Disenchanted World: Bonhoeffer's 'Discipline of the Secret' and Adorno's 'Strategy of Hibernation.'" *Journal of the American Academy of Religion* 53, no. 3: 384–410.

Taleb, N.N. 2007. *The Black Swan*. New York: Random House.

Taylor, Charles. 2007. *A Secular Age*. Cambridge, MA: Belknap Press.

Thirouin, Laurent. 1991. *Le hasard et les règles: Le modèle du jeu dans la pensée de Pascal*. Paris: Vrin.

–––. 2011. *Pensées sur la justice*. Paris: La Découverte.

van Fraassen, Bas. 1980. *The Scientific Image*. Oxford: Clarendon Press.

van Inwagen, Peter. 2006. "Philosophical Failure." Lecture 3 in *The Problem of Evil*, 37–55. Oxford: Clarendon Press. http://dx.doi.org/10.1093/acprof:oso/9780199245604.003.0003

Voltaire. 1958. "Sur les *Pensées* de M. Pascal." Twenty-fifth letter (incipit). *Lettres philosophiques*. Oxford: Blackwell.

von Balthasar, Hans Urs. 1991. *The Glory of the Lord: A Theological Aesthetics*. San Francisco: Ignatius Press.

–––. 1994. *Pascal and Disbelief: Catechesis and Conversion in the Pensées*. Washington, DC: Catholic University of America Press.

Whelan, Ruth. 1992. "From Christian Apologetics to Enlightened Deism: The Case of Jacques Abbadie." *Modern Language Review* 87, no. 1: 32–40.

Wright, William Kelly. 1941. *History of Modern Philosophy*. New York: Macmillan.

Zwierlein, Eduard. 2001. *Existenz und Vernunft: Studien zu Descartes, Pascal und Nietzsche*. Würzburg: Königshausen und Neumann.

# Index